CROSS-NATIONAL PERSPECTIVES:
UNITED STATES AND CANADA

INTERNATIONAL STUDIES

IN

SOCIOLOGY AND SOCIAL ANTHROPOLOGY

General Editor

K. ISHWARAN

VOLUME XXIV

CROSS-NATIONAL PERSPECTIVES:
UNITED STATES AND CANADA

LEIDEN
E. J. BRILL
1977

CROSS-NATIONAL PERSPECTIVES:
UNITED STATES AND CANADA

EDITED BY

ROBERT PRESTHUS

LEIDEN
E. J. BRILL
1977

ISBN 90 04 05238 0

PRINTED IN THE NETHERLANDS

CONTENTS

Introduction: Some Conditions of Comparative Analysis in the United States and Canada

ROBERT PRESTHUS

York University, Toronto, Canada

FOR REASONS which are subtle and varied, Canada remains *terra incognita* in the United States. Canadians, moreover, maintain that their own politics and culture are inadequately known *inside* Canada. After five years of inquiry, the (Symons) Commission on Canadian Studies (1976) reports in its first volume, *To Know Ourselves*, that "few other countries in the world with a developed post-secondary educational system pay so little attention to the study of their own culture, problems and circumstances in the university curriculum". The Commission finds several reasons for this condition. In the face of a pervasive cultural nationalism, it resolutely concludes, "the dearth of Canadian content in the curricula cannot be attributed solely or even primarily to the influence of non-Canadian professors and administrators." Instead, the major responsibility is said to rest with Canadian members of the university community. In such words, the Commission seems to take what is perhaps the first essential step toward its goal.

On the other hand, perhaps an outsider may be pardoned for asking whether Canadians are really this deeply concerned about knowing themselves. Two recent items come to mind. After a decade of fervent nationalism centered in the universities and the mass media, the Canada Council recently announced (1976) two huge grants, one for $450,000, the other for $250,000, to Canadian scholars. The purpose of these impressive sums is to prepare annotated editions of the letters of Sir Benjamin Disraeli and of Emile Zola. Although I am personally grateful for the Council's support, this situation contrasts dramatically with my own experience, almost a decade ago, when I had considerable difficulty securing an initial grant of some $35,000, and a subsequent one of some $30,000, to carry out the first systematic analysis of Canadian interest groups and their interaction with legislators and bureaucrats. The generally hostile reception in Canada of the two books resulting from the study reinforces my judgment that Canadians remain ambivalent regarding self-knowledge.

Among possible explanations one must surely include the role and recruitment of intellectuals in Canadian society. Although striking exceptions exist, their role has often included governmental consultancy and nation-saving.

The penetrating critical style found in the work of Frank Underhill, A. R. M. Lower, S. D. Clark, John Porter and most recently, Wallace Clement, remains exceptional. That the capacity for excellent research, disinterested criticism, and scholarly commitment devoted to vital issues of political, economic, and bureaucratic power exists in contemporary Canada is beyond question. The work of Clement, a young sociologist trained at Carleton University under the direction of John Porter, provides an impressive recent example. Yet, my own view is that such conceptions of the academic role are exceptional, to the extent that those who hold them might well be systematically analyzed to determine precisely what conditions are responsible for their uniqueness. To some extent, the problem is a dual one, including not only the paucity of Canadian Studies, but also the paucity of definitive, serious social research generally.

It is fascinating to speculate on explanations for this condition. Canada is one of the wealthiest societies in the world, so it seems reasonable to conclude that lack of research funds is not involved. Nor can inadequate preparation for serious research be an explanation, since most Canadian academics have been educated at the best American and British universities. It is true that most of them have been trained in "traditional", as opposed to behavioral methods, but this is not directly germane to the issue of *how much* research is done. It may, however, contribute to the neglect of Canadian Studies by focussing attention on the problems of the two "parent" countries.

The underlying causes seem to include social and cultural factors, and notably certain aspects of Canada's British heritage. Some of them rest generally in Canada's colonial status, as suggested in Wilson's analysis of the conditions of "hard" scientific research in Canada, as perceived by natural scientists. The colonial experience may also underlie any attending conclusions that Canadian institutions and behaviors are less deserving of attention than those of older societies. Perhaps, too, there is some latent feeling that Canadian scholarship is too young to attempt large scale analyses. Such attitudes may reflect and inspire what seems to be a highly developed, often negative, critical strain among Canadian *literati*. If this is so, it must be one of the most tragic aspects of the colonial burden. It may be, too, as a Canadian colleague has suggested, that settlement by defeated people, Empire Loyalists, Irish, and *Canadiens*, encouraged the strain of negativism that remains visible today.

Educational elitism, however, is perhaps the most dysfunctional aspect of the British heritage, and it also bears heavily upon the present condition, fostering as it has, the dominance of university appointments, research resources, and university offerings by a small, class-selected elite which too often succumbed to a somewhat idealized version of most things British. Their "more means worse" philosophy often meant that anything produced domestically was suspect, that criticism became more honored than creativity, and that young scholars must at times have felt that silence was preferable to disinterested inquiry in the social sciences. Meanwhile, their pervasive conservatism fostered a resistance to behavioral methods of research, denying to young scholars one set of analytical tools that might have expanded the parameters

of social research. Following the British model, ascriptive criteria of performance competed with those of achievement, again blunting the incentive to
"drill hard boards", in Weber's phrase. In the event, substantial reservoirs of
human energy were diverted to ceremonial aspects of scholarship.

Educational elitism and the resultant production of a very small cadre of
certified intellectuals may have had a limiting effect upon individual aspira-
tions simply because the mere achievement of even a first university degree
enabled one to present himself as a vast reservoir of knowledge. Given this
comfortable illusion, it became less likely that a Ph.D. might feel any compelling obligation to contribute new knowledge to his discipline. When this
perspective is attached to the pervasive bureaucratic norms characteristic of a
financial and commercially-oriented economy, a further displacement of scholarly values becomes even more understandable. As I have remarked elsewhere,
the extent to which young Canadian academics gravitate toward administrative posts within the university and in government is striking. In such a milieu,
it is perhaps not surprising that Canadian Studies have not evolved at the
expected pace.

The Symons report courageously faces some of these institutional and
conceptual dysfunctions, which is surely a cause for hope. Yet, so strong is the
appeal of projecting one's misadventures upon others that, in reviewing the
Commission's findings, the *Toronto Star* and at least one university newspaper
ran headlines proclaiming "Dearth of Canadian Studies Attributed to Foreign
Professors", or some such comfortable but inaccurate rationalization. Instead,
it seems that while the money and the problems have long been available for
critical inquiry and original research in Canadian Studies, the incentives, the
reward structure within academia and in the larger Canadian society, have
often been inapposite to such activity.

Recently, cultural nationalism, although it has sometimes provided a surro-
gate for academic research, has brought a welcome focus upon Canadian
economic affairs, as suggested by McKie's analysis of branch-plant managers in
Canada. In the process, we are provided a view of the extent to which Canadian
economic culture is influenced by American industrial penetration. If nationalism could inspire serious research rather than endless Conferences, Commissions
and essentially negative pamphleteering—it might have a greater therapeutic
effect. But the incentive and reward structures within academia must change,
and this requires a redefinition of the relative social value of creative work.
Such a change runs against the defensive core of cultural nationalism which
deflects criticism away from domestic motes to the behavior of outsiders.

As always, the solution is one of more education in the long-term. Certainly,
until the base of Canadian higher education is broadened to include individuals,
both in number and diversity, who can cut through the prevailing complacency,
change will continue to be difficult. Here, the expansion of opportunity in
higher education following World War II is all to the good. The nation moved
from only 5 per cent of youth aged 18–24 being in university to about 13 per
cent in 1971. In the process, the social parameters of admission must have

changed dramatically. Economic dislocation, inflation, and public disenchantment with the vast costs of such programs are now causing cut-backs, but these are probably temporary. Thus a quarter-century of flat-out support is beginning to redress the pre-1945 myopia of political and economic leaders regarding the critical role of higher education in national development.

Despite such gains, certain problems remain. The conservatism and ambivalence of the general public is sometimes shared by those within academe, which aggravates the problem of achieving change in the required directions. The questionable premise that technology and science are eventually destructive and that economic life will become simpler, motivates many young people and their academic mentors. That investment in *human development* is required to create the national wealth upon which rest academia, the arts, Expo 67's, Olympic Games, Canadian Opera and Ballet Companies – this seems only dimly perceived. And political leaders are often at fault for creating and sustaining the illusion that endless borrowing can provide the economic development upon which such essential social delights rest. Meanwhile, industrial productivity grew by only 0.4 per cent in 1975. National public indebtedness is some 60 billions of dollars, adding a permanent inflationary factor to the national balance sheet. Canada, we are told, has been the foremost borrower in world money markets in the recent past, and its credit position is reflected in the hard fact that such loans now require rather high interest rates.

Yet, resistance to economic reality remains passionate. When Pierre Elliott Trudeau observed that Canada has perhaps never been a "free enterprise" economy, a fact widely recognized by sane men across the nation, a battery of flatulent dissent arose from public relations mills and economic leaders. Government grows irresistibly and some academics insist that it "produces" in a way similar to basic industry. In a city containing some of the worse slums in North America, Mayor Drapeau confirms that he never considered curtailing the lavish design of the 1976 summer Olympics site, merely because huge cost over-runs were becoming evident. Thus yet another deficit of at least one billion dollars will be fastened upon Canadians, adding again to inflationary pressure that must have substantially reduced standards of living over the recent past, while encouraging the "brain drain" treated in Cuneo's analysis of the migration of Canadian managers to the United States.

To Know Ourselves

It is my hope that the comparative analyses brought together here will contribute *inter alia* to Canadian Studies, and to easing the gap found by the Symons Commission. Although structural-functionalists insist that all social analysis is comparative, it seems equally certain that not all analysis is *cross-national*. Cross-national perspectives sometimes result in one's comparing apples and oranges, but they can be especially fruitful, if only because critical elements of the political and economic structure of two or more national systems can be held constant, providing a foil against which differences among elements within each system can be explained. Such variations include Canada's parliamentary system, which contrasts so sharply with the separation of powers apparatus in the United States. Campbell's essay considers one aspect of such differences: the institutionalization of the Canadian committee system along the lines of the American legislative committee structure.

The behavior of such critical elements as interest groups can profitably be set against variations in political structures, providing a useful diagnosis of precisely where power rests. Here the article by Presthus and Monopoli analyzes various aspects of interaction and influence between bureaucratic elites and interest groups. Again, as shown in the analysis by Pierce and Beck, Canadian political culture seems to have levels of participation very similar to those of the United States. But here again the stronger traditions of secrecy and centralized power that characterize the Canadian parliamentary system can help us understand why some variations exist. Certainly, regarding lobbying and interest group activity, fewer centers of power provide fewer avenues of access, which culminates in less participation, all else being equal.

When the analysis regarding participation is pushed to another level, explanations may be found in differing theories of education in the two systems. The almost pathetic faith that Americans have had in higher education, contrasted with Canada's philosophy of educational scarcity, has generally meant that the potential for political activism is widely-held in the United States. We know that political activism is positively associated with educational achievement: so once again a broad cross-cultural norm, tropism toward education, may provide an explanatory variable of utility in explaining different styles and degrees of participation in the two political systems.

It is for such reasons that the studies reported here often attempt to tie their empirical generalizations to the underlying social, political, and economic cultures of the two societies. My own premise is that any political system is to some substantial extent an epiphenomenon of demographic, class, and economic variables. In Canada, deferential patterns of authority and the tendency to assign considerable autonomy and legitimacy to political elites, have resulted in a system of governance which may be called "elite accommodation". As my article on legislative values and behavior suggests, sharp cleavages of ethnicity, religion, class, and region have fostered a style in which divisive subcultural groups have been kept isolated, while critical issues (e.g., English-French dualism and federal-provincial power struggles) have been reconciled in concert by elites representing such interests. This imperative has given Canadian federalism its distinctive cast, in which Quebec's special position and strong regional identities elsewhere, have meant that the system of national dominance over the states characteristic of the United States is countered in Canada by a relatively balanced power equilibrium between Ottawa and the provinces.

A precariously-integrated political culture, usually attributed to the absence of a revolutionary tradition and weak patterns of political socialization in the schools and elsewhere, provides another cultural incentive for elite accommodation in Canada. In the United States, on the other hand, the early surgical detachment from Britain and the tragic sacrifices of civil war have inspired a pervasive sense of national identity and a relatively more highly-integrated political culture, extending perhaps to all groups except the blacks. In this context, Landes' comparative analysis provides a test of the conventional assumption that political socialization has been somewhat less self-conscious and effective among Canadian, compared with American, youth.

Relatively suggestive cross-national variations exist regarding civil rights, the social context of the constitutional and statutory measures concerning them, and their interpretation by the courts. Monopoli's essay traces the historical evolution of "equality before the law" and "equal protection of the law", with special emphasis upon the role of the judiciary in treating the Canadian Bill of Rights (1960).

The substantive areas covered in the following chapters thus include electoral behavior, legislative and scientific values, socialization among Canadian and American youth, executive behavior in two industrial contexts, namely, branch-plant managers in Canada and Canadian managers who have emigrated to the United States, comparative values among senior bureaucrats, recent institutional changes in the Canadian legislature, and national experiences regarding civil rights and the courts. My aim has been to include essays based upon comparative, quantitative research, despite the difficulty of finding analyses done cross-nationally, using similar concepts and methods. One hopes that the studies presented here will suggest avenues for further research, while providing new information and understanding regarding continuity and diversity in American and Canadian behavior and institutions.

Aspects of Political Culture and Legislative Behavior: United States and Canada

ROBERT PRESTHUS

York University, Toronto, Canada

THE CONCEPT of political culture has been widely used as an independent dimension in explaining variations in political behavior in several political systems (Almond and Verba: 1963).[1] Political culture may be described as the orientations of individuals toward the political system including the extent to which they accept government as legitimate, feel politically efficacious, identify with the "rules of the game" governing the system, and thus participate in politics. Insofar as the structure of political institutions shapes and is shaped by these variables, it seems valid to include such structures as a part of political culture. This approach emphasizes the vital fact that political institutions and behavior tend essentially to be products of the socioeconomic framework in which they exist. It is especially helpful in comparative politics, not only by its attempt to factor out a small number of critical independent variables, but also by demonstrating that significantly different political behaviors may occur in very similar types of political structures. Thus the impact of religious or ethnic cleavages may vary significantly across multi-party parliamentary systems, despite similarities in the scope and intensity of such cleavages (Lijphart: 1970; Rae and Taylor: 1970). Again, the political culture concept is useful in forcing one to confront the issue of the extent and the conditions under which attitudes are associated with behavior (Edinger and Searing: 1967). This problem is especially salient in the analysis of political elites because the pragmatic, bargaining context of policy making seems to increase the probabilities that such continuity will not always occur.

In the following analysis, several highly generalized aspects of American and Canadian political culture will be set down, from which certain hypotheses will be drawn and tested using data from a cross-national study of legislators in the House of Commons and three provinces (N-269) and the House of

---

1 Gabriel Almond and S. Verba define political culture as the "frequency of different kinds of cognitive, affective, and evaluative orientations toward the political system in general, its input and output aspects, and the self as political actor," p. 16.

Representatives and three states (N-249) (Presthus: 1974). It should be emphasized that such variations occur along a continuum and that they must be dealt with here in a mercilessly abbreviated way.

Some Aspects of American and Canadian Political Culture

For our purposes, a particularly salient aspect of the two political cultures is their diverse institutional frames, which shape political recruitment and behavior in the formal system and, at the same time, reflect and reinforce relevant cultural norms, values, and political behavior. The Canadian parliamentary system has such well-known characteristics as a highly powerful Cabinet and senior bureaucracy, reinforced by strong party discipline and a jejune role for backbenchers, a weak legislative committee system, and in recent times, a tendency toward minority Governments which augments party discipline but undercuts somewhat the assumed autonomy and dispatch of Cabinet government. These attributes reflect and reinforce certain social and institutional conditions in Canadian society, including deferential patterns of authority; an organic or corporatist social philosophy; an attending and rather pervasive dependence upon government; and finally, a quasi-participative condition insofar as the citizen's role in politics is concerned (Presthus: 1973).[2] These mutually-reinforcing conditions are associated with certain historical and structural facets of Canadian national development, including the French fact and the British legacy (transmitted initially through the Empire Loyalist migration following the American Revolution) of class, conservatism, and the resultant tendency toward the survival of ascriptive as opposed to achievement-oriented criteria of recruitment into strategic institutional roles. Bureaucratic norms and behavior tend to compete with entrepreneurial ones in most institutional sectors, again reflecting and reinforcing these conditions.

With many exceptions, such conditions are often different from those existing in the United States. Certainly, the respective national ideals of the two societies are often inapposite, even though differences in practice may be less apparent. At the institutional level, the well-known structural variations between the parliamentary and presidential systems are clearly germane. The presidential system disperses power more widely; the role of the individual legislator is more significant; the political system tends to be more "open," in the sense that access is facilitated by the existence of more centers of power and influence.

In the normative sphere, the organic, collectivist drift of Canadian social philosophy contrasts sharply with the highly individualistic, competitive thrust of American social thought and behavior. Respect for authority and hierarchy have not been as characteristic of Americans, nor have government and politics been accorded the legitimacy they have enjoyed in Canada. Canada's "evolutionary" path of national development, contrasted with the American revo-

---

2   For details and documentation regarding Canadian political culture, see ch. 2.

lutionary experience, has nevertheless culminated in a tendency among Canadians to grant only a limited legitimacy to their national government, and to produce a much less well integrated political culture than that of the United States. This fragmentation has of course been aggravated by the highly self-conscious French-Canadian society, which has remained estranged from the dominant English-Canadian presence.

Finally, despite many similar demographic and geographical continuities, the nominally "middle-class" social structure of America, based initially upon the availability of free and fertile land and the rise of an independent farmer class, was not duplicated in Canada. Instead, a rather small middle class has often found its careers in large bureaucratic structures, in banking, commerce, education, and government (Clark: 1968, 234).

Hierarchical norms and deferential patterns of authority in Canada have been augmented by elitist and restrictive attitudes toward higher education which have meant that only a small minority of Canadians have university degrees. The occupational consequences have included an historical dependence upon immigration to supply the skill demands of an industrializing society. By 1970, only 13 per cent of Canadian youth, age 18–24, were in university, and only 6 per cent of all Canadians had a university degree (Dominion Bureau of Statistics, 1971). As late as 1961, in the relatively affluent province of Quebec, only 50 per cent of youth in the 15–19 age group were in school, while 86 per cent of Quebec farmers and farm workers had less than nine years of education (Tremblay and Anderson: 1966, 65). Among the consequences was a tendency for opinion formation and political leadership to be monopolized by a rather small proportion of highly-educated men and women. Symbolic of the persistence of hierarchical, conservative norms is the appointive Senate in the federal political system, comprising almost exclusively men representing finance, industry and law. One result of these conditions is governance by a process of "elite accommodation," whereby divisive ethnic, religious and regional cleavages in Canadian society are reconciled through decisions made at the summit by elites representing the various subcultures and regional interests. More will be said of this condition later.

Certain hypotheses regarding political recruitment and behavior in the two legislative systems are suggested by these conditions. (1) The hierarchical and ascriptive norms of Canadian society, contrasted with the more egalitarian achievement orientation of the American, should result in more recruitment of legislators on a generalist, amateur basis in which previous political experience and length of tenure should be significantly lower than in the American system. (2) The American separation of powers system should be characterized by a higher degree of "openness" in the political system, defined by the extent of penetration by private interest groups. Our data enable us to test whether the attitudes of legislators toward the openness of the system are associated with relevant behavior, i.e., the extent to which they interact with interest group directors. A critical assumption here is that legislators have the initiative in such interactions – they typically determine whether a group agent will gain access.

(3) Canadian legislators should rank higher on an index of "welfare capitalism", defined as a relatively more positive acceptance of government intervention in the economy. Although it is well known that all Western legislators are composed of highly advantaged individuals, one might expect (4) Canadian members to rank *higher* on socioeconomic status and to have experienced *less* class mobility than their American peers. However, since education (along with occupation) is one of the two indexes used here to determine class status, and since educational opportunity and achievement have been greater in the United States, this prediction must be hedged. Given the amateur bases of recruitment, relatively high turnover, and the weak role of backbenchers, we should expect (5) to find Canadian MPs ranking somewhat lower on political efficacy than their American peers. Finally, following the theory of elite accommodation (Presthus: 1973), we assume (6) that the Canadian legislative elite will be more cohesive than its American counterpart regarding certain political values. Some specification will be provided throughout by analyzing the samples cross-nationally by region and by party.

"Amateur" v. "Professional" Conceptions of the Legislative Role

We turn first to any variation in political experience and tenure as a reflection of underlying social norms and institutionalized differences in the legislative role in the presidential and parliamentary systems. One putatively valid test of political experience is the number of party positions (whip, secretary of cabinet, caucus chairmen, chairman of a local party, etc.) which legislators have held and which seem to differentiate amateurs from professionals. When the data are analyzed, however, we find that no significant differences exist between either federal or state and provincial members. In the latter case, only about 10 per cent have held such positions. Among federal samples, a slightly larger proportion of Canadian members have held such positions. Possible explanations include the fact that appointment to party positions in the Canadian system is not typically based upon seniority or political experience. Instead, and partly reflecting high rates of turnover, a novice is apparently equally eligible for leadership posts. Here again, perhaps, the generalist tradition is at work. A related explanation may be that insofar as such party positions are a necessary component of all party and legislative systems, they must be filled, despite the fact that incumbents do not displace equal amounts of influence and power in such roles. In effect, party position may not be a valid test of political amateurism v. professionalism.

Perhaps a better test of the hypothesis is provided by a comparison of tenure. It has often been said that politics in Canada is a temporary interruption in a career devoted to business, industry, law or the professions. In the United States, parties are more bureaucratized, thus "politics as a vocation" is more likely to be the norm. If this is so, we would expect to find dramatic variations in tenure between the two samples. Table 1 tests this hypothesis.

Table 1

Comparative political tenure, United States v. Canadian legislators, in per cent

	United States		Canada	
Tenure*	Federal	State	Federal	Provincial
High	16	3	1	4
Medium	27	22	20	25
Low	57	75	79	70
	(100)	(146)	(142)	(112)

Federal-state: X^2 = 12.96207 with 2 d.f. = .0015
  Gamma = .39066
Federal-provincial: X^2 = 2.49145 with 2 d.f. = .2877
  Gamma = .20156
Federal-federal: X^2 = 22.1854 with 2 d.f. = .0000
  Gamma = .48901
State-provincial: X^2 = .53088 with 2 d.f. = .7669
  Gamma = −.07181
  * "High" = 20 + years; "medium" = 9–19; "low" = 0–8.

Regarding the "amateur" quality of Canadian legislative recruitment, insofar as this is indexed by brief tenure, these data suggest that the hypothesis holds only at the federal level where some 16 times as large a proportion of U.S. legislators rank at the high (20-34 years in office) level. This finding is reinforced by other data indicating that turnover for each federal parliament is about 40 per cent in the Canadian system, compared with 25 per cent in the United States. The striking variation between federal and state legislators indicates, as noted elsewhere, that American state legislators are fully as "amateur" as their Canadian peers. Tenure patterns among state and provincial members are virtually identical with about 70 per cent of each system having served only from 1–8 years.

"Openness" of the Political System

As noted, the parliamentary system has been characterized as less open to penetration by external interests, including groups and individual citizens. Both structural and cultural factors may explain this divergence. Cabinet government centralizes power, restricting the points of access available to exogenous interests, compared with the separation of powers system. Deferential patterns of authority and hierarchy also tend to inhibit access, as rank-and-file citizens may be more prepared to delegate power and influence to political elites. These conditions are reinforced by a tradition of official secrecy in political and bureaucratic affairs[3] (Albinski: 1973, 356).

Comparative attitudes of legislators are measured by an "index of openness." The extent to which attitudes seem to be associated with behavior will

---

3 Henry Albinski, for example, states, " . . . a mania for stamping nearly every internal document in sight with some classified grade remains very much in evidence."

be tested in this specific context by an analysis of the frequency of interaction between legislators and interest group executives. The data on perceived openness indicate a strong cross-national difference as 63 per cent of American state and federal legislators rank high, compared with 42 per cent of the Canadian sample. The items used here (not shown) actually evoke broader issues than group penetration, including philosophical conceptions of the "proper" role of the legislator in determining policy. Perhaps backbenchers are influenced by the fact that, even though they are official members of the system, their own role is mainly confined to mediating the claims of their constituents. Some supporting evidence is available in data showing that the highest single proportion of provincial members (40 per cent) rank their own riding as the *major* focus of their representational role. Federal members, however, have a broader conception of their role, since fully two-thirds rank the nation as their most salient reference.

If Canadian and American legislators vary significantly in openness, as defined here, and if attitudes are associated with behavior, one might assume that their interaction with interest groups would vary similarly. Before testing this hypothesis, it seems useful to present an analysis of cross-national rates of interest group interaction (Table 2).

Table 2

Comparative frequency of interaction with interest groups, United States v. Canadian legislators, in per cent

Interaction*	United States		Canada	
	Federal	State	Federal	Provincial
High	72	94	42	58
Medium	25	5	29	32
Low	3	1	29	11
	(100)	(149)	(141)	(127)

Federal-state: $X^2 = 22.80962$ with 2 d.f. $= .0000$
     Gamma $= -.70847$
Federal-provincial: $X^2 = 14.05877$ with 2 d.f. $= .0000$
     Gamma $= -.33954$
Federal-federal: $X^2 = 31.93622$ with 2 d.f. $= .0000$
     Gamma $= -.59214$
State-provincial: $X^2 = 52.25348$ with 2 d.f. $= .0000$
     Gamma $= -.83343$
 * "High is defined as "frequently" (twice a week); "medium" as "occasionally"; and "low" as "seldom or rarely".

The striking finding here is the significantly higher rates of interaction existing among the American sample, at both federal and state levels. In each system, interaction is also significantly higher at the state-provincial level, but the intensity of interaction is sharply higher among state legislators. This controverts one theory which holds that interest groups focus on those points in the political system where the stakes are highest, at the federal level. Perhaps the finding can be explained in terms of "professionalization," which assumes that group activity flourishes most where legislative resources in staff, information, and research are marginal, as is probably more likely in state-provincial systems. Insofar as the personal resources of legislators tend to be weaker at such levels (see Table 5), this tendency might be reinforced.

Assuming that legislators mainly determine the extent of interest group penetration, by agreeing to see or not to see directors, most of whom contact legislators by formal appointment, our data suggest that behavior may at times reflect attitudes: American legislators who, as a group ranked substantially higher on perceived openness, interact at a significantly higher rate with interest group agents, especially at the state level.

Attitudes Toward Etatisme

As indicated earlier, the Canadian organic or corporatist philosophy of society, in contrast to the American ideal of laissez-faire, suggests that the two legislative elites should rank quite differently on an "economic liberalism" index, defined as a positive valence toward government intervention in the private economy. Here again, it is important to stress that both systems are welfare capitalist regimes and that variations occur along a continuum. Nevertheless, their ideological positions may be quite different, and it can be shown that the United States spends considerably less of GNP on all government

Table 3

Economic liberalism, United States v. Canadian legislators, in per cent

Economic Liberalism*	United States		Canada	
	Federal	State	Federal	Provincial
High	21	25	56	63
Medium	55	53	43	37
Low	24	22	—	—
	(90)	(147)	(722)	(117)

Federal-state: X^2 = .68741 with 2 d.f. = .7091
    Gamma = .03790
Federal-provincial: X^2 = .85141 with 1 d.f. = .3562
    Gamma = −.133863
Federal-federal: X^2 = 45.70766 with 2 d.f. = .0000
    Gamma = .71306
State-provincial: X^2 = 50.44708 with 2 d.f. = .0000
    Gamma = .70495
 * "Economic liberalism" is defined here by the following items: 'That government which governs least governs best' (reverse scored); 'Economic security for every man, woman and child is worth striving for, even if it means socialism'; 'If unemployment is high, the government should spend money to create jobs'; 'A national medicare plan is necessary to ensure that everyone receives adequate health care'; 'More federal aid to education is desirable if we are going to adequately meet present and future educational needs in this country.'

(about 30 per cent v. 44 per cent in the case of Canada) and that a substantially smaller part of her federal budget is allocated to welfare, in the usual connotation of the term. As a result, one would expect Canadian legislators to rank significantly higher on the acceptance of "big government." Table 3 tests the hypothesis.

Here, in line with expectations based upon differences in political culture, we find striking cross-national variations. Both federal and provincial legislators in Canada rank significantly higher than Americans on economic liberalism. This preference reflects the Canadian historical experience in which, from Confederation onward, a close partnership has often existed between government and industry in promoting economic development. The prolificacy of Crown corporations and huge government investments in oil exploration agencies such as Syncrude, launched jointly with private oil companies, suggest the continuity of this tradition.

On the other hand, in the American case the data suggest that attitudes do not necessarily reflect behavior as strongly as one might expect. American legislators rank relatively low on economic liberalism, yet as noted it is surely fair to characterize both the U.S. and Canada as welfare capitalist societies in which vast and sustained government subsidies for private interests are visible in every sector[4] (Branch: 1972, 9).

The data indicate considerable cohesion on this value *within* each system, since differences are not significant between federal and state-provincial legislators. Some observers have characterized Canada as a society in which capitalism and free enterprise are among the dominant values (Porter: 1965, 270). Yet, insofar as legislators may be included among national elites, which does not seem unreasonable, one may question how pervasive or intense this ideal really is. Certainly, an American observer is impressed with the extent to which all institutional sectors in Canada rely on government to cushion the shock of the marketplace. Moreover, the strong "bureaucratic ethos" in Canada suggests that security orientations and noncompetitive behavior might be somewhat more widespread than in the American milieu.

Despite the nation-wide cohesion found in Canada on this dimension, it seems important to check for any differences between major parties, in both systems. Insofar as "big government" provides a major instrument for achieving national political stability through a generous allocation of public largesse among contending social interests, economic liberalism is a crucial variable. Table 4 presents the distribution.

It is immediately apparent that Canadian MPs have a strikingly stronger valence toward positive intervention by government, and despite the free enterprise rhetoric that characterizes some political and most economic elites across the society. Here, as suggested, a pervasive dependence upon government,

---

4   Although it is impossible to determine with any precision, the total annual amount of federal subsidies in the United States has been estimated at over 60 billion (1972).

Table 4

Comparative economic liberalism, United States and Canada, by party, in per cent

Economic liberalism	United States		Canada	
	Democrats	Republicans	Liberals	Conservatives
High	35	9	62	40
Medium	54	52	38	60
Low	11	39	—	—
	(142)	(94)	(97)	(67)

United States: Democrats v. Republicans, $X^2 = 35.75037$ with 2 d.f. $= .0000$
    Gamma $= .64428$
Canada: Liberals v. Conservatives, $X^2 = 6.55355$ with 1 d.f. $= .0105$
    Gamma $= .41218$

anchored in an organic conception of society brought from Britain, is probably a major explanatory variable.

Despite the dramatically higher ranking of both Canadian parties on this dimension, a significant difference exists between them, with Conservatives, not surprisingly, much less inclined to support government intervention in the so-called private economy. Although the nexus is somewhat tenuous, this condition supports the generalization that the Conservative Party is much less inclined to accept the ongoing system of elite accommodation, which requires vigorous government spending to encourage national political integration by placating Quebec, equalizing regional economic disparities, and launching "nation-saving" programs such as the Bicultural-Bilingual Commission, Expo 1967, and more recently, the summer Olympics.

In line with conventional perceptions of policy differences between the major American parties, Republicans are significantly more likely to oppose large-scale government programs in the areas of welfare and education, unless adequate provisions for tax revenue are built directly into such proposals.

There is some indication that *étatisme* is now quite strongly held in Quebec, in the sense that working-class *Québécois* seem to have rejected the traditional assumption of such recent political leaders as Duplessis, Johnson, Lesage, and Bourassa that economic development and higher living standards could be achieved through essentially private means by huge infusions of foreign, largely American, capital. Recent events in Quebec indicate that blue- and white-collar workers are combining in militant industrial and political action in a fashion that may herald the development of a new class politics in Quebec. Although at present this movement seems to be provincial, with no visible attempt to combine forces with working-class elements in English-Canada, it is possible that Quebec may become a model for the emergence of a radical politics in Canada, which would displace its traditional brokerage style. Canadian sociologists have argued persuasively that such a party system is necessary to ensure political dynamism and change in Canada (Porter: 1965; Clement: 1975).

Comparative Socioeconomic Status and Mobility

Although it is well known that parliaments in all Western societies are highly advantaged in occupational and educational terms compared with rank-and-file members of society, it seems useful to differentiate American and Canadian legislators along these dimensions. If political recruitment and party organization in Canada tend to remain less bureaucratized than in the United States, in the sense that politics is less likely to be a "vocation," in Weberian terms, and more likely to exhibit residues of control by "notables," variations in class status and mobility should appear. We have seen that significant differences regarding length of legislative service exist, although variations in party positions held were minimal. From this we would expect to find that Canadian legislators have somewhat higher SES levels, especially since the effect of education, which has not been as fully available in Canada, has been reduced by weighting it $\times 3$, compared with occupation at $\times 7$. Table 5 presents the distribution.

Table 5

Comparative socioeconomic status and mobility, United States v. Canadian legislators, in per cent

Socioeconomic Status*	United States Federal		Canada Federal		United States State		Canada Provincial	
	Respondent/	Father	Respondent/	Father	Respondent/	Father	Respondent/	Father
I	79	24	54	14	31	10	32	11
II	15	17	20	14	38	19	35	13
III	6	37	23	27	30	34	28	36
IV	—	22	4	45	2	38	4	41
	(100)	(83)	(142)	(132)	(149)	(144)	(127)	(121)

Federal-state; respondent: $X^2 = 21.02460$ with 3 d.f. $= .0000$
    Gamma $= -.53444$
Federal-provincial; respondent: $X^2 = 2.83548$ with 4 d.f. $= .5800$
    Gamma $= -.00163$
Federal-federal; fathers: $X^2 = 13.77$ with 5 d.f. $= .0100$
    Gamma $= -.33630$
State-provincial; fathers: $X^2 = 4.20662$ with 4 d.f. $= .3700$
    Gamma $= -.03275$
 * This index is based upon occupation and education, weighted $\times 7$ and $\times 3$, respectively. See A. B. Hollingshead and F. Redlich, *Social Class and Mental Illness* (New York: Wiley, 1958).

Turning first to socioeconomic status among federal legislators, we find a significant variation, with 79 per cent of the American sample ranking at the highest (I) point in the scale, compared with 54 per cent of the Canadian. Since the weight of educational achievement has been reduced, it seems the hypothesis that Canadian party recruitment brings a comparatively greater proportion of highly advantaged individuals into political office at the federal level, must be abandoned. Such recruits are probably more likely to be amateurs but they are not as likely, it seems, to be "notables." Indeed, just over one-quarter of the sample is found in the III and IV categories, which translate roughly into middle- and lower-middle-class strata.

Regarding comparative social mobility among the two federal samples, we speculated that Canadian members would have experienced *less* mobility, under the assumption that they represented, *en bloc*, a more advantaged segment of Canadian society, Here, it seems that social mobility has been marginally different, with the American federal members experiencing somewhat lower rates since, if we combine categories I and II, the ratio between the present class status of American legislators and their fathers is less than that found among the Canadian sample. This finding suggests, then, that any vestige of an hierarchical, deferential style in the formal political system rests upon class differences that are apparently meaningful within the context of Canadian society, but are not objectively based when compared across national boundaries. To some extent, perhaps, as said of the American South, there exists an aristocratic style without an aristocracy (Cash: 1960).

The state-provincial distributions are quite different. None of the variations are significant. Compared with their federal counterparts, the status rankings of legislators are dramatically lower for both samples, as only slightly less than one-third fall in the I category. Not surprisingly, although perhaps less explicably in Canada given the relatively greater influence of provincial governments *vis-à-vis* Ottawa, state-provincial legislators are not as advantaged as the federal group.

Combining each national sample, some broader cross-national generalizations are possible. If one considers only the occupations of both federal and state-provincial members, 46 per cent of Canadians fall in the top "high executive' category, compared with 53 per cent of the American sample. One-quarter fall in the second-level "lesser executives" category, compared with 16 per cent of the American; and another quarter are in the "small business" category, compared with 30 per cent of the United States sample. Another piece of evidence, voluntary group membership, reinforces this variation in occupational status. Since group membership is positively associated with class status, we would expect the Canadian sample to rank somewhat lower on membership. Analyzing membership in 3-or-more voluntary groups, we find only 27 per cent of all Canadian members in this category, compared with over four-fifths of the American sample. This is a remarkably significant difference, especially considering that overall rates of group membership in the two societies are very similar, with about 16 per cent of national samples belonging to 3-or-more groups (Curtis: 1971, 876). Insofar as multiple group memberships are functionally necessary for a professional politician who needs wide exposure to win elections, it may suggest again the amateur character of Canadian MPs.

Despite such variations, it is important to emphasize how distinct both samples are in socioeconomic terms from their respective populations. Whereas legislators, both national and state-provincial cluster around the top 3 categories in the scale, the majority of citizens cluster in the lower sector (not shown). Only in the middle (III) category does any substantial overlapping occur, excepting in the U.S. federal sample.

Comparative Political Efficacy

Political efficacy, defined as the belief that one is capable of influencing political affairs, has been found to be positively and strongly associated with social factors such as education and occupation. Given their advantaged socio-economic status and their formal role in the political system, one would expect North American legislators to rank high on this attitude. At the same time, the influence of national political structure and norms upon political efficacy might be expected to vary cross-nationally. If, as in the parliamentary system, some dissonance exists between personal attributes and role, on the one hand, and the influence potential of the individual member on the other, we may find that political efficacy is not as strongly associated with personal political resources as one might expect. Any tension between the political role and the expectations of those in it may result in reduced feelings of political efficacy. Our data enable us to test this hypothesis, which holds that despite generally impressive personal political resources and formal position, Canadian members will tend to rank lower on efficacy than their American counterparts (Table 6).

Table 6

Comparative political efficacy, United States v. Canadian legislators, in per cent

	United States		Canada	
	Federal	State	Federal	Provincial
Political efficacy*				
High	57	35	28	36
Medium	41	56	53	43
Low	2	9	19	21
	(92)	(147)	(135)	(118)

Federal v. federal: $X^2 = 25.94218$ with 2 d.f. $= .0000$
    Gamma $= .57612$
Federal v. state: $X^2 = 12.18858$ with 2 d.f. $= .0023$
    Gamma $= .41547$
Federal v. provincial: $X^2 = 1.76081$ with 2 d.f. $= .4146$
    Gamma $= .04274$
State v. provincial: $X^2 = 8.33759$ with 2 d.f. $= .0155$
    Gamma $= .16574$
  * "Efficacy" is based upon the following items: 'The old saying, "You can't fight city hall" is still basically true'; 'Most decisions in business and government are made by a small group that pretty well runs things'; 'The average man doesn't have much chance to get ahead today'; 'Anyone in this country who wants to, has a chance to have his say about important issues.' Although the 'average man doesn't have . . .' item is often used as an alienation item, it emerged as part of this index through cluster analysis.

As assumed, the combined effects of parliamentary institutions and resultant norms such as strong party discipline and the "Old Tory theory of leadership" tend to be reflected in significantly lower rankings on political efficacy among Canadian federal members, compared with their American peers. There are, of course, some differences between them in personal political resources, but within each national context, members of both Houses enjoy disproportionate amounts of the kinds of properties that have been found to correlate strongly and positively with efficacy (Verba and Nie: 1972, 95–101).

Some reinforcement for this generalization is provided by an analysis (not shown here) of variations between Cabinet ministers and backbenchers, which indicates that 57 per cent of the former (N-42), compared with only 38 per cent of the latter (N-211) rank high on efficacy (Presthus: 1973, 292). In effect, there is less dissonance between the ministerial role and the incumbent's personal political sources than in the backbencher's case. It seems probable that substantial interparty variation exists among the Canadian federal sample, which may help explain their low ranking. Analyzing Liberal and Conservative members, who provide about four-fifths of the entire sample, the differences on political efficacy are not significant ($X^2 = 15.24325$, 14 d.f. $= .36$), although Liberals rank somewhat higher. The explanation in part thus rests upon the New Democratic Party, fully 80 per cent of whose federal members (N — 17) rank low on this dimension.

When we turn to the state-provincial sample, a similar continuity appears. The explanation is reasonably clear. Although the national samples rank substantially higher at the "medium" level, the global difference (.01) is significant, and unknown factors must produce this condition, which seems to be in line with cross-national differences in influence in the legislative role. Regional variations (not shown) appear in both national contexts. In Canada, Ontario members rank highest, while those in Quebec rank lowest. In the United States, Michigan ranks highest, followed not very closely by legislators in Washington state.

Looking next at cross-national variations by party, Liberals and Conservatives rank very similarly. In the United States, the variation is close to significance (.10) with Republicans expressing higher feelings of efficacy than Democrats. When both national samples are combined, the difference is again close to being significant (.08), with the American sample ranking substantially higher.

Several explanations may be offered for the dramatically lower ranking of state-provincial v. federal legislators. The former, as we have seen, possess fewer political (i.e., occupational and educational) resources than federal members. But this does not explain why the rates are virtually the same between federal and provincial sets. Perhaps party discipline is weaker at the provincial level, which might tend to increase the felt efficacy of backbenchers.

In two of the American states, moreover, Washington and Louisiana, the legislatures are not highly "professionalized."[5] They meet biannually, have

5 The usual criteria of legislative "professionalization" include length of session, pay, research support of legislators, laws passed, etc.

rather limited committee and staff research resources, and to this extent legislative politics is a part-time role with marginal influence. Such conditions
probably reduce feelings of efficacy among them. Meanwhile, in the over-all scale
of political prestige, the state legislative role suffers greatly by comparison with
the federal role. Given the relatively stronger position of provincial government
in Canada and the fact that our sample covers the three most affluent and
populous provinces, Quebec, Ontario and British Columbia, it is perhaps not
unexpected that provincial members rank somewhat higher than federal, and
yet lower than American state legislators.

Cross-National Cohesion and Elite Accommodation

Our final hypothesis suggests that Canadian legislative elites will tend to be
more cohesive than their American counterparts along certain ideological and
property dimensions. The theoretical basis for this judgment rests upon the
assumption that Canada is a "consociational" society, in which strong ethnic,
religious and regional cleavages have been reconciled by a relatively pervasive
level of social and normative cohesion among its political elites. A "relatively
pervasive level of cohesion" means *an absence of statistically signifcant variations
on selected variables among the legislators across party and region*, and especially upon
the "economic liberalism" dimension. Such cohesion has been instrumental in
overcoming fragmentation in Canadian society. An historical policy of distri-
buting governmental largesse among the several provinces has also encouraged
an often uneasy equilibrium among contending groups and regions. This
instrument for attaining democratic stability is called "elite accommodation"
(Presthus: 1973; Lijphart: 1970; Girod: 1964). Explosive subcultures, in effect,
are kept isolated, while conflicts are reconciled at the summit by elites representing the various divergent groups.[6] Such groups must be integrated and
disciplined enough to grant a conclusive mandate for action to their respective
leaders. Their leaders, in turn, must possess a "nation-saving" attitude and the
political skills required to bargain effectively with leaders of other ethnic, geographical and institutional sectors. They must share a consensus regarding the
need to maintain national integration, despite strong centrifugal forces. The
uncertain place of Quebec in Confederation and attending concessions by Ottawa to maintain a national political equilibrium – these provide the most
obvious examples of the problems and solutions characteristic of consociational
societies.

A necessary element in the process of accommodation would seem to be a
relatively high level of social, behavioral and ideological cohesion among

---

6 Other instruments of accommodation exist, of course, including federal-provincial
conferences, proportionality in appointments to the federal civil service and the courts,
royal commissions designed in part as a cathartic, and so on, but my research focus has
been upon the routine "between-elections" shaping of public policy by interaction among
legislators, high bureaucrats, and articulate interest groups, which is the major, continuous
and neglected instrument of elite accommodation.

political elites, including legislators, senior bureaucrats, and the leaders of articulate interest groups who play a critical role in shaping public policy at the provincial and federal levels. Comparing the Canadian legislative elite in this context, it seems that its members share a great deal of social propinquity, as seen earlier when their educational and occupational backgrounds were analyzed (Table 5). There is also impressive evidence that they interact frequently with another segment of the political elite, interest group leaders (Table 2). Regarding the most salient ideological preference, we found that the Canadian *federal* parties, which are a critical instrument of accommodation, do not vary significantly on "economic liberalism." More important, perhaps, no significant variation exists between all federal legislators and powerful senior bureaucrats on the dimension called "openness"; on cognitive perceptions of the tactical role of interest groups; and on the ideological dimension, political liberalism (Presthus: 1973, 317). When compared on political efficacy, the two major parties are again strongly cohesive ($X^2 = 15.27495$ with 15 d.f. $=. 43$). Only when the two parties are compared on political liberalism, defined as a pro-civil liberties-free speech dimension, do we find a significant difference, with Liberal members ranking much higher. Another exception is the sharp disparity between MPs and senior bureaucrats on economic liberalism, where only 15 percent of the latter rank high. Regarding the American sample, elite cohesiveness is generally lower, especially in a cross-regional context (Presthus: 1974, 398, 424).

A final test of cohesion among the Canadian parties is provided by analyzing them on the three ideological dimensions *across* regions to determine whether intra-party cohesion still persists. Beginning with Conservatives, no significant differences appear among the sample on political efficacy nor upon political and economic liberalism. The respective chi-square values are .20, .10, and .91.

Turning to the Liberal Party across regions, political efficacy does not vary significantly, nor do political or economic liberalism, although the latter is fairly close. The chi-square values are .40, .72, and .10, respectively.

In sum, it seems that inter-party cohesion is substantial across behavioral, social class, and ideological dimensions, providing part of the necessary requisites of political stability in a consociational society.

REFERENCES

ALBINSKI, Henry
    1973   *Canadian and Australian Politics in Comparative Perspective.* New York and London: Oxford University Press.
ALMOND, Gabriel and S. VERBA
    1963   *The Civic Culture.* Princeton: Princeton University Press.
BRANCH, Taylor
    1972   "Government Subsidies: Who Gets the 63 Billion." *Washington Monthly*, 4, 9–27.
CASH, W.J.
    1970   *The Mind of the South.* New York: A. Knopf.

CLARK, S. D.
    1968   *The Developing Canadian Community.* Second edition. Toronto: University of Toronto Press.
CLEMENT, Wallace
    1975   *The Canadian Corporate Elite.* Toronto: McClelland & Stewart.
CURTIS, James
    1971   "Voluntary Association Joining: A Cross-National Comparative Note". *American Sociological Review*, 36, October.
EDINGER, Lewis J. and D. SEARING
    1967   "Social Background and Elite Analysis." *American Political Science Review*, 61, 428–45
GIROD, R.
    1964   "Geography of the Swiss Party System," Eric Allardt and E. Littunen, eds., in *Cleavages, Ideologies and Party Systems.* Helsinki: Academic Bookstore.
LIJPHART, Arend
    1970   *The Politics of Accommodation.* Berkeley: University of California Press.
    1969   "Consociational Democracy." *World Politics*, 21, January.
PORTER, John
    1965   *The Vertical Mosaic.* Toronto: University of Toronto Press.
PRESTHUS, Robert
    1973   *Elite Accommodation in Canadian Politics.* New York and London: Cambridge University Press.
    1974   *Elites in the Policy Process.* New York and London: Cambridge University Press.
RAE, Douglas W. and M. TAYLOR
    1970   *The Analysis of Political Cleavages.* New Haven: Yale University Press.
TREMBLAY, M. A. and W. J. ANDERSON
    1966   *Rural Canada in Transition.* Agricultural Research Council of Canada.
VERBA, Sidney and N. NIE
    1972   *Participation in America: Political Democracy and Social Equality.* New York: Harper and Row.

Political Involvement and Party Allegiances in Canada and the United States[1]

NATHANIEL BECK and JOHN C. PIERCE

Washington State University, Pullman, U.S.A.

Introduction

THIS PAPER presents an overview of major public attitudes and behaviors in Canada and the United States. The publics of the two countries are compared in terms of political involvement (participation, efficacy, and trust) and the role of political party allegiances.

Political involvement and party identification are chosen as the bases for comparison for several reasons. First, they are central to any description of the basic orientations of citizens in a polity. The extent to which individuals participate in a country's politics is one important indicator of that public's role in decisions which affect them. Citizens' feelings that their participation has some impact on policy (a sense of efficacy) and that government is worthy of support and confidence (political trust) have important implications for the stability and integration of the political system. Political parties can be important links between the public and government; they compete for the right to govern, they offer policy cues to the public, and they are objects of personal political allegiance. The extent to which parties are stable foci of political allegiance for the public has considerable potential for impact on the stability of a party system and the continuity in electoral outcomes (Converse and Dupeux 1966).

Second, the questions of political involvement and party allegiances and their differences among the two countries are the objects of considerable study, particularly in that literature taking Canada as its focus. Compared to Americans, for example, Canadians have been described as "quasi-participative" and less politically efficacious (Presthus 1974: 6, 34). Also, there currently exists disagreement as to the relative importance of party identification when compared to the United States (Sniderman, *et al.* 1974; Jenson 1975; Jacek 1975). While we do not examine exhaustively each of these problems, our findings do serve to alter some of the previous conclusions about differences between the publics of the two countries.

---

1   The authors wish to acknowledge the assistance of Kathleen M. Beatty.

Third, most present comparisons of the Canadian and American publics are based on survey data from the 1950's and 1960's, or are based in local or regional studies in Canada. In addition to some of the earlier nationwide studies, this paper employs data from the 1970's in each country. Some of the alterations in conclusions noted above stem from the ability to employ data sources both more recent and more comparable in content and time. However, just as the available data provide some opportunities for more direct comparisons, they also impose some limitations. The concerns examined in this paper obviously are not the only ones which are important in comparing the citizens of the two countries. They are, however, the major topics which appear in the data in sufficient substance to allow for comparative analysis.

The general content of the political structures and cultures of the two countries have been described in other sources (Presthus 1974; Porter 1956; Alford 1963) and in the other contributions to this symposium. The two cultures obviously share a great deal. Alford, for example, argues that "since the Anglo-American countries share a common culture, a comparative study of the association of class and vote is not complicated by widely varying political values and traditions" (1967: 72). At the same time, there is much which distinguishes the two systems. Canada's parliamentary form of government, multiparty system, and regional, cultural and language divisions are widely acknowledged as distinct from the United States. Rather than comment in detail on the comparable and distinct characteristics of the two countries, we will introduce them when they are most germane to the analysis and explanation of the data.

The American data for this analysis came from the 1964, 1968, and 1972 election studies of the Center for Political Studies of the Institute for Social Research at the University of Michigan.[2] The Canadian data are derived from the 1965 and 1968 national election studies headed by John Meisel, and the 1974 national election study conducted by Clarke, Jenson, Leduc, and Pammett.

---

2   The 1964, 1968, and 1972 American data utilized in the paper were made available by the Inter-University Consortium for Political Research. The data were originally collected by the Center for Political Studies of the Institute for Social Research, the University of Michigan. Neither the original collectors of the data nor the consortium bear any responsibility for the analyses or interpretations presented here.

3   The 1965 and 1968 Canadian data were made available by the Inter-University Consortium for Political Research. The 1965 data were collected by John Meisel, Philip Converse, Maurice Pinard, Peter Regenstreif and Mildred Schwartz. The 1968 study was headed by John Meisel. Neither the original collectors nor the Consortium bear any responsibility for the analyses or interpretations presented here. The 1974 Canadian National Election Study was made available by the York University Data Archive. The Data were originally collected by Harold Clarke, Jane Jenson, Lawrence Leduc and Jon Pammett. Neither the Archive nor the original collectors of the data bear any responsibility for the analyses or interpretation presented here.

Political Involvement

Based on the 1965 Canadian election study, Rick Van Loon concluded that:

> The Canadian political culture, both French and English, and without regard for most of the major lines of cleavage, may be described by the term "spectator-participant." . . . relative to most democratic countries, Canadians do have a high level of political participation; only in the United States is it considerably higher (1970: 396).

Robert Presthus, as previously noted, characterized the Canadian political culture as "quasi-participative" (1974: 34), and presented evidence which "suggests that an average of about 60 per cent of Canadian citizens rank 'low' on political efficacy, compared with some 50 per cent of Americans" (1974: 359). These conclusions, as well as those by other writers (Schwartz, 1974), suggest that Canadian and American patterns of political involvement should differ. In particular, based on past studies one would expect to find greater participation and greater levels of political efficacy in the United States.

The overall comparison of the level of participation in the two countries is presented in Table 1. The complete American data are available for all three elections, while the comparable Canadian results are found only in the 1974 study. These data for the most recent elections do not support the contention that the Canadians are less active politically than are the Americans. Canadians are slightly more likely than Americans to "often" follow the election in newspapers, they report higher rates of voting, they are more likely to have attended a political rally or meeting, they are more likely to have engaged in party work, and they are as likely to have engaged in attempts to convince others about politics.

Table 1

Reported Political Participation in the United States and Canada*

Political Activity	United States			Canada		
	1972	1968	1964	1974	1968	1965
Read Newspapers often	37%	49%	47%	43%	—	—
Tried to Convince Others	32%	32%	31%	23–34%**	—	23%
Attended Rally, Meeting	9%	9%	9%	19–32%**	—	15%
Did Party Work	5%	5%	5%	11–17%**	—	5%
Displayed Sticker	14%	15%	16%	16–21%**	—	—
Voted	75%	76%	78%	85%	86%	86%

*   The entry in each cell is the percentage of the sample in that year reporting that they engaged in that political activity.

** On these activities the questions in the two countries were asked differently. In the Canadian study, individuals were given the opportunity to indicate the *frequency* with which they participated in the activity, while in the American studies the response alternatives were simply yes or no. The first figure in the Canadian percentages excludes respondents saying they "seldom" or "never" participated in the activity. The second figure excludes only those individuals who said they "never" participated in the activity.

Do these country-wide patterns hold up when taking other variables into account? Table 2 presents a comparison of voting rates and campaign activities in Canada (1974) and the United States (1972) controlling for education in both countries and for region and language in Canada. Philip Converse has placed education at the head of his list of priority variables in comparative research (1974: 730). Education is thought to have special significance in explaining differences in Canadian and American political behavior. Presthus notes a wide disparity in the level of education in Canada and the United States and suggests that "generally lower educational levels in Canada probably account for part of (the) difference" in participation levels found in earlier studies (1974: 3). Welch has found education to have a substantial impact on Canadian voting and campaigning (1975: 558) and Van Loon has observed its relationship to voting (1970: 385–386). The impact of education on participation in the United States also has been widely shown (Milbrath 1965; Verba and Nie 1972). For bases of comparison, each country's respondents have been grouped into three levels of education: low (0–8 years in the U.S. and 0–9 in Canada), medium (9–12 in the U.S. and 10–13 in Canada), and high (more than 12 years in the U.S. and more than 13 years in Canada).[4] Likewise, the impact of regionalism and language differences in Canada has

Table 2
Political Participation in Canada (1974) and the United States (1972), with Controls*

		Political Activity			
		Voting		Campaigning	
		Canada	U.S.	Canada	U.S.
Education**	Overall	85%	75%	22%	11%
Low		80%	58%	19%	4%
Medium		87%	70%	23%	10%
High		87%	87%	25%	19%
Region					
Maritimes		85%		36%	
Quebec		81%		26%	
Ontario		88%		17%	
Prairies		83%		21%	
British Columbia		87%		14%	
Language					
English		87%		20%	
French		81%		26%	

*   The entry under "campaigning" includes the percentages reporting having participated in campaign or party work or having attended a political meeting.
** The education groupings are reported in the text.

4   The differences in the grouping of education levels is due to differences in the two countries' educational systems. For a discussion of the problems in classifying education in Canada, see Schwartz (1974: 590).

received wide comment (Van Loon 1970: 387–388; Simeon and Elkins 1974; and, Schwartz 1974: 571–574). As Simeon and Elkins argue, "Canadian politics is regional politics . . ." (1974: 397). Thus, for Canada only, we also have introduced controls for region and language.[5]

In differentiating among levels of voting turnout, education is substantially more important in the United States than it is in Canada. At the highest level of education there is no difference in reported rates of voting. However, at the lowest level of education substantial differences appear. In Canada, the voting turnout difference between the lowest and highest education groups is only 7 per cent, while the American difference is 29 per cent. Similar patterns appear when the level of campaign activity is controlled by education. Differences in campaigning narrow at the highest level of education; however, unlike voting, at all education levels Canadian campaign participation exceeds that of the Americans.

The control for region in Canada has very little impact on voting turnout. Although voting turnout in Quebec is slightly lower than in the other provinces, it still surpasses the American overall figure. The control for region does have a substantial impact on participation in campaign activities. Reported campaign participation is markedly higher in the Maritimes provinces than in Ontario and British Columbia. The overall figure for the United States approaches the campaign level of only the least active of the Canadian provinces. Language differences in participation are relatively small in Canada. English speaking Canadians are slightly more likely to participate in voting than Canadians who speak French, while the French speaking Canadians are slightly more likely to participate in campaign activities.

These 1974 results on the impact of region and language in Canada are in general agreement with those reported in Simeon and Elkin's study of regional political culture in Canada which employed 1965 data (1974). Simeon and Elkins found that "French Canadians and Maritimers rank at least as high as the others, despite a much more pervasive cynicism about politics and a sense that there is little the individual can do to influence government" (1974: 414). It is to the questions of efficacy and political trust that the paper now turns.

Political efficacy and political trust are two of the most crucial elements of a country's political culture (Devine 1974). Political efficacy is the individual's feeling that political participation has some impact on political outcomes. Political trust is the extent to which the individual feels that government is competent, honest and worthy of support. Together, they represent the public's perceptions of the system's responsiveness and the acceptability of its outputs. A sense of political efficacy has been shown to be productive of political participation. People who feel more efficacious are more likely to participate in

---

5 Unlike Canada, the United States exhibits no consistent regional differences unexplained by the group compositions of the regions (Erikson and Luttbeg 1973: 199–202). No regional differences in the United States were found in the concerns of this study. Thus, we have omitted regional controls for the United States.

politics, to acquire political information, and to discuss political issues (Lane 1959: 152; Almond and Verba 1963: 257; Dahl 1961: 286; Campbell, *et al.* 1960: 105). The importance of political trust is indicated by Arthur Miller:

> A democratic political system cannot survive for long without the support of a majority of its citizens. When such support wanes, underlying discontent is the necessary result, and the potential for revolutionary alteration of the political and social system is enhanced (1974: 951).

Efficacy and trust, therefore, are important bases for comparing the publics of two countries. /

In both Canada and the United States, political efficacy has been argued to be related to the individual's level of education. The lower sense of efficacy previously discovered among Canadians has been linked to the overall lower levels of education in that country. Within Canada, however, significant variations in political efficacy have been discovered along dimensions other than education. In Canada, political efficacy varies among the provinces, differences which are not eliminated by controls for class, education, or party affiliation (Simeon and Elkins 1974). Indeed, the effect of the additional controls varied among the provinces, pointing up the regional differences. Thus, in addition to comparing the levels of efficacy and trust in the two countries, the following analysis also controls for education in both countries and for region in Canada.

/ The comparison of political efficacy and political trust in the two countries is based on responses to items with the following content. /

Political Efficacy

1. "Generally, those elected to parliament (congress) soon lose touch with the people."
2. "Sometimes, politics and government seem so complicated that a person like me can't really understand what's going on."
3. "I don't think that the government cares much what people like me think."
4. "People like me don't have any say about what the government does."

Political Trust

1. "Do you think that people in government waste a lot of the money we pay in taxes, waste some if it, or don't waste very much of it?"
2. "How much of the time do you think you can trust the government in Washington (Ottawa) to do what is right?"
3. "Would you say the government is pretty much run by a few big interests looking out for themselves or that it is run for the benefit of all of the people?"
4. "Do you feel that almost all of the people running the government are smart people who know what they are doing, or do you think that quite a lot of them don't seem to know what they are doing?"
5. "Do you think that quite a few of the people running the government are a little crooked, not very many are, or do you think hardly any of them are crooked at all?"

The distributions of the samples in the two countries at the different time periods are shown in Table 3. The entries are the percentage giving the *efficacious* response to the efficacy questions, and the *cynical* response to the political trust questions.

Table 3

Political Efficacy and Trust in Canada and the United States*

Political Efficacy (% Efficacious)

	Canada			United States		
	1974	1968	1965	1972	1968	1964
Leaders Soon Lose Touch	35%	39%	40%	32%	44%	—
Government Complicated	35%	28%	29%	29%	28%	32%
Government Doesn't Care	42%	54%	52%	50%	56%	63%
People Like Me Have No Say	45%	51%	49%	64%	59%	70%

Political Trust (% Cynical)

	Canada		United States		
	1968	1965	1972	1968	1964
Government Wastes Money	46%	38%	68%	61%	48%
People in Government Crooked	27%	27%	38%	20%	30%
Government Run By Big Interests	90%	83%	59%	44%	30%
People in Government Smart	49%	57%	42%	39%	28%
Trust Government to do Right	39%	39%	46%	37%	22%
Average	50%	49%	51%	40%	32%

* For the political efficacy questions, the entry in each cell is the percent giving an *efficacious* response. For the political trust questions, the entry in each cell is the percent giving a cynical response. No political trust questions were asked in the 1974 Canadian study.

The citizens in the two countries are roughly similar on the questions of whether politics is too complicated to understand and whether leaders lose touch once they are elected. Differences do appear on the two questions which more directly tap political responsiveness. Americans are slightly less likely to say that government officials don't care about "what people like me think," and they are substantially less likely to agree that "people like me don't have any say about what the government does." These figures support earlier findings only partially. That is, the Americans' greater efficacy is not uniform across all of the questions. Rather, it can be traced primarily to one of the items. But, it is this item, of all of those in the efficacy group, which most directly confronts the meaning of the concept of efficacy – the individual's perception of an ability to impact government.

Unfortunately, the opportunity to compare political trust in the two countries is attenuated somewhat by the availability of data. The questions on political trust were not asked in the 1974 Canadian study. This would be of little trouble, except that the American figures show rather substantial change in the period between 1968 and 1972 – there is an increase in cynicism in the American public in that period. We cannot know if similar changes in Canada occurred after 1968. Given this limitation, the differences between the two countries are mixed. Americans are substantially more likely than the Canadians to think that people in government waste a lot of money, slightly less likely to trust the national government to do what is right, and slightly more likely to think that the people in government are crooked. On the other hand, Canadians are far more likely to think that government is run by big interests rather than for the benefit of all of the people. At the same time, however, the American figures on that question evidence a big increase in cynicism between 1968 and 1972. The *average* level of cynicism is about the same in the two countries, but the cynicism seems to come from different perceptions of the operation of the government. The Americans are critical of the efficiency with which the government is operated. The Canadians reject the notion of the government responding to the interests of all of the people. This difference in cynicism mirrors the differences in perceptions of governmental responsiveness found in the political efficacy questions.

Table 4 presents the responses on some of the efficacy items and an average political cynicism score for the two countries, controlling for level of education in both countries and region and language in Canada. For the efficacy items the entry in the table is the proportion giving the *efficacious* response; for political cynicism, the score is the average number of cynical responses. The govern-

Table 4

Political Efficacy and Cynicism in Canada and the United States, Controlling for Education, Region, and Language: 1968*

Education	Government Too Complicated		Government Responsiveness		Political Cynicism Index	
	Canada	U.S.	Canada	U.S.	Canada	U.S.
Low	.18	.09	.29	.33	2.7	2.3
Medium	.36	.25	.50	.54	2.3	1.9
High	.62	.50	.57	.75	2.0	1.9
Region						
Maritimes	.28		.43		3.0	
Quebec	.34		.32		2.4	
Ontario	.37		.50		2.4	
Prairies	.22		.42		2.4	
British Columbia	.44		.60		2.2	
Language						
English	.34		.49		2.4	
French	.33		.31		2.5	

*   For the two efficacy scores, the entry in the cell is the proportion giving the efficacious response. The government responsiveness scores are the result of summing the proportion efficacious on the item of the public having no say in government and the item saying that public officials do not care what the people think, and dividing by two. The cynicism score is the average number of cynical responses given by individuals in that control category.

ment responsiveness scores are an average of the items on whether the government cares what the people think and whether the public has any say in government.

In both the United States and Canada there are very large differences among education groups in the proportion saying that the government is too complicated to understand. Yet, at each level of education the Canadians are more likely to give the efficacious response – to say that government is *not* too complicated to understand. Likewise, on the government responsiveness index education affects the level of efficacy in both countries. However, only at the high education level do substantial differences appear between the two countries. The highly educated Canadians are much less likely than their American counterparts to view their government as responsive. Thus, the overall differences in efficacy between the countries cannot be explained by differences in the level of education. In fact, it is the most highly educated in each country which account for the overall difference.

A contrary pattern appears on the index of political cynicism. At the highest education level, there is little difference in the level of cynicism in the two countries. However, at the lower education levels the Canadians exhibit greater cynicism than do the Americans.

The regional differences generally correspond to those observed by Simeon and Elkins (1974). The Maritimes and Prairie provinces are most likely to see government as too complicated to understand, while Quebec residents are least likely to see the government as responsive to the public. Respondents from British Columbia show up as the most efficacious on both of the measures. The Maritimes exhibit the greatest level of cynicism while British Columbia shows the greatest trust in the national government. French speaking Canadians are much less likely to view the government as responsive, a finding which corresponds to the observed regional differences.

Controlling for education on the responses to the individual trust items has different effects on different items. Perhaps the most significant difference between the citizens in the two countries comes in the perception of whether the government is run for the general public or for the big interests. Very large differences exist between the two countries at all education levels (data not shown here), with the Canadians the more cynical. Education has very little impact on that perception in Canada, with 89 percent of the high education group and 87 percent of the low education group agreeing that the big interests run the country. On the other hand, in the United States, education has a more substantial impact. Only 37 percent of the high education group perceives big interests as dominant, while 52 percent of the low education group agrees with that perspective.

In summary, it appears from the most recent data available that the characterization of the Canadian electorate as less participative than the American electorate no longer is accurate. Canadians may indeed be "quasi-participative" (to use Presthus' term) or spectator oriented (as described by Van Loon), but that is a status they share with Americans. The overall lower level of efficacy in Canada stems from the Canadians' perceptions of an absence of government responsiveness, not from seeing the government as too complex or from perceptions of the leaders losing touch. The Canadians' overall lower trust in government stems primarily from their greater perception that government is run for the benefit of big interests rather than for the benefit of the public. Canadians are less likely than Americans to see their government as wasteful.

The differences between the two countries are attenuated only partially by controlling for the respondents' level of education; in many instances the country level differences remain. Within the Canadian sample, people from the Prairies and Maritimes provinces are more likely to see government as too complicated, but people from Quebec are less likely to see the government as responsive. The British Columbians are both the most efficacious and the most trustful of government. This supports the Simeon and Elkins (1974) conclusion that regional political cultures exist in Canada. Indeed, variations among regions in Canada approach the size of the differences between Canada and the United States.

Party Allegiances

Substantial disagreement presently exists as to the nature, source, and stability of party identification in the Canadian electorate. Unlike their American counterparts, Canadians' party loyalties have been pictured as volatile, transient, and lacking in independent influence on the individual's vote. This view of the Canadian voter has been labeled the "textbook theory" by Sniderman, et al. (1974). Sniderman and his colleagues reject the textbook theory. In a recent study they have concluded that:

> ... the vote in Canada is no more volatile than the vote in the United States or United Kingdom. Similarly, most Canadians think of themselves as supporters of a particular party, just as most Americans and most Britons do. Equally important, this sense of identification with a party tends to reflect a long-term commitment, not a passing preference (1974: 285–286).

Jane Jenson has challenged the Sniderman conclusions. She argues that much of the textbook theory is indeed correct:

> Canadians do alter their party ties more frequently and more easily than do voters elsewhere; they do abandon the loyalties of their fathers; and they do search out new parties (1975: 553).

There is little disagreement about the willingness of Canadians to identify with a political party. Both sides of the argument admit that Canadians are quite ready to profess allegiance to a party. The question is whether party identification reflects a long-term psychological commitment. The meaning of party identification in the Canadian context has been dealt with in terms of the stability of an individual's party identification through time, the stability of party identification through generations within families, and the stability of the individual's vote preference through time. This section of the paper examines those questions in the light of more recent data. It also introduces several additional concerns, with particular focus on the impact of the strength of party identification on other attitudes and behaviors.

The role of party identification in a country is important because of its implications for long-term stability or volatility in electoral politics. Party identification has been central to the major studies of democratic electorates (e.g., Campbell, *et al.* 1960). Allegiance to a party has been argued to develop quite early in life, at least among Americans (Greenstein 1965), to act as a core orientation for the organization of other political beliefs (Pomper 1972), and to be an important and independent influence on voting behavior (Flanigan and Zingale 1975). Party identification has received the greatest attention in the study of the American electorate, but variations in the role of party identification have been demonstrated in the study of other electorates (Converse and Dupeux 1966; Campbell and Valen 1966; Butler and Stokes 1969; Alford 1963; Rose 1974).

What is it about the Canadian political system that *might* generate a different role for party identification? A set of interrelated answers are available.[6] It has been argued that the differences among the two major parties in Canada (the Liberals and the Progressive Conservatives) are more blurred than the differences among the two major parties in the United States (Scarrow 1965). Schwartz suggests that the diversity of interests (region, class, language, religion etc.) represented *within* each party makes any comprehensive distinction unlikely (1974: 556). This blurring, then, would provide an opportunity for (a) the expression of regional points of view in minor parties, (b) a relatively effortless movement of both the individual's vote and allegiance between the two major parties, based on relatively transient forces such as candidate personality or short-term but salient issues, (c) less transmission of party identification between generations in a family, and (d) less impact of variations in the strength of the individual's party identification itself. Yet, there is not complete consensus that the parties' differences are blurred, at least in the perceptions of the Canadian electorate. Elkins, for example, has found that there is general agreement in the electorate on the ordering of the three central parties, moving from the NDP on the left, to the Liberals, and then to the Progressive Conservatives on the right (1974: 510). Much greater confusion exists, however, when the peripheral parties are located in such a party space. We now turn to an analysis of some data which reflect on the disagreement as to the relative role of party allegiances in the two countries.

Table 5 presents the baseline information comparing the stability of party identification and voting behavior in the two countries. The Canadians are more likely to express an identification with a political party. In 1974 for

---

6 Much has been written about the nature of the party systems in the two countries, although not usually within the context of direct comparisons. For one lucid discussion of the Canadian party system the reader is referred to Schwartz (1974).

Table 5
The Stability of Party Identification and Voting Behavior in Canada and the United States

	Canada			United States		
	1974	*1968*	*1965*	*1972*	*1968*	*1964*
Percent Independents	20%	16%	17%	37%	30%	24%
Percent Strong Identifiers	66%	69%	67%	26%	29%	38%
Partisan Change*	34%	37%	38%	21%	25%	22%
Intergenerational Change**	48%	—	46%	43%	—	—
Vote Change***	22%	—	—	27%	—	—

  *   The partisan change figure is the percent presently having a party identification who report having a different party identification at some other time.

 **   The intergenerational change figure is the percent having a party identification different from the party identification of their father, given that the father had an identification.

***   The vote change figure is the percent reporting having voted for different parties in the last two elections.

example, only 20 percent of the Canadians classify themselves as "independent" compared to 37 percent of the Americans. At the same time, however, the Canadian voter is more likely than his American counterpart to have changed party identification (34 percent for the Canadians compared to 21 percent for the Americans). This suggests greater instability in party identification within generations in Canada and with that, apparently greater potential for parties to capture the followings of their competitors.

The stability of party systems has been linked to the strength of the socialization of party identification (Converse and Dupeux 1966). One source of stability is argued to be the degree to which party identification has been transmitted across generations within families. If the family is successful in transmitting party identification to its offspring, the long range distribution of party preferences in the system will be more stable and the electoral support for the parties will be more consistent. As the results in Table 5 show, the Canadians also are more likely to have a party identification different from that of their fathers. In 1974, the intergenerational change figure for Canada is 48 percent, while for 1972 in the United States it is 43 percent. The gap between the two countries is narrowing from that reported by Jenson, who relied on figures from the more stable fifties in which only 20 percent of the Americans switched from their father's party (1975: 551). Does this suggest that Jenson is wrong in characterizing the Canadians' party choices as less stable than those in the United States? Only in a minor sense. The differences between the two countries *are* less than thought, but not because the Canadian electorate is any more stable across generations than characterized. Rather, the American electorate is itself becoming more volatile. This is reinforced by comparing the stability in vote choice between the last two national elections in each country. The Canadian vote volatility (1972–1974) actually is less than the American vote volatility (1968–1972), due primarily to the influence of George Wallace in the 1968 American election.

In Canada, the greater instability is primarily the result of the decline of the Progressive Conservative party (only 60 percent of the old PC identifiers have remained in the party) and shifts from the NDP and Social Credit parties to the Liberal party. Stability is higher among Canadian strong identifiers, especially for those identifying with the Liberal party. Even the Progressive Conservative party does well among its English speaking strong identifiers. This suggests that variations in the strength of party identification have some behavioral consequence in Canada. Nevertheless, when comparing across countries, the stability of party identification is considerably higher among the American strong identifiers than among the Canadian strong identifiers. In the United States, 87 percent of the strong identifiers have remained stable, while the comparable figure for the Canadian strong identifiers is 74 percent. Indeed, the stability of party identification among the Canadian strong identifiers is comparable to that of the weak identifiers in the United States (also 74 percent). In Canada, the stability figures for the "fairly strong" identifiers drops to 62 percent, and to 61 percent for the "not very strong" identifiers.[7]

Table 6

Intergenerational Transmission of Party Identification in Canada and the United States*

| Canada (1974) | Father's Party | Respondent's Party | | | | | |
		LIB	PC	NDP	SC	Total	N
	Liberal	77%	12	8	3	100%	(565)
	Progressive Conservative	41%	47	9	2	99%	(443)
United States (1972)	Father's Party	Respondent's Party					
		Republican		Democrat		Total	N
	Republican	80%		20		100%	(452)
	Democrat	16%		84		100%	(904)

*   This table includes only those respondents whose fathers had a party identification and who themselves identify with a political party.

The intergenerational stability of party identification (from father to respondent) in the United States and Canada is shown in Table 6. This analysis controls for the party identification of the father and includes only those respondents whose father had a party identification and who themselves identify with a political party. The source of the intergenerational instability in Canadian party identification has been the decline of the Progressive Conservative party. Almost as many children of the PC fathers have moved to the Liberal party as have remained in the PC party. Indeed, the Liberal party's continuity is almost as great as that for the two American parties. The intergenerational decline in identification within the Progressive Conservative party occurs most strikingly among French speaking Canadians. Only 13 percent of the French

---

7   These data are not displayed in a table.

speaking Canadians whose fathers identified with the PC presently identify with the PC.

We now turn to some considerations of the impact of party identification in the two countries. One element of the nature of partisan allegiances in a country is the degree to which supporters of a party evaluate their own party more favorably than they evaluate opposition parties. The magnitude of the differences between the evaluation of one's own party and the evaluation of opposition parties may reflect the intensity of partisan conflict in the country. Competing expectations come from the previously presented patterns. The greater movement from one party to another in Canada might suggest that Canadians evaluate all of their political parties favorably, particularly if that movement does not, as some suggest, reflect true *partisan* attitudes. On the other hand, that the Canadians are more likely to strongly identify with the party of their choice indicates greater intensity of commitment to that party and greater rejection of other parties. One measure of support for all parties in the two systems is available for both the Canadian and the American data. This measure is the "fever thermometer." The respondent is asked to evaluate the object of the attitude (in this case each of the parties in the respective systems) on a scale from zero – extremely negative – to one hundred – very positive. Table 7 presents the average ratings given each of the parties in the United States and Canada, controlling for the party identification of the respondent.

Table 7
Fever Thermometer Ratings of the Political Parties in Canada and the United States,
*Controlling for Party Identification**

Canada	Party	Political Party			
	Identification	LIB	PC	NDP	SC
	LIB	.77	.47	.40	.36
	PC	.45	.74	.38	.37
	NDP	.45	.42	.78	.32
	SC	.46	.44	.35	.79
	IND	.54	.51	.41	.36
United States	Party	Political Party			
	Identification	Democrat		Republican	
	Democrat	.75		.61	
	Republican	.56		.74	
	Independent	.62		.58	

*   The fever thermometer is an evaluation of the attitude object on a scale from zero to one hundred, where zero is extremely negative and 100 is extremely positive. The entry in each cell is the average evaluation for a political party by the respective group of party identifiers.

/ In both Canada and the United States, party identifiers evaluate their own party at about the same level. In the United States, the average ratings are .74 and .75, while in Canada they range from .74 to .79. The two countries' citizens differ substantially, however, in the evaluation of the opposition parties. In the United States, Republicans and Democrats both evaluate their counterparts rather favorably, with respective scores of .56 and .61. On the other hand, the Canadian party identifiers are substantially more negative toward parties other than their own, with average ratings ranging from .32 to .46. The least favorable ratings in Canada appear when the followers of the two minor parties evaluate each other's parties. The NDP identifiers rate the Social Credit party on the average of .32, while the Social Credit identifiers give the NDP an average rating of .35. Moreover, the American independents are relatively favorable toward both parties (.62 and .58), while the Canadian independents rate the parties with averages from .36 to .54. Thus, Canadian and American identifiers are similar in the support they give their own parties, but the Canadians are substantially less favorable to parties other than their own, particularly when those other parties are the minor parties.

An additional test of the importance and meaning of party identification in a system is the relationship of variations in the *strength* of that identification to other kinds of attitudes and behavior. For example, if party identification and variations in the strength of that identification are meaningful concepts, strong identifiers should be more likely to participate in political activities, to see differences among the parties and should be more likely to perceive their own party as closest to themselves. We examine those expectations on the basis of the 1972 election study in the United States and the 1974 Canadian election study. This comparison presents problems because of different codings in the two countries. The measure of strength of party identification in the American study allows for three categories: strong identifiers, weak identifiers, and independents. However, the Canadian study provides four groups: very strong identifiers, fairly strong identifiers, not very strong identifiers and independents. Thus, direct comparison of the two countries requires some interpolation and a focus on the differences among the extremes of the two measures.

Generally, variations in the strength of party identification are as strongly related to the level of political activity in Canada as in the United States, and in some cases the relationship is even stronger in Canada.[8] While at all levels of party identification the Canadians are more likely to participate in political campaigns, the difference in the extremes also is larger in Canada. In the United States, 16 percent of the strong identifiers campaign, while 10 percent of the weak identifiers campaign. In Canada, however, 28 percent of the very strong identifiers campaign but only 14 percent of the not very strong identifiers do so. A similar patterns obtains for political media usage and voting turnout. Fifty-two percent of the strong identifying Americans rank high on media usage, while only 39 percent of the weak identifiers are high. In Canada, however, 68 percent of the very strong identifiers are high on media usage, while only 43 percent of the not very strong identifiers are high users of the media. Eighty-three percent of the American strong identifiers vote, while 74 percent of the

---

8 These results are not presented in a table.

weak identifiers report voting. In Canada, 91 percent of the very strong identifiers vote, while 81 percent of the not very strong identifiers vote. On interest in the campaign the figures are about equal in the two countries. In the United States, 49 percent of the strong identifiers express high levels of interest, but only 25 percent of the weak identifiers do so. In Canada, the figures are 45 percent for the very strong identifiers, and 25 percent for the not very strong identifiers.

The relationship of the strength of party identification to political participation, then, is the same in the two countries. In both countries, as the strength of identification increases, the behavioral and psychological (interest) involvement of the individual in politics increases. This suggests a similarity in the concept of party identification in the two countries.

Respondents in the two countries were asked to indicate whether there exists any differences among the parties on the issue they consider the most important and which party took the best position on that issue. Again the concern is whether the strength of party identification makes any difference. If party identification is a valid concept then differences in the strength of identification should be related to the perception of the differences in the parties themselves. Strong party identifiers should be more likely to see differences among the parties and they should be more likely to see their own party as having the best position on the relevant issue. The results are shown in Table 8.

Table 8
*Strength of Party Identification and Perceptions of Party Issue Differences**

Percent Seeing Party Difference On Most Important Issue	Canada (1974)	United States (1972)
Identification		
Very Strong	90%	
Strong		61%
Fairly Strong	83%	
Weak, Not Very Strong	72%	47%
Independent	59%	37%
Percent Seeing Own Party As Best on Most Important Issue		
Identification		
Very Strong	82%	
Strong		53%
Fairly Strong	68%	
Weak, Not Very Strong	53%	34%

* The entry in each cell is the percent of the respondents who (a) see a party difference on the issue they perceive as the most important, and (b) see their own party as having the best position on that most important issue.

Once more distinct differences appear between the countries and among the levels of party identification. At all levels of party identification the Canadians are more likely to perceive differences among the parties on the issue the respondent holds to be most important. The Canadians also are more likely to see their own party as having the best position on that most important issue. Yet, in both countries as the strength of party identification increases so does the perception of party differences and the perceptions of one's own party having the best position. Thus, the impact of party identification on issue perceptions is the same in the two countries, but the Canadians are more likely to see differences among the parties at all levels of party identification.

The patterns just described are buttressed by the impact of controlling for strength of party identification on the thermometer ratings of the parties (not shown here). In both countries, the stronger identifiers are more likely to rate their own party higher than are the weak identifiers. However, the difference between the strong and weak identifier ratings is greater in Canada than in the United States. In Canada, the very strong identifiers rate their own party an average of 84, while the not very strong identifiers rate their party an average of 65, a difference of 19. In the United States, however, the strong identifiers rate their own party 80 while the weak identifiers rate their own party 72, a difference of only 8. Likewise, at each level of party identification, the Canadians rate the opposition parties lower than the Americans rate their opposition party, although the strength of identification has little impact on that rating. Again, then, variations in the strength of party identification have greater impact in Canada than in the United States.

Conclusions

This paper has compared the American and Canadian electorates in terms of their political involvement and their partisan allegiances, employing national election studies from the mid-sixties through the mid-seventies. Earlier studies have concluded that Canadians both participate less in their country's politics and also feel less efficacious about that participation. There likewise has been considerable disagreement as to the nature of partisan allegiances in the two countries, with party identification thought by some to be more volatile in Canada.

This analysis found no difference in the levels of political participation in the two countries. Canadians are less likely to feel that their participation has an impact on government – that is, they are less efficacious. However, the lower rates of efficacy in Canada stem from perceptions of the absence of governmental responsiveness, rather than from viewing the government as complicated or the leaders as losing touch with the people. Canadians also are more cynical than the Americans, but again the difference comes from a feeling that government is run for the big interests and not for the general public. The Americans, on the other hand, are more likely to see the government as wasteful. Although earlier studies had explained Canadian/American differences in terms of lower levels of education in Canada, we found that the differences in the two countries were altered only partially by controlling for education. As in other studies, however, we find considerable differences in efficacy and trust among the Canadian provinces.

Canadians are both more likely to express a party identification and to have altered party identifications. The greater instability of Canadian party allegiances occurs both within the lifetimes of the respondents and between generations. Differences in stability in the two countries remain even when controlling for party identification. Canadians and Americans both evaluate their own parties quite favorably. However, the Canadians are much less positive toward other parties in their own system than are the Americans. The relationship of the strength of party allegiance to participation is the same in both countries. As the strength of identification increases, so does the involvement of individuals in the political process. In both countries, the strength of party identification is related to the perception of differences among the parties, even though Canadians are more likely to perceive differences at all levels of identification. In both countries, strong identifiers are more likely to rate their own party high than are weak identifiers, although the differences are greater in Canada. Thus, while there are differing levels of partisan attachment and differing levels of partisan stability in the two countries, variations in the strength of partisan attachments are similarly associated with other variables.

The two most interesting findings of the paper are:

(1) Canadians, in spite of their higher cynicism and lower sense of governmental responsiveness, participate as much or more than do Americans; and

(2) Canadians, in spite of their greater volatility of party identification, see the parties more distinctly than do the Americans and are more likely to use party as an ideological organizing device than are Americans.

Both of these findings appear explicable, although we cannot as yet present hard evidence to support the following speculation.

The high rates of cynicism and participation and the low sense of governmental responsiveness in Canada are most evident in the Maritimes and Quebec. Simeon and Elkins (1974: 433–4) argue that the Maritimes and Quebec may be viewed as "small town in mass society." Hughes has suggested that the Protestant ethic and "capitalist values" have failed to take hold in Quebec (1943: Chapter 7). Both of these factors suggest that the Maritimes and Quebec have suffered considerably less than the rest of Canada and the United States from what Verba and Nie have called "decline of community" (1972: 229–247). Verba and Nie have found a strong relationship in the United States between "decline of community" and decreased political participation. High cynicism, high participation, and low efficacy have been found in France and Italy in areas similar to the Maritimes and Quebec (Tarrow 1971; 1972). Apparently, high participation, high cynicism and low efficacy are all related outside of modern capitalist culture.

The second finding has two separate explanations. We can explain the higher volatility of the Canadian electorate by the major realignment of the Canadian party system; we can explain the greater clarity of the Canadian parties by appealing to Downs' theory of party competition.

The United States has not had a major party realignment since the election of Franklin Roosevelt in 1932 (Key 1955; Campbell 1966). The same is not true in Canada. In the last half century, the Progressive Conservative Party has been essentially eliminated from French Canada. The last twenty years have also seen the birth of a new party (The NDP) and the growth of a previously insignificant party (SC). These factors are sufficient to explain the greater volatility of Canadian party identification relative to American party identification. Possibly, had we compared Canadian and American party identification in the first part of the twentieth century, when the American party system was undergoing realignment, we might have found considerably higher American volatility.

In spite of this difference in volatility, Canadians have a much clearer perception of differences between the parties. Downs predicts that in a two party system, both parties should converge toward the center of the electoral arena (1957). This accounts for the relative "fuzziness" of American's perceptions of their parties. However, in a party system like Canada's, the existence of two small, ideological parties should keep the two large centrist parties from converging toward each other. For example, if the Liberal party moved rightwards towards the PC, then presumably, the left wing of the Liberal party could desert to the NDP. On the other hand, American Left-liberals who perceive a rightward drift of the Democratic Party have no alternative party available. Consequently, in spite of the greater volatility of Canadian party identification, party is as important (if not more important) in explaining Canadian political behavior as it is in explaining political behavior in the United States.

REFERENCES

ALFORD, Robert R.
  1963   *Party and Society: The Anglo-American Democracies*. Chicago: Rand McNally.
  1967   "Class Voting in the Anglo-American Political Systems," pp. 67–93, in Seymour
          M. Lipset and Stein Rokkan (eds.), *Party Systems and Voter Alignments: Cross-National Perspectives*. New York: The Free Press.
ALMOND, Gabriel and Sidney VERBA
  1963   *The Civic Culture*. Princeton: Princeton University Press.
BUTLER, David and Donald E. STOKES
  1969   *Political Change in Britain: Forces Shaping Electoral Choice*. New York: St. Martin's Press.
CAMPBELL, Angus
  1966   "A Classification of Presidential Elections," pp. 63–77, in Campbell, *et al.*, *Elections and the Political Order*. New York: John Wiley and Sons.
CAMPBELL, Angus and Henry VALEN
  1966   "Party Identification in Norway and the United States," pp. 245–268, in Angus
          Campbell, *et al.*, *Elections and the Political Order*. New York: John Wiley and Sons.
CAMPBELL, Angus, *et al.*
  1960   *The American Voter*. New York: John Wiley and Sons.
CONVERSE, Philip E.
  1974   "Some Priority Variables in Comparative Research," pp. 727–745, in Richard
          Rose (ed.), *Electoral Behavior: A Comparative Handbook*. New York: The Free Press.
CONVERSE, Philip E. and Georges DUPEUX
  1966   "Politicization of the Electorate in France and the United States," pp. 269–291,
          in Angus Campbell, *et al.*, *Elections and the Political Order*. New York: John Wiley
          and Sons.

DAHL, Robert A.
    1961   *Who Governs? Democracy and Power in an American City.* New Haven: Yale University Press.
DEVINE, Donald J.
    1972   *The Political Culture of the United States: The Influence of Member Values on Regime Maintenance.* Boston: Little, Brown and Company.
DOWNS, Anthony
    1957   *An Economic Theory of Democracy.* New York: Harper and Row.
ELKINS, David J.
    1974   "The Perceived Structure of the Canadian Party Systems," *Canadian Journal of Political Science* VII (September), 504–524.
ERIKSON, Robert S. and Norman LUTTBEG
    1973   *American Public Opinion: Its Origins, Content, and Impact.* New York: John Wiley and Sons.
FLANIGAN, William H. and Nancy H. ZINGALE
    1975   *Political Behavior of the American Electorate.* Boston: Allyn and Bacon.
GREENSTEIN, Fred I.
    1965   *Children and Politics.* New Haven: Yale University Press.
HUGHES, E. C.
    1943   *French Canada in Transition.* Chicago: University of Chicago Press.
JACEK, Henry A.
    1975   "Party Loyalty and Electoral Volatility: A Comment on the Study of the Canadian Party System," *Canadian Journal of Political Science* VIII (March), 145–146.
JENSON, Jane
    1975   "Party Loyalty in Canada: The Question of Party Identification," *Canadian Journal of Political Science* VIII (December): 543–553.
KEY, V. O.
    1955   "A Theory of Critical Elections," *Journal of Politics* 17 (February), 3–18.
LANE, Robert E.
    1959   *Political Life: Why and How People Get Involved in Politics.* New York: The Free Press.
MILBRATH, Lester
    1965   *Political Participation.* Chicago: Rand McNally.
MILLER, Arthur H.
    1974   "Political Issues and Trust in Government: 1964–1970," *The American Political Science Review* LXVIII (September), 951–972.
POMPER, Gerald M.
    1972   "From Confusion to Clarity: Issues and American Voters, 1965–1968," *The American Political Science Review* LXVI (June), 415–428.
PORTER, John
    1956   *The Vertical Mosaic.* Toronto: University of Toronto Press.
PRESTHUS, Robert
    1974   *Elites in the Policy Process.* London: Cambridge University Press.
SCARROW, Howard A.
    1965   "Distinguishing Between Political Parties – The Case of Canada," *Midwest Journa of Political Science* IX (February), 61–76.
SCHWARTZ, Mildred A.
    1974   "Canadian Voting Behavior," pp. 543-617, in Richard Rose (ed.), *Electoral Behavior: A Comparative Handbook.* New York: The Free Press.
SIMEON, Richard and David J. ELKINS
    1974   "Regional Political Cultures in Canada," *Canadian Journal of Political Science* VII (September), 397–437.
SNIDERMAN, Paul A., *et al.*
    1974   "Party Loyalty and Electoral Volatility: A Study of the Canadian Party System," *Canadian Journal of Political Science* VII (June), 268–288.

TARROW, Sidney
    1971 "The Urban-Rural Cleavage in Political Involvement: The Case of France," *The American Political Science Review* LXV (June), 341–357.
    1972 "The Political Economy of Stagnation: Communism in Southern Italy," *Journal of Politics* 34 (February), 93–123.
VAN LOON, Richard
    1970 "Political Participation in Canada: The 1965 Election." *Canadian Journal of Political Science* III (September), 376–399.
VERBA, Sidney and Norman H. NIE
    1972 *Participation in America: Political Democracy and Social Equality.* New York: Harper and Row.
WELCH, Susan
    1975 "Dimensions of Political Participation in a Canadian Sample," *Canadian Journal of Political Science VIII* (December), 553–559.

American Managers in Canada

A Comparative Profile

CRAIG McKIE

The University of Western Ontario, London, Canada

IN THE PERIOD of its economic development, Canada has experienced a substantial and continuing influx of foreign investment, both direct and portfolio. With it have come the attendant features of international business activity including the immigration of managerial personnel. Kindleberger (1969), for instance, has argued that foreign investment can best be understood as a blend of incoming economic resources, managerial[1] and technological skills, and technical properties. These inflows (and the price paid for them) have habitually been analyzed in terms of the economic consequences for the receiving country (for example, by Safarian, 1973; Watkins, 1968; Levitt, 1970; and Fayerweather, 1974) and for the metropolitan country as well. The political aspects of the process, where raised, have generally involved inter-national frictions (Vernon, 1974; Wilkins, 1974) or obvious abuses of national sovereignty, such as in Chile. One seldom finds discussions of the effects of the importation of foreign nationals to manage subsidiary operations on host countries' normal civic life.

Evidence has been presented in the literature (Safarian, 1973) that the proportion of foreign-born managers in a subsidiary operation tends to decline with time after incorporation. Nevertheless, in a country such as Canada, in which the level of foreign ownership of manufacturing and mining assets reached 55.8 percent and 64.7 percent respectively in 1972 (Statistics Canada, 1975: 132-3), substantial numbers of foreign-born (predominantly U.S.-born) senior managers continue to be employed.

While one could argue that modern management skills are sufficiently general in incidence now that there should be few if any differences between foreign-born managers and native Canadian managers in Canada, there are persistent indications that, at least in the matter of educational attainment, native Canadian managers are at a comparative disadvantage (Economic Council, 1965: 62; Daly, 1972: 53). In addition, because of the immigration of management personnel to Canada, the aggregate characteristics of managers in Canada, taken as a group, are different from what they might have been in

---

1   Kindleberger does say however: "Superiority of management may be the advantage that many companies bring to foreign investment . . . [but] the nature of that superiority is illusive (1969: 16).

the absence of this type of immigration. Possibilities for upward social mobility are to some extent affected, and hypothetically, the tone and tenor of business life in Canada may have been altered as a result of the introduction of exogenous behavioural and attidudinal sets.

In this paper, we propose to examine the characteristics and attitudes of a group of senior American managers employed in positions in large firms in Canada, in comparison to their native-born counterparts. In so doing, we raise both the question of national differences between Canadians and Americans, and the question of the nature of the non-economic component of the foreign direct investment process as it has unfolded in Canada.

The Development of Dependent Industry in Canada

There is every indication that from the inception of industrialization in Canada, foreign capital investment (together with foreign management and technology) has played a dominant role. Prime Minister Macdonald's nineteenth century "National Policy" fostered the branch plant as the modal form of industry in Canada and the kind of development which has subsequently taken place can be interpreted as congruent with that longstanding policy. Numerous studies (Watkins, 1968; Levitt, 1970; Safarian, 1973; Nelles, 1974) have shown how the construction of a dependent industrial base has progressed to the present.

During the process, substantial amounts of entrepreneurial skill have entered the country. Whole towns appear to have been established as virtual colonies of American metropoli. Paris, Ontario, for instance, was established by entrepreneurs and craftsmen from Buffalo, New York. In contemporary terms, Galt, Ontario, has recently been described as the American enclave 'Galt U.S.A.' by Robert Perry in a book of the same name (1971).

Entering the Canadian scene as immigrants in the nineteenth century, American entrepreneurs established themselves as prominent actors on the Canadian industrial scene. Many of Canada's leading industries were established by such persons during this period. Massey-Harris (farm machinery), Hiram Walker, and Gooderham and Worts (distillers) were all founded, for instance, by immigrant American entrepreneurs. The penetration was so great that " . . . the leading industry in Canada for most of the nineteenth century in terms of employment, and capital invested, was introduced by Americans who imported them with the capital, the machinery, and the skilled workers (Naylor, 1975: II-40)." One result was that the Canadian consumer became attuned to American goods, styles, and predilections. Another was the necessity for Canadian entrepreneurs and inventors to emigrate, taking their energies and inventions elsewhere, as has been described by J. J. Brown in *Ideas in Exile* (1967).

In twentieth century Canada, the process has continued apace. Licensing and patent pool arrangements have led to greater integration of the consumer economies; and the two-way flow of management personnel has been established.

The deep-rooted financial and technological dependence of Canadian industry has ensured an immigration of management personnel. Simultaneously, considerable numbers of native Canadian managers, their upward mobility blocked in Canada, have chosen to leave for greener fields abroad.

The International Migration of Managers

The reliance of Canadian industries on highly qualified personnel from abroad in the management field is by no means an isolated phenomenon. Canadian immigration policy has for many decades been based on the notion that the immigration of highly qualified persons to Canada represent a windfall benefit. Special arrangements for persons in selected occupational categories (the 'waiver list') have been made to allow such persons into Canada to work by completely circumventing the normal immigration control procedure. This freedom facilitates intra-company international movements of management personnel into Canada. There are no statutory reasons, in short, why senior Canadian management personnel should be developed and promoted though many companies choose to do so for other reasons.[2]

As part of the reverse flow, Canadian managers must sometimes leave the country in order to advance with the international corporate structure of a firm beyond the Canadian branch plant level. In some companies, this type of mobility is actively encouraged or made semi-obligatory, perhaps on the ground that corporate ties can in this way be made stronger than national ties. But for whatever reason, the international flow of senior managers is significant, and Canada as a result has a substantial number of foreign-born senior managers. This inflow has the tacit blessing of the Canadian government; and in previous eras, was actually promoted by various bonus schemes funded by Canadian municipalities anxious to create employment at any cost. The practice continues today at the Provincial level.

In light of the importance, and the volume of the international flow of managers, it is surprising that the literature on the subject is not more extensive than it is. Canadian businessmen themselves have long been aware of this process. Turn of the century Canadian business views, as exemplified by the public statements of the Canadian Manufacturers' Association, are unequivocal on this matter. An 1893 statement for example suggests that:

> Whenever a man comes to Canada to live and to contribute in any manner to the material success of the country, he may very properly be considered a Canadian. His birth place may be in Europe, Asia, Africa, an isle of the sea, or even in the land of the Yankee, and

---

2 Safarian writes for example that such firms have an interest in developing national management because:
> ... success will depend over time on familiarity with the laws and customs and economic conditions of the country in which the subsidiary is located; [and] partly because competent managerial and technical personnel are scarce and worth developing or acquiring in their own right; [and] partly also for reasons of public relations. (1973: 51)

protectionists will be ready and willing to acknowledge him a Canadian. There will be no objection to him whatever because of his nationality. And the same as regards his money (cited in Naylor, 1975: II-69).

Or in another passage:

It is of small moment where the capital comes from that may be employed in developing our industries. When it is invested it at once becomes Canadian capital . . . we gladly welcome all American capitalists who desire to join our procession in our march to industrial greatness and national greatness (cited in Naylor, 1975: II-71).

Given this openness to American companies and their national managers, it is perhaps not surprising that there have been significant flows of managers across national boundaries. A study of 176 U.S.-based multinationals carried out in 1969 showed for instance that offshore management ranks were dominated by U.S. nationals, though with an increasing third country component (Wilke, 1972). Parai's survey of the two-way flow between Canada and the United States showed a net loss of 4000 managers to the United States between 1958 and 1963, largely as the result of extraordinary numbers of Canadians leaving the country (Parai, 1965: 57). Emigrant Canadian managers show up in studies of American managers in an over-representation of Canadians with reference to the Canadian-born population of the United States (Newcomer, 1955: 42). This outflow is, however, almost entirely made up of English-speakers and is therefore not representative of the group of Canadian managers as a whole.

Tepperman has recently attempted to explain this uneven two-way flow in terms of the structure of opportunity in Canadian society. He writes, for example, that the large scale immigration of highly qualified persons:

. . . manages to answer the work force needs of Canada but at the same time keeps the upward mobility of native Canadians at a low level . . . so emigration to the United States in particular serves as a safety valve to reduce the discontent of socially immobile workers . . . High rates of emigration always indicate a rigid system of stratification, low mobility and little receptivity to social innovation (Tepperman, 1975: 142).

Thus, perhaps the international flow of managers may help sustain the Canadian elite structure, a possibility entirely consistent with current research on the exclusive nature of that venerable set of institutions (eg. Clement, 1975).

If foreign-born managers are useful to Canadian elite members in that they are not aspirants to elite status in Canada, the presumption must be that such immigrants remain attitudinally and behaviourally distinctive for a long while after entry into the country. But whether the incoming American managers are different from their Canadian counterparts is an empirical question on which little light has yet been shed. Evidence presented by Bass and Eldridge (1973) suggests that there may well be differences. They conclude that:

. . in countries like the United States, the United Kingdom and West Germany, those managers who move up fastest tend to make choices which suggest preference for or acceptance of the profit maximization objective. But such results fail to hold in [9] other countries (1973: 169).

Unfortunately for our purposes, Canada was not one of the included countries.

If offshore employment is an upward step for U.S. executives, then, on the basis of Bass and Eldridge's work, a more single-mindedly profit-preoccupied manager might be found in Canada compared to those who fail to be promoted abroad and remain in the United States. If, on the other hand, the American manager sent abroad is a misfit, as Fayerweather (1959: 6) seems to suggest, a quite different personality type might be found in Canada. Citing Perlmutter (1954) on the prevalence of the xenophilic personality, Fayerweather suggests that some American managers leaving the United States view the leaving as an opportunity to discard conformity to conventional business standards in the United States. He writes for instance:

> Probably many left the United States because they did not like its culture. Their conduct abroad may therefore be a true expression of their personalities which, while in the United States, were forced into a degree of conformity to our ideology by social pressure (1959: 171).

Vernon suggests in contrast that "the popular caricature – a relatively incompetent, shunted off by a benign headquarters to an obscure sinecure – has little to do with the facts" (1971: 148). He states that the expatriate American executive's most singular characteristic is high educational attainment (higher even than that of his domestic counterparts) followed by a firmer than usual attachment or loyalty to his employer.

Still, we cannot assume that U.S.-born managers fit quickly or easily into the receiving society. Dissimilarities of personal values, social background, and possibly business goals are all logically possible in comparisons between American and Canadian managers in Canada.[3]

The Social Integration of American Managers in Canadian Society

American managers in Canada keep a low profile. They are not visible as foreign nationals. Nor are the companies they work for (predominantly American-owned) conspicuous in the Canadian environment. As Kindleberger has put it:

> Corporations want profits. They also want peace and quiet. As much as possible they want to become citizens of the home country, invisible to the public eye, fading into the background, so long as it gives them peace and quiet at not too large a price in profits (1969: 198).

The threat of incipient anti-Americanism is a persistent reality in Canada – and not one of recent vintage. The first Prime Minister of Canada, Sir John A. Macdonald – an Imperial nationalist, saw American industry and immigrants

---

3   Based on a survey of 254 senior international executives of U.S. corporations, Duerr and Greene (1968: 18) reported that the biggest source of displeasure with foreign nationals was "unfamiliarity with U.S. business practices". Second most often mentioned was "lack of education or technical competence."

both as a source of prosperity for Canadians, and a source of political danger. Writing to a colleague in 1856, for instance, he stated that "the peninsula (southern Ontario) must not get control of the ship. It is occupied by Yankees and Covenanters, in fact the most yeasty and unsafe of populations" (cited in Landon, 1967: 232). There has been, in short, a lingering suspicion that 'flag follows trade'.

Ambivalence towards American industry and culture has continued to the present time. Canadian industrialists, no less than ordinary citizens, report an ambivalent stance (see Fayerweather, 1974: 18–19). On the one hand, Canadian prosperity is seen to depend in large measure on continued foreign investment, but on the other hand, non-economic influences are seen in a somewhat less favourable light.

American managers in Canada would thus seem to occupy a delicate position. They could hardly fail to be aware of the antagonisms and resentments; yet must at the same time deliver the economic benefits which their firms are widely assumed to provide. Under these circumstances, at least superficial acculturation would seem to be a prudent course of action. In practice, this may prove difficult.

Elite studies of Canadian society (for example: Porter, 1965; Clement, 1975) have presented a view of a relatively closed business elite. Access to exclusive private schools, social clubs, and positions of industrial leadership is often seen as highly selective. Even given the willingness to integrate, the obstacles facing the foreign executive may be substantial. It may well not be possible for him, in that he may not possess the requisite social background characteristics, to gain entry to standard elite institutions and activities. Since these characteristics are not of the sort which lend themselves to fabrication, he might well be forced to rely more heavily on the stature which his company by association, confers on him as its senior executive in Canada. If the view presented in Canadian elite studies is correct, and if ease of access to positions in the Canadian economic elite is *declining*, then it would be reasonable to expect both a lack of success on the part of the American managers in attempts to participate in the 'normal' activities of their Canadian counterparts; and a persistence of any attidutinal differences which might have existed upon their arrival in Canada, since the institutional settings for changing these attitudes are relatively closed to him. In short, therefore, we might expect that owing to the highly exclusive nature of the Canadian economic elite, American managers in Canada would not be as integrated in the system of industrial power as their native-born colleagues in community affairs; nor would their attitudes on matters of public importance be identical to those held by their Canadian counterparts.

The American-born Manager as Immigrant

As an immigrant, the senior manager arrives in a new country with a pre-existing relationship with a company. Though the Canadian branch may have some unique operating rules and regulations, it is nevertheless a strong source of continuity and positive reinforcement. The community institutions are, in contrast, much more likely to be foreign to him, more demanding of progressive re-socialization, and less likely to recognize the importance of his company ties. Elite institutions present an even greater discontinuity since he usually lacks the social background characteristics traditionally valued in Canadian elite circles (which are by definition Canadian in content). Daly has argued that U.S. managers who come to Canada often lack even the characteristics associated with membership in the American industrial elite (such as attendance at Ivy League universities) (1972: 50). In such a context, it is thus reasonable to expect less involvement in Canadian institutions, at least initially, and thus less opportunity for the learning of new views or the re-thinking of old values.

In practice, one might expect to find less evidence of a full range of inter-company relationships and associations, particularly with Canadian interest groups, which might in the extreme, work to the detriment of the employing company. If it is important to 'know the ropes' (and the important people) in the Canadian business world, then foreign managers could well be at an initial disadvantage in Canada. Compensating for this initial liability might take the form of a rapid buildup of community ties and involvements, and commitments of the sort which do not require the possession of standard Canadian elite characteristics or which do not involve highly selective recruitment procedures (eg. active work for the United Appeal, Kiwanis, etc.).

If such compensatory techniques are followed, a pattern of relatively heavy involvement would emerge in due course – but it would be one which did not touch on the central institutions of Canadian elite selection and status affirmation (such as the exclusive men's clubs in all major Canadian cities). Extensive re-socialization and redefinition of status, the fabrication of new views and attitudes, and the building up of the appropriate social ties would necessarily take considerable time before entry into elite institutions would be a practical possibility. Easy entry would only be possible into those institutions which valued a man's connections to a large and important company to the extent that deficient credentials could be overlooked.

If the executive is in Canada for only a period of time and not permanently, he is unlikely to be willing to undergo such a prolonged re-socialization process nor might he see the benefits of it. For these reasons, one would expect senior executives of foreign origin to retain many of the attitudes and dispositions to behaviour which he brought with him to Canada.

Data

Most surveys of managers in Canada have sought a representative sample and have not been concerned with foreign nationals. As a result, we do not have a large-scale survey of American managers in Canada with which to work. Rather, we have survey material within which the U.S.-born form a proportionate minority. This restricts the scope of analysis which can be done with the data from the American-born but nevertheless builds in a direct comparability with Canadian-born managers.

Place of birth is almost always taken as the relevant indicator of nationality. Using such a measure, a fairly consistent proportion of U.S.-born managers in Canada is obtained. Heidrick and Struggles Inc. (1973: 7) report that 12.5 percent of the managers of 136 of "Canada's largest companies" were U.S. born. Similarly Daly (1972: 36) reports that 16.3 percent of the senior executives of 332 large Canadian firms were born in the United States. Finally, in the dataset which will form the basis of this analysis, a stratified random sample of Ontario firms, 13.7 percent of the *seniormost* executives proved to have been born in the United States.[4] While not identical, the proportions of the U.S.-born in each sample are both substantial and consistent in size. We may thus conclude that American-born managers in Canada continue to form an important minority. This minority of managers is, in fact, far out of proportion to the 1.4 percent of the Canadian population which in 1971 reported birth in the United States. (Statistics Canada, 1974: 167).

In using the Ontario data here, it was decided to provide comparisons both between the American-born (N=24) and the Canadian-born managers as a group (N=114); and between the American-born managers and a sub-sample of Canadian-born managers matched with the American-born in terms of two company characteristics: size of firm and sector of industry (N=24). In the latter case, we are thus comparing respondents with these two important characteristics of companies controlled for.

Because of the small sample size, which is the direct result of a design not intended specifically to capture the American-born, and the inclusion of repetitive sub-samples, no statistical tests are included. We can however be satisfied that the proportion of U.S.-born in the overall sample is correct. From time to time in the analysis, data from Daly (1972) will be introduced for comparative purposes.

Analysis

The findings in Ontario industries concerning the comparative characteristics of Canadian and American managers and their companies can be summarized under four major headings: the structure and functioning of their firms; the personal characteristics of the respondents; the extent and form of business and community involvement of respondents; and finally, the attitudes held by Canadian and American managers on matters of public importance. We will deal with each in turn.

---

4   Data were drawn from extensive structured interviews with 176 seniormost executive officers of a random sample of Ontario industrial firms employing 100 or more persons, stratified by size of firm and sector of industry, conducted in 1970 and 1971. Full sampling details are to be found elsewhere (McKie, 1974).

A. Canadian and American Managers: Their Firms

The companies in which American managers find themselves working are, in some respects, atypical of Canadian businesses in general. These differences arise directly from the direct foreign investment process. Of the 24 American nationals in the sample, all but one works in a subsidiary of another company. Seventeen of the *parent* companies were incorporated in the United States, five in Canada, and one was controlled by European owners. In contrast, in the matching sub-sample of 24 Canadian managers, only 11 proved to be employed in subsidiaries.

Other differences of both structure and function are to be found in firms managed by American-born persons. These are summarized in Table 1. Many of the differences appear to be the result of the subsidiary status of firms managed by American respondents and thus have little to do with the nationality of the senior executive.

Table 1

Structural and Functional Characteristics of Employing Firms
Canadian and American Managers in Ontario

| | | Matched Sub-Samples | |
Item	Canadian-born Managers	U.S. born Managers	Comparable Canadian-born Managers
A. Company incorporated after W.W. II	17.5%	33%	20.8%
B. Company is in a currently expanding industrial sector	39.7%	66.7%	not applicable
C. Company produces a "modern" high technology product	59.5%	70.8%	not applicable
D. Board of directors meets semi-annually or less often	27.5%	50%	36.3%
E. Most time-consuming activity reported by respondent: long-range planning and setting norms	40%	63.6%	43.4%
N =	(114)	(24)	(24)

Since many foreign-owned subsidiaries in Canada are relatively tightly tied to the single profit centre located in the United States (Litvak *et al.*, 1971), they are thus morphologically different from autonomous firms. We see in Table 1 that the American-born managers are more often to be found in firms whose characteristics are consistent with subsidiary status and with the known outline of the direct foreign investment process in post-war Canada. They are more likely to work in recently incorporated companies (33 percent, as opposed to 17.5 percent of the Canadian-born managers and to 20.8 percent of the matched sub-sample). Also consistent are the findings that the U.S.-born managers are in the currently expanding sectors of industry (66.7 percent in contrast to 39.7 percent of the Canadian managers), and in firms producing "modern" high technology products (50 percent to 27.5 percent of Canadian managers). These results are entirely consistent with those reported by Daly (1972).[5]

With respect to internal decision-making functions (as reflected in Item D of Table 1), we find that again consistent with the subsidiary status of firms managed by Americans, the board of directors tends to be relatively inactive (meeting less often than semi-annually in a greater proportion of the firms managed by Americans).[6]

Thus most of the findings in Table 1 indicate that the nationality of the manager matters little. Rather the institutional form of the company, its corporate history, and its ties and associations with a parent company appear to be the relevant explanatory dimensions. There is however, one clear exception to this pattern.

This is the matter of the "most time consuming activity" of the respondents (Item E, Table 1). Here, even in comparison with the matched sub-sample of Canadian-born managers, the U.S. nationals report much more often that they spend the greatest part of their time on long-range planning and setting norms (63.6 percent in contrast to 40 percent of the Canadian-born group, and 43.4 percent of the matched sub-sample of Canadians). This does appear to be a distinct difference of style of management (since "giving orders" is the prominent alternative activity). One American-born president of a machinery manufacturing company typifies the approach which more American-born managers appear to have. He said: "I don't give many orders, that's for sure. I have lots of men in this company who could do my job "

As would be expected, the variation is in the direction of a more 'conservative' mode of managerial activity on the part of the Canadian managers. While not an enormous difference, it does lend some credence to the view previously discussed that the American manager abroad does suffer or benefit from a distinctive style of work.

B. Canadian and American Managers: Personal Background Characteristics

As mentioned previously, the literature leads us to believe that American managers in Canada are possessors of at least one advantageous characteristic,

---

5   Daly writes:
       It would appear that big business in Canada has imported technical knowledge and organizational experience from the United States, particularly if control was owned outside Canada. Many of the American-born leaders were in industries which have experienced great expansion in Canada during the past 20 years: oil, chemicals, and cement. Almost a third (25 out of 80) were employed by firms that have been in operation in Canada less than 20 years. Generally they were more highly educated than the average respondent, particularly in the fields of business administration and engineering. Consequently it appears that many were brought into industries where Canada had neither time nor facilities to develop its own experts. (1972: 41).

6   In other data relating to the internal operations of firms not presented here, though, the nationality of managers proved not to be related to the functioning of the management committee of companies, nor to the way in which corporate goals are defined.

higher educational attainment, in comparison to their Canadian-born counter-parts. Our data confirm this impression but further suggest that other social background characteristics are not important grounds for differentiation. Some of these are summarized in Table 2.

Table 2

Personal Background Characteristics.
Canadian and American Managers in Ontario

Item		Matched Sub-samples			Daly (1970)*	
		Canadian-born Managers	U.S.born Managers	Comparable Canadian-born Managers	Canadian-born	U.S.born
A.	Educational attainment:					
	High school or less	34.8%	25%	25%	20.7%	16.1%
	Some university or Bachelor's degree	47.0	45.8	58.3	58.2	56.3
	Graduate studies	18.2	29.2	16.7	21.0	27.5
	Totals	100.0%	100.0%	100.0%	99.9%	99.9%
B.	Attended private secondary school	25%	0%	8.7%		
C.	Religious affiliation					
	Anglican	23.3%	16.7%	20.8%		
	Roman Catholic	5.2	16.7	—		
	Other Protestant	40.5	41.7	45.9		
	Jewish	6.0	—	4.2		
	Other	0.9	8.2	—		
	None	24.1	16.7	29.1		
	Totals	100.0%	100.0%	100.0%		
D.	Father's occupation					
	Professional	21.1%	27.3%	21.7%		
	Manager or owner of large business	21.9	22.7	17.4		
	Owner of small business or skilled worker	46.5	40.9	52.2		
	Other manual and un-skilled occupations	10.5	9.1	8.7		
	Totals	100.0%	100.0%	100.0%		
	N =	(114)	(24)	(24)	(344)	(80)

Source: Daly (1972: 54)

We can see that educational attainment is indeed higher in the group of American-born managers (and consistent with Daly's 1972 figures which are also included for the purposes of comparison). We find for instance that about 29 percent of the American-born group had undertaken graduate studies in contrast to only about 18 percent of the whole group of Canadian-born managers and about 17 percent of the matched sub-sample of Canadian managers though the differences in achievement are only those of the level attained in university, not in university attendance itself. This finding would seem to indicate that the differences observed are to some extent a function of the sector and the size of the firm worked for. Since the American-born tend to work in "modern" high technology sectors, the requirement for greater technical expertise would be more obvious. Still, it does seem to be the case that the American-born managers do tend to have superior educational attainment, as the literature suggests, particularly in the matter of graduate training.

Another education-related finding is reported in Item B of Table 2. Put simply, the traditional Canadian reliance on the private secondary school as a source of potential elite members is not reflected in the backgrounds of the American-born. In fact, *none* of the American managers had attended such a school (in contrast to fully 25 percent of the Canadian-born group as a whole, and about nine percent of the matched sub-sample). The lower proportion found in the matched sub-sample again probably reflects the over-riding importance of expertise to the firms which employ both Canadians and Americans in the sectors of industry represented.

In terms of religious affiliation, another dimension shown to be important in Canadian elite studies, the comparative distributions are not markedly different. In each panel, the under-representation of Roman Catholics is striking. In 1971, Roman Catholics made up 46 percent of the Canadian population (Statistics Canada, 1974: 146), but a much smaller proportion of each managerial group is of this faith. The under-representation is noticeably lower in the American-born group however. An over-representation of Anglicans is also noticeable in each classification.[7] Thus we can conclude that the religious affiliation of the American-born managers does *not* represent a radical departure from the (unrepresentative) pattern established in Canadian business.

Finally, it has been suggested that the class origins of American managers in Canada might be different from (and lower than) those of Canadian-born managers. Item D of Table 2 presents comparative data bearing on this matter using father's occupation as a measure. The notion that the class origins of American managers in Canada might be lower is not sustained. The distributions are quite similar, and if anything, the American-born are of marginally higher status. For example, we find that about 27 percent of the American-born managers had a father whose occupation was a profession (in contrast to 21.1 percent of the Canadian managers as a group, and 21.7 percent of the matched sub-sample).

Thus, in terms of the selected social background characteristics, the differences between Canadian-born and American-born managers are minor. No difference which could be considered disruptive of existing (inequitable) Cana-

---

7 Anglicans represented 11.8 percent of the Canadian population in 1971 (Statistics Canada, 1974: 167).

dian patterns of incidence of characteristics is to be found.[8] This confirms virtually intact the view presented in the literature that the American-born manager in Canada has an advantage principally in terms of marginally higher educational attainment. The view of the American-born managers as misfits (at least in terms of their personal characteristics) is clearly not sustained. The lack of private secondary school education may be a detriment in the integration of the American-born manager into the Canadian elite structure, but it is a detriment shared by a majority of Canadian-born managers.

C. Canadian and American Managers: Involvement in Business and Community Organizations

We have argued that as a result of the nature of the elite structures in Canadian society, American managers in Canada might have difficulty in integrating themselves within business and community organizations. Table 3

Table 3

Involvement in Business and Community Organizations
Canadian and American Managers in Ontario

		Matched Sub-samples	
Item	*Canadian-born Managers*	*U.S. born Managers*	*Comparable Canadian-born Managers*
A. Number of External industrial directorships:			
none	60.2%	75.0%	54.2%
one	6.1	4.2	4.2
two	8.0	12.5	20.8
three +	25.7	8.3	20.8
Totals	100.0%	100.0%	100.0%
B. Mean number of industrial interest group positions held	4.87	4.57	4.75
C. Respondent approaches government officials regularly or occasionally	54.3%	68.2%	58.3%
D. Community activities:			
i) held charitable organization position	32.8%	33.3%	37.5%
ii) held position in civic group	24.1%	29.2%	29.2%
iii) on board of non-profit foundation	27.6%	25.0%	29.2%
iv) held position in religious organization	20.7%	33.3%	25.0%
N =	(114)	(24)	(24)

8   One Canadian-born president of a large machinery firm put his views this way. "New blood," he said, "is a good thing but not at very top management."

presents some selected findings in this regard. The findings tend to confirm a lower level of participation in business organizations, but again, the differences are not overwhelming in magnitude. With respect to community organizations, entree to which we assume to be easier, there are few meaningful differences, indicating a standard incidence of participation, irrespective of national origin.

Taking business-oriented associations first, in Item A of Table 3, we note that American-born managers have a much lower number of industrial directorships external to their firms. Fully 75 percent have no such directorships (in contrast to about 60 percent of the Canadian-born managers as a group, and about 54 percent of the matched sub-sample). At the other end of the scale, holding three or more such external directorships we find far greater proportions of the Canadian-born (25.7 percent of the Canadian-born as a group, only 8.3 percent of the American-born, and 20.8 percent of the matched sub-sample of Canadian-born managers). Assuming that participation on the board of directors of another firm is both a meaningful activity and a recognition of the importance of the individual concerned, it is apparent that the American-born managers are not as well integrated as their Canadian counterparts.

Similarly, in Item B, the American-born have a slightly lower mean number of industrial interest group positions held, though the differences are not of major proportions (Canadian-born 4.87; U.S.-born 4.57; matched sub-sample of Canadians 4.75).

Another dimension of extra-company involvement is concerned with relationships with government officials. Perhaps because of this relatively lower level of integration, the American-born managers tend to approach government officials *directly* more often (as is shown in Item C) in preference to using the facilities of industrial interest groups. We find that 68.2 percent of the American-born managers regularly or occasionally contact government officials in contrast to 54.3 percent of the Canadian-born managers as a group, and 58.3 percent of the matched sub-sample of the Canadian-born. Again, though, the differences are those of minor degree only and do not indicate distinct patterns.

In the matter of participation in community organizations, there are almost no differences in the patterns of activity reported. Four types of such activity are reported in Item D of Table 3. Only in the case of holding office in a religious organization is there a marked difference, with the American-born managers reporting a higher incidence (33 percent) in contrast to the group of Canadian-born (20.7 percent) and the matched sub-sample of Canadians (25 percent).[9]

In summary, then, it does appear to be the case that American-born managers in Canada are less heavily involved in extra-company business organizations (and particularly as board members of other firms). It seems

---

9   This finding contradicts those of Daly (1972). He writes for instance that "over-representation in executive ranks by [the] United States born was not reflected in community action where their participation rate was slightly less than for Canadian-born" (1972: 83).

likely that this finding is, again, at least partly the result of working in the subsidiary of another firm. Participation in community organizations is, on the other hand, much more the result of individual initiative and there is little evidence of different patterns of participation, a finding consistent with our view that these organizations may proved "open" compensatory outlets for the energies of potentially less well integrated American-born managers in Canada.

D. Canadian and American Managers: Attitudinal Differences

It has been asserted in the literature that there are important attitudinal differences between Canadians and Americans reflecting the differences in the political development of the two countries. The general attitudes held by American managers in Canada are of course a matter of legitimate enquiry but we are here concerned principally with those attitudes which bear directly on the industrial world in Canada. In this respect, the data available are not extensive. In Table 4 are presented the results of two questions administered to the sample of managers in Ontario which are relevant to the dependent nature of industry in Canada.

Table 4
Attitudinal Differences
Canadian and American Managers in Ontario

Item	Canadian-born Managers	Matched Sub-samples	
		U.S.-born Managers	Comparable Canadian-born Managers
A. "American investment makes Canada politically dependent on the U.S.A." agreeing	40.4%	30.4%	45.0%
B. "Do you think the participation of foreign capital in Canadian industry should be admitted without limitations?" agreeing	40%	52.2%	47.8%
N =	(114)	(24)	(24)

These questions address the issues of the political dependency which some presume is a result of heavy foreign investment; and the issue of further foreign investment. At least on these two issues, there are noticeable though small differences between the American-born managers and the Canadian-born. Perhaps as is to be expected, the American-born managers are much more sanguine about the foreign investment process.

In response to the assertion that "American investment makes Canada politically dependent on the U.S.A.", a lower proportion of the American-born managers agree (about 30 percent) in contrast to about 40 percent of the Canadian-born managers as a group, and 45 percent of the matched subsample. What is perhaps more remarkable is the generally low level of agreement with this assertion indicating the non-threatening nature of the foreign direct investment process to the respondents overall. A slightly higher proportion of the American-born managers also believe that foreign capital should be admitted to Canada without limitations (52.2 percent, as opposed to 40 percent of the Canadian-born managers as a group, and 45 percent of the matched sub-sample of Canadians).

Specific comments from the interviews highlight the mixture of opinion. For instance, the Canadian-born president of a food manufacturing firm said unequivocally: "American capital should be admitted without limitations, so long as they invest and spend in Canada and follow Canadian government guidelines." A contrasting view was given by the American-born president of a firm of similar characteristics. He said: "American investment can translate into unfavourable investment decisions. Our labour force in Canada used to be 3000. Now it's 1800. There's also a constant influx of 'advisory personnel' from New York."

The possession of contentious and unfashionable political views on other subjects is not the exclusive property of one group either. Consider the parallel between the remarks of the Canadian-born president of a giant petrochemical firm who said: "French is not a good language in which to conduct business", with the views of an American-born president of a large chemical firm who said: "some of my best friends are French-Canadian but bilingualism is a lot of crap."

While we cannot place too much burden on these data, it is interesting to note that the attitudes registered by the American-born managers are not truly distinctive in any sense; quite the opposite, there is a fairly consistent pattern of attitudes in each sub-group of the sample. We cannot therefore expect to find that the nationality of the manager in Canada is a guide to attitudes held, just as previously, we have shown that it is not a good predictive guide in terms of the respondents' social biographies, or their community and business activity. The alternative to this type of explanation is clearly an institutional approach which focuses on *the characteristics of firms*.

Conclusions

There now seems little doubt that the form which economic development has taken in Canada (and indeed the development of institutions in Canada generally) has been different from that experienced in the United States. These differences should not be understood as variations of degree only. Clark (1968), Lipset (1968), and more recently Presthus (1973, 1974) have argued that Canadians have adhered to a more collectivist, conservative path of institution building and remain, as individuals, more disposed to caution, conservatism, and introspection.[10] On the individual level of analysis, however, there is

10   As Levitt has put it, "Canada was an ordered, stable, conservative and authoritarian society, based on transplanted institutions" (1970: 142–3). Vernon's description of British

little direct support for this view, in this study or in others.[11]

The results of the survey analysis presented here point only to minor differences between Canadian-born and American-born managers in Canada. Those that do exist (eg. slightly greater educational attainment, a different style of work, and less integration into the Canadian business world by the American-born) are not central to the managerial role. Why then are there so many American-born managers in Canada?

The answer to this question must ultimately lie in the corporate subsidiary-parent relationship. There seems to be a feeling that the interests of a parent firm are best upheld by a national manager. Such feelings have already been well documented by Duerr and Greene (1968) and appear persistent. There seems to be no other reason, given the virtual interchangeability of Canadian-born and American-born managers in the respects dealt with here.

One result of the decision to use an American national in the senior-most position in a Canadian subsidiary is the inhibiting effect on upward social mobility in Canada discussed previously; another is the pressure on Canadians with ability to leave the country. As the Canadian-born president of a very large food processing company put it: "a bright man between 30 and 40 is a fool to stay in Canada – he should go to the United States."

In his discussion of the outmigration of Canadians which we touched briefly upon before, Lorne Tepperman pointed out that this flux ultimately helps to preserve Canadian elite structures. He concludes that such a result is "unhealthy" (1975: 141).

It would surely be excessive to blame foreign-born managers, or their employers for such resultant blockages in Canadian mobility patterns; since the migration process was clearly mandated by the "National Policy". Still, further work on highly qualified manpower is clearly warranted, particularly with reference to the process of social mobility in Canada.

The data discussed here carry the implication that there are few rational grounds for preferring American-born managers to Canadian-born managers in Canada either in terms of superior social background characteristics (either achieved or ascribed), or in terms of their attitudes. Ultimately each manager must contend with the same institutional reality.[12]

---

business elite members closely corresponds to the image presented by Canadian elite analysts of Canadian industrialists. He writes, for instance, of the "limited character of their emotional and intellectual commitment to their business activities." (1971: 217)

11 Arnold and Tigert (1974) present inconclusive evidence based on comparative consumer data on Canadians and Americans which suggests in sum that differences, at least on an individual level, have been overstated. Their peculiar data base and even more peculiar interpretation of results (failure to agree that "Communism is the greatest peril in the world today" is characterized as "socialistic" (1974: 82)), however, diminish the value of their conclusions and the question of cross-national individual differences must remain moot. Suffice to say that many Canadians believe themselves to be different from Americans in this characterological sense; and indeed there is some marginal support for this notion.

12 One American-born president of a large foreign-owned transportation equipment firm

Therefore, rather than making managerial differences based on country of birth central to any argument, it appears more appropriate to search out and understand the real differences in institutional life between Canada and the United States. For example, the virtual monopoly position of the five major Canadian chartered banks must perforce have an effect on the behaviour of firms far in excess of any based on the nationality of the senior manager. It is evident, however, that the foreign-born manager who fails to grasp the nature of such institutional differences would be at a distinct disadvantage.

If, in such a setting, foreign-born managers persisted in acting and thinking in a manner unmodified from their previous metropolitan experience, some strains and tensions with national institutions and national subordinates might be expected. But contrary to Fayerweather's views on the American 'misfit' manager abroad, there is little evidence that such a situation has developed in Canada. Rather, differences of an institutional nature between autonomous Canadian businesses and the Canadian subsidiaries of multinational firms could well form the central foci of further comparative studies in this field. Certainly the progressive internationalization of business would make such investigations timely and of great relevance.

REFERENCES

ARNOLD, Stephen J., and Douglas J. TIGERT
    1974   "Canadians and Americans: A Comparative Analysis," *International Journal of Comparative Sociology* XV, 68–83.
BASS, Bernard H., and Larry D. ELDRIDGE
    1973   "Accelerated Managers' Objectives in Twelve Countries," *Industrial Relations* 12 (May), 158–171.
BROWN, J. J.
    1967   *Ideas in Exile.* Toronto: McClelland and Stewart.
CLARK, S. D.
    1968   *The Developing Canadian Community*, 2nd ed. Toronto: University of Toronto Press.
CLEMENT, Wallace
    1975   *The Canadian Corporate Elite.* Toronto: McClelland and Stewart.
DALY, W. G.
    1972   *The Mobility of Top Business Executives in Canada.* University of British Columbia: unpublished M.B.A. thesis.
DUERR, Michael G., and James GREENE
    1965   *Foreign Nationals in International Management.* New York: National Industrial Conference Board.
Economic Council of Canada
    1965   *Second Annual Report.* Ottawa: Queen's Printer.
FAYERWEATHER, John
    1959   *The Executive Overseas.* Syracuse: Syracuse University Press.
    1974   *Foreign Investment in Canada.* Toronto: Oxford University Press.

---

appears to acknowledge the implications of this argument when he said: "I'm dedicated to putting Canadians into jobs as fast as possible. There were 35 before, now there're only 15 U.S. citizens and in five years, there will only be one or two."

HEIDRICK and STRUGGLES Inc.
    1973   *Profile of a Canadian President.* New York.
KINDLEBERGER, Charles P.
    1969   *American Business Abroad.* New Haven: Yale University Press.
LANDON, Fred
    1967   *Western Ontario and the American Frontier.* Toronto: McClelland and Stewart.
LEVITT, Kari
    1970   *Silent Surrender.* Toronto: Macmillan of Canada.
LIPSET, S. M.
    1968   "Revolution and Counterrevolution: The United States and Canada," pp. 31–63,
            in Lipset (ed.), *Revolution and Counterrevolution.* New York: Basic Books.
LITVAK, I. A., C. J. MAULE, and R. D. ROBINSON
    1971   *Dual Loyalty: Canadian U.S. Business Arrangements.* Toronto: McGraw-Hill.
McKIE, D. C.
    1974   *An Ontario Industrial Elite: The Senior Executive in Manufacturing Industry.* University
            of Toronto: unpublished Ph.D. thesis.
NAYLOR, R. T.
    1975   *The History of Canadian Business 1867–1914,* Volumes 1 and 2. Toronto: James
            Lorimer.
NELLES, H. V.
    1974   *The Politics of Development.* Toronto: Macmillan of Canada.
NEWCOMER, Mabel
    1955   *The Big Business Executive.* New York: Columbia University Press.
PARAI, Louis
    1965   *Immigration and Emigration of Professional and Skilled Manpower during the Post-War
            Period.* Ottawa: Queen's Printer.
PERLMUTTER, H. V.
    1953   "Some Characteristics of the Xenophilic Personality," *The Journal of Psychology* 38,
            291–300.
PERRY, Robert
    1971   *Galt, U.S.A.* Toronto: Maclean-Hunter.
PORTER, John
    1965   *The Vertical Mosaic.* Toronto: University of Toronto Press.
PRESTHUS, Robert
    1973   *Elite Accommodation in Canadian Politics.* Toronto: Macmillan of Canada.
    1974   *Elites in the Policy Process.* London: Cambridge University Press.
SAFARIAN, A. E.
    1973   *Foreign Ownership of Canadian Industry.* Toronto: University of Toronto Press.
Statistics Canada
    1974   *Canada Year Book.* Ottawa: Queen's Printer.
    1975   *Corporations and Labour Unions Return Act for 1972,* Part 1 – *Corporations.* Ottawa:
            Queen's Printer.
TEPPERMAN, Lorne
    1975   *Social Mobility in Canada.* Toronto: McGraw-Hill Ryerson.
VERNON, Raymond
    1971   *Sovereignty at Bay.* New York: Basic Books.
    1974   *Big Business and the State.* Cambridge: Harvard University Press.
WATKINS, Melville *et al.*
    1968   *Report of the Task Force on the Structure of Canadian Industry.* Ottawa: Queen's Printer.
WILKE, Gerd
    1972   "Multinational Managers: Overseas Positions no longer a dead end," *New York
            Times* CXXI (March) 12, F-5.
WILKINS, Mira
    1974   *The Making of Multinational Enterprise.* Cambridge: Harvard University Press.

Political Socialization Among Youth:

A Comparative Study of English-Canadian and American School Children

RONALD G. LANDES

Saint Mary's University, Halifax, Canada

THE RAPID GROWTH in the field of Comparative Politics in the past decade and a half has not only resulted in a major increase in the amount of comparative data available, but, perhaps more significantly, it has also produced a growing concern with and attention to the methodology of comparative political analysis (see, for example, Scarrow, 1969; Holt and Turner, 1970; Przeworski and Teune, 1970; Mayer, 1972). Unfortunately, the connection between these two elements has not always been immediate. While we would agree with Blondel (1972: 5) that "any analysis of government is, in the deepest reality, either implicitly or explicitly comparative," much of what passes for comparative research seems to be of the implicit genre. This criticism is particularly true, we feel, of the literature which purports to compare various segments of the Canadian and American political systems. While the comparative literature on these two systems spans three decades, it appears that few definitive answers are supported by empirical research (Arnold and Tigert, 1974: 68).

Such a perspective is particularly evident in relation to the possible comparative studies between Canada and the United States in the political socialization area. To this point such research is almost nonexistent. While several research collections on the political socialization process in Canada are now becoming available (Zureik and Pike, 1975; Whittington and Pammett, 1976), the only article that seeks to provide a comparative analysis of the process in Canada and the United States is the work of Jon Pammett (1971). However, even this article could be classified in the implicit genre in that the focus of Pammett's (1967: 12) study of Kingston, Ontario was an attempt to discover "the effect the factor of religion has in producing differential patterns of political socialization in children." His original purpose (Pammett, 1967: 21) was not to make a comparative study of Canadian and American children, although in his later article (Pammett, 1971: 139–140) he does suggest some interesting, speculative hypotheses about the similarities and differences between the United States and Canada in the political socialization area.

Thus, the following article is a brief summary of some of the major findings from the first explicitly comparative study of the political socialization process in Canada and the United States (Landes, 1973). Using a purposive sample of approximately 600 children in grades four through eight in both Belleville,

Ontario and Watertown, New York,[1] the following areas will be investigated in this comparative analysis: the child's affective response to government, the child's cognitive perception of the political structure, the development of political knowledge, the acquisition of partisan orientations, and the perception of similarity between Canadians and Americans.

The Child's Affective Response to Government

In considering the child's developing perception of the political system, one of the first problems encountered by the analyst is the focus of the child's attention on the political world. In an early and important article in the political socialization field, David Easton and Jack Dennis (1965: 42) suggested that it is "through the idea of government itself that the child seems able to reach out and at a very early age to establish contact both with the authorities and with certain aspects of the regime." In investigating the child's developing affective image of the polity in the American system, Easton and Dennis (1965: 55) came to the conclusion that the child "begins with deep sympathy for government, and this early aura of approval is likely to remain at the base of his acceptance of the government . . ."

In reviewing the comparative literature on Canada and the United States, several major themes of their respective political cultures led us to expect tha: the level of political affect expressed for government in Canada would be higher than that found in the United States (Lipset, 1967; Hartz, 1955; Presthus, 1973). In particular the significance of the factor of elitism, among others, was the basis for John Meisel's (1975: 244–245) conclusion that "the total effect . . . has been to make Canadians less deferential than the British, and more so than the Americans." In a significant comparative study of interest groups in Canada and the United States, Robert Presthus (1974: 3–39) also suggests that certain elements of Canada's political culture (i.e. the mosaic philosophy of acculturation, a corporatist theory of society, deferential patterns of authority, and a quasi-participative politics) may help to explain the "differential perceptions of legitimacy regarding government in each society." Particularly the greater role of government in the economic sphere in Canada than in the United States,

---

1 The assumption underlying the city selection process for this comparative analysis was the idea of choosing two cities which were reasonably similar on a number of important economic and social characteristics. In other words, we followed the "most similar systems" method of comparison which seeks to minimize the effects of such variables as town size, geographical setting, occupational makeup, and ethnic-racial composition in our data. Using general classiffication schemes and census data comparisons, Belleville, Ontario and Watertown, New York were viewed as appropriate cities for such a comparison.

The sample utilized can be described as one of "purposive" design selected from the children in grades four through eight in Belleville and Watertown. In consultation with the schoolboards and principals we chose schools which were "representative" of each city and comparable between cities. Schools from several sections of each town and from both the separate and public school systems were included. Approximately 600 questionnaires were administered in each city in late 1971 and early 1972.

such that nearly 40 percent of the Gross National Product was spent by all governments in Canada in 1971 (Van Loon and Whittington, 1976: 1), would provide a basis for inferring that acceptance of government, and thus a more positive view of government, would perhaps characterize Canadian rather than American attitudes. An additional line of reasoning which supports this interpretation is the work of Paul Abramson and Ronald Inglehart (1970), in which they argue that the idealization of political authority should be higher in democracies which are also monarchies than in democracies with only elected political figures.

In considering the child's affective response to government, three indicators of the child's perception of the image of government will be investigated in this comparative study: benevolence ("Would want to help me if I needed it"), dependability ("Makes mistakes"), and leadership ("Makes important decisions").[2] By first of all analyzing the "don't know" alternative we can see to what extent the children in both cities are at least vaguely aware of the concept of "government." Only in grade four do a significant number of children indicate that they do not know what the word "government" means (17 and 18 percent in Belleville and Watertown, respectively). These percentages drop to 7 and 3 percent, respectively, by grade five and to 2 percent by the grade eight level in both cities. Thus, on these data, it is apparent that over 90 percent of the children by the grade five level have an early recognition of the concept of the government, with nearly total recognition (98 percent) by the time they reach junior high school.

In relation to our first indicator regarding the benevolence of government (Table 1), the "high" benevolence rating is equal in grade four in Belleville and Watertown (37 percent), and although there is some fluctuation over the grade span, the percent of Canadian children in the "high" category remains relatively stable, except for grade six, while the percentage of American children declines noticeably in grades six through eight. Thus, by the grade eight level, nearly twice as many Canadian children (38 percent) than American children (20 percent) feel a "high" level of benevolence toward their government.

Perhaps even more significant is the pattern of development for the "low" benevolence comparison in Table 1. For both the Canadian and American children the view of government as benevolent declines sharply over the grade span. In other words, the percentages in the "low" columns for both cities

---

2   The indicators utilized were taken from those developed by David Easton and Jack Dennis (1969: 168). Of their original 14 indicators, 5 were selected, on the basis of a pretest, for inclusion in the final format for the students in Belleville and Watertown. Due to space limitations only 3 of these items are presented in this particular analysis.

Each item originally contained six possible answers, plus a "don't know" alternative. For Tables One through Three, we have collapsed the six answer categories down to three, producing a high, medium, and low split for each variable. The "don't know" column is not included in the Tables. In addition, a "no answer" column was eliminated from the Tables, and this, along with rounding errors, accounts for the fact that the row percentages may not add up to 100 percent.

Table 1

The Benevolence of Government
"Would want to help me if I needed it"
(percent agreeing)

Grade	High Benevolence "Always" and "Almost Always"			Medium Benevolence "Usually" and "Sometimes"			Low Benevolence "Seldom" and "Not Usually"		
	Can.	Amer.	E & D	Can.	Amer.	E & D	Can.	Amer.	E & D
4	37	37	57	34	25	36	12	18	7
5	40	37	48	40	35	44	12	26	8
6	27	21	48	47	44	44	17	32	7
7	45	17	45	32	50	47	22	33	9
8	38	20	43	37	41	48	21	36	9

nearly double between grades four and eight, such that one-fifth of the Canadian students and over one-third of the American students feel that government would only "seldom" or "not usually" want to help them if they needed it. Such comparisons as these based on Table 1 are consistent with our view expressed above that the level of political affect would be higher in Canada than in the United States.

In Table 1 we have also included the results from the Easton and Dennis (1969) study, so that a comparison of the image of government among American children using data collected a decade apart could be presented.[3] In contrast to our data from Watertown, the Easton and Dennis work found a very large segment of children scoring in the "high" benevolence column (57 percent in grade four, which declines to 43 percent in grade eight) and very few children ranking "low" in their perception of governmental benevolence. The comparison of these two sets of data is striking and significant, in that by the grade eight level four times as many students in Watertown (36 percent) expressed a "low" level of benevolence than did the students studied a decade earlier (9 percent).

Our second indicator for comparing the children's view of government concerned the dependability of government in relation to how often it was perceived as making mistakes. In Table 2 we see that while relatively few of either the Canadian or American children view government as ranking "low" on the dependability rating, the Canadian children do give a much larger response to this item in terms of perceiving their government as ranking "high" in terms of "almost never or rarely" making mistakes. For example, by the grade eight level nearly twice as many Canadian students (37 percent) as American students (20 percent) ranked government "high" on the dependability evaluation. While in both groups of children there is an increasing pattern of viewing the government as "sometimes and often" making mistakes,

---

3   The data from the Easton and Dennis study (1969: 132–133) were also collapsed into our 3 groupings for the purposes of comparison. The Easton and Dennis study is referred to as the E & D column in Tables One through Three.

Table 2

The Dependability of Government

"Makes mistakes" (percent agreeing)

Grade	High Dependability "Almost Never" and "Rarely"			Medium Dependability "Sometimes" and "Often"			Low Dependability "Usually" and "Almost Always"		
	Can.	Amer.	E & D	Can.	Amer.	E & D	Can.	Amer.	E & D
4	44	35	73	37	40	26	3	6	2
5	52	35	70	33	54	30	7	9	0
6	43	25	70	47	63	29	2	7	1
7	45	24	66	50	72	34	2	3	0
8	37	20	59	60	72	40	3	6	0

such an image begins slightly higher in the American sample and increases at a faster rate across the grade span than in the Canadian sample (i.e. the "medium" category in Table 2). Again this pattern is congruent with our expectations concerning the image of government between these two countries.

In comparing the American data from Watertown with the Easton and Dennis study, we are again struck by the large differences in the results of the studies conducted a decade apart. For example, by grade eight nearly three times as many students (59 percent) in the Easton and Dennis study ranked government as highly dependable than did the American students in Watertown (20 percent). A plausible explanation, we suggest, for these differences on our first two indicators is that the turmoil of American politics in the 1960's, both in foreign and domestic affairs, is reflected in the later data from Watertown. Such an interpretation would be consistent with recent studies on American adults which have found, for example, that "there has been a significant growth in mistrust of government and in pessimism over the ability of government and political leaders to cope with current problems and issues" (Dawson, 1973: 50; see also Dahl, 1976: 111; Miller, 1974).

A third and related factor in the child's image of government is what we have labeled the leadership of government in terms of making important decisions. As indicated above, the greater role of government in Canada would lead us to expect that it would be perceived as making more important decisions than the American government, despite, we suggest, the greater significance of the role played by the United States in world affairs. The results in Table 3 do indeed confirm our expectations. While very few students in either city rank government in the "low" category on the leadership rating, the Canadian children, particularly in the later grades, rate government more highly than their American counterparts. For example, in grade eight 89 percent of the children in Belleville and 73 percent of the children in Watertown rate government as making important decisions "all and a lot of the time." Correspondingly, more of the American children rank their government in the "medium dependable" category than is true for the Canadian students. As with our previous two indicators these findings were consistent with our prediction that

Table 3
The Leadership of Government
"Makes important decisions" (percent agreeing)

Grade	High Leadership "All" and "A Lot of the Time"			Medium Leadership "Sometimes" and "Seldom"			Low Leadership "Almost Never" and "Never"		
	Can.	Amer.	E & D	Can.	Amer.	E & D	Can.	Amer.	E & D
4	53	50	83	25	22	16	4	7	1
5	69	56	86	20	38	14	4	4	0
6	73	50	88	18	36	11	2	8	0
7	89	76	89	7	22	10	3	1	0
8	89	73	93	8	19	7	2	5	0

the child's affective response to government would be greater in Canada than in the United States.

The comparison of the Watertown and the Easton and Dennis data in Table 3 also shows the pattern evident on our other two indicators. The level of "high" leadership in Watertown is significantly below that of the earlier study (73 *versus* 93 percent, respectively, at the grade eight level). Once again these data probably reflect the political conflict and vast changes which took place in the American political system between the Easton and Dennis survey (1961–1962) and the Watertown data collected in January, 1972.

In concluding our discussion of the child's affective response to government in these two communities, several major points should be emphasized. First, as previous research led us to expect, the political affect expressed for government by children in these two cities is higher in Canada than in the United States for our three indicators of benevolence, dependability, and leadership.[4] Secondly, in comparing our American data from Watertown with the American data collected a decade earlier by Easton and Dennis, we have witnessed significant differences in the child's image of American government. The lower scores on the rating of governmental qualities by the American children in 1972 than in 1962 could be explained, we suggested, by the conflict and turmoil evident in the American political system throughout the period between the two surveys. As a result of the pre-Watergate data from Watertown, we would suggest a need for a possible revision in the conclusion that "in the United States a positively supportive image of the general structure of authority is being widely and regularly reproduced for young new members" (Easton and Dennis, 1969: 138).

---

4   If the mean scores on these indicators are compared by grade level, using a difference of means test, the Canadian children have lower scores (higher affect) in all 15 cases, 13 of which are statistically significant at the .05 level using a one-tailed test.

The Child's Perception of the Political Structure: A Presidential and a Parliamentary System

The rating items discussed in the previous section provided us with an indication of the level of affect felt by the child for the general political structure in the Canadian and American systems. However, the child relates to his political system not only on an affective base, but also in relation to his developing cognitive perceptions of the specific structures of the polity. In other words, the developing recognition by the child of the more detailed aspects of the political system is a key ingredient of what Easton and Dennis (1969: 288) have called the institutionalization of political authority. Therefore, our concern in this section will be twofold: first, to consider the extent of the institutionalization of political authority and secondly, to compare the effects that a presidential or a parliamentary structure has on the child's perception of the polity. These effects will be judged by the responses to two questions: "Who makes the laws?" and "Who does the most to run the country?"

In Table 4 we see the Canadian children's responses to the lawmaking question. The "don't know" category is revealing in that approximately 20 to

Table 4

Awareness of Chief Lawmaker
("Who Makes the Laws?")

Grade	Don't Know	Queen	Percent of Canadian children selecting		Senate	Cabinet
			Prime Minister	House of Commons		
4	20	24	39	16	1	1
5	17	18	27	28	4	5
6	19	10	26	33	2	8
7	26	13	15	36	4	6
8	25	6	5	46	6	11

Grade	Don't Know	Supreme Court	Percent of American children selecting		Senate	Cabinet
			President	House of Representatives		
4	26	16	39	12	4	2
5	23	17	20	34	6	0
6	19	34	9	22	13	4
7	19	13	14	20	27	8
8	16	6	8	38	23	9

25 percent of the students at all grade levels admit that they cannot select the political institution that is responsible for making the laws of the country. More importantly, the data in Table 4 clearly reveal the early personalization of the political system by the Canadian children and the growing institutionalization of political authority as the children mature. For example, note the predominance of the Prime Minister and the Queen, the two faces of the divided

political executive in Canada, at the grade four level and their subsequent and large decline across the grade span in relation to the lawmaking function. Correspondingly, across the grade span the House of Commons increases sharply in the child's view of the political system, from 16 percent in grade four to 46 percent in grade eight. Here we have some initial evidence that the process of the institutionalization of political authority is applicable to the Canadian as well as to the American political system.

The data for the American children are also presented in Table 4. The patterns found in the Watertown data are similar to those previously reported by Easton and Dennis (1969: 118–121). For example, although the President dominates at the youngest grade level, he is quickly overtaken in the law-making function by the House of Representatives in grade five and even by the Senate in grade six. While in the Easton and Dennis study, 44 percent of the children in grade four viewed the President as the chief lawmaker, a percentage which declined to 5 by the grade eight level, in our Watertown findings the corresponding percentages are 39 percent in grade four and 8 percent in grade eight. These findings in Table 4 support the Easton and Dennis view that as children mature there is an increasing institutionalization of political authority.

Our second major theme in this section, the effects of the parliamentary or presidential structure on the child's perception of the political system, can be investigated by comparing the two sections of Table 4. In relation to the Cabinet, the impact of the political structure in these two systems appears to be beyond the view of our sample children in grades four through eight. While important differences exist in the role of the Cabinets in these two systems, such distinctions are not yet an element of the child's cognitive perception of the political system. However, some interesting differences are evident regarding the structures responsible for the lawmaking function. For example, the difference in the role of the Senates in both systems is quite apparent, with the American children perceiving their Senate as an important part of the law-making function, while the Canadian children attach little importance to their own Senate.

Probably more significant is the difference in the view of the role of the executive and legislative branches in the lawmaking function evident in Table 4. For example, the executive branch (Prime Minister and Queen) dominates among the younger Canadian children, but is replaced by the legislative branch (House of Commons plus the Senate) by the grade seven level. Likewise, the American executive (President) is seen as the chief lawmaker in grade four, but is overtaken in this role by the legislature (House of Representatives plus the Senate) in grade five. Thus, in the American presidential system the lawmaking function is more readily transferred to the legislative branch at an earlier age than in the Canadian parliamentary system. This pattern is perhaps a reflection of the fusion of executive and legislative power in a parliamentary political system.

Having considered the child's perception of the lawmaking function in both political systems, we now turn to our second indicator respecting the child's perception of who runs the country (Table 5). While the American children selected the President about 63 percent of the time (except for grades five and seven), the Canadian children chose the Prime Minister as running the country in grade four 54 percent of the time, a figure which declines to 24 percent by the grade eight level. Conversely, the choice of Parliament increases from 13

Table 5

Awareness of Who Runs the Country

| | ("Who does most to run the country?") | | | |
| | Percent of Canadian children selecting | | | |
Grade	Don't Know	Parliament	Prime Minister	Supreme Court
4	18	13	54	15
5	11	33	42	13
6	14	33	43	10
7	16	40	31	12
8	11	54	24	9

| | Percent of American children selecting | | | |
Grade	Don't Know	Congress	President	Supreme Court
4	12	15	63	7
5	7	13	76	4
6	4	30	62	4
7	7	32	57	4
8	9	24	63	3

percent in grade four to 54 percent in grade eight among the Canadian children while the legislature (Congress) is selected by 15 percent of the American children in grade four, a figure which only increases modestly to 24 percent by the grade eight level. The effects of the presidential-parliamentary structure are clear, we feel, in the data in Table 5. The American President totally dominates in regard to running the country, a view which has a basis in political reality.[5] By contrast, in the Canadian parliamentary system, the Prime Minister does not dominate (except in grade four) and is displaced by Parliament in the child's view by the grade seven level.

In regard to both of our indicators, therefore, the structure of the political system, whether a presidential or a parliamentary setup, does appear to have an impact on the child's developing perception of the polity. In both systems a developmental pattern of the institutionalization of political authority was evident across the grade span. Also, the children increasingly associate the legislative structures with the lawmaking function. However, there were also

---

5   The data from Watertown on this indicator are very similar to the Easton and Dennis (1969: 120) results. For example, in grade five 72 percent and in grade eight 58 percent of the children in the Easton and Dennis study viewed the President as the one who runs the country, while the corresponding figures in Watertown are 76 percent in grade five and 63 percent in grade eight.

some differences between the two systems in relation to lawmaking: for example, the different ratings given to the two Senates.

With regard to our second indicator ("Who runs the country?"), in the American system the children view the President as the one who runs the country, while in Canada the older children view Parliament as both making the laws and running the country. Such findings as those presented above are congruent, we feel, with the distinction between the presidential structure of the American system and the parliamentary structure of the Canadian system. These results also seem to suggest that future research in the political socialization area should deal more explicitly with how differences in political structure (i.e. whether it is presidential or parliamentary, federal or unitary) influence the child's developing perception of his polity.

The Development of Political Knowledge

The third major area of analysis in this comparative study is the development of political knowledge among the students in our Canadian and American samples. Our concern will be twofold: first, with the level of political information acquired by the children and secondly, with the developmental pattern of political learning, in particular, the age at which political knowledge is acquired. As an indicator for the level of political information we will use the child's ability to name particular political figures. Of course, our indicator is a low level abstraction for the more sophisticated concept of political information. However, given the age of our respondents, we feel that knowledge about political leaders is a suitable indicator for this comparison.

In Table 6 we present our data concerning the acquisition of knowledge

Table 6

The Development of Political Information

Grade	Percent of Canadian Children Correctly Naming Political Leaders		
	Mayor of City	Premier of Ontario	Prime Minister of Canada
4	26	13	37
5	47	45	66
6	66	56	79
7	69	69	82
8	68	73	94

Grade	Percent of American Children Correctly Naming Political Leaders		
	Mayor of City	Governor of New York	President of the United States
4	16	21	79
5	32	50	90
6	42	52	96
7	72	67	99
8	85	74	99

about the major political leader at each level of government for both the Canadian and American children. In both groups the level of political information, as expected, shows a marked and steady increase across the grade span. For example, among the Canadian children in grade four 26, 13, and 37 percent can correctly name the Mayor, Premier, and Prime Minister, respectively, while in grade eight the corresponding percentages have increased to 68, 73, and 94 percent. It is evident in these data that the Prime Minister is the most salient in the child's perception of these three political authority figures. At all grade levels the Prime Minister is the leader that is correctly named the most often. Except in grade four, the children can correctly name the Mayor and Premier about the same percent of the time at all grade levels.

A similar pattern of results is also apparent in the American data summarized in Table 6. The predominance of the President in the American political system is evident. At grade four 79 percent of the children in Watertown can correctly name the President, and this correct perception becomes virtually complete by grade seven. This predominance is especially noticeable at the younger grade levels, where only 21 and 16 percent of the children in grade four can correctly name the Governor and Mayor, respectively. In grades four through six more children can correctly name the Governor than the Mayor, but this pattern reverses itself among the older children.

In comparing the levels of political information evident in our Canadian and American data in Table 6, we can see that the active head of the national government, particularly among the younger children in both systems, predominates over other authority figures in the child's developing cognitive image of the political system. Moreover, in a comparison of the political leaders at the same level of government, it is apparent that the level of knowledge about the American President is greater at each grade level than the knowledge Canadian students have of their Prime Minister. This knowledge differential is particularly striking among the younger students.

The comparison regarding local and state or provincial leaders shows a mixed pattern of responses. The American children can more often name their Governor in grades four and five than the Canadian children who can name their Premier. In the later grades the children in both cities are about equal in their ability to name their state or provincial political leader. For the local level of government the younger Canadian children can more often name their Mayor, but by grades seven and eight the older American children have a higher level of correct information.

On the basis of the kind of data presented in Table 6, we would have to conclude that the levels of political information acquired by the Canadian and American children in these two cities are quite similar. Only on the Prime Minister-President comparison is there a large and persistent difference across the entire grade span. This particular finding is not surprising, considering the presidential *versus* parliamentary structure of the American and Canadian political systems discussed in the previous section of this paper. However, in relation to our two other indicators of political knowledge, the comparisons show a mixed pattern of responses. On a number of possible comparisons concerning the levels of political information between the Canadian and American children, (data not presented here), the differences are either small or show a mixed pattern, as with the data in Table 6.

Our second major focus in relation to political information concerns the age at which political orientations are acquired. For example, Jon Pammett (1971: 140), on the basis of his study of Kingston, Ontario, suggested the following hypothesis:

> The socialization of political orientations in many Canadian children takes place in adolescence rather than at earlier stages of development. In the United States, for comparison, many more political orientations are learned in pre-adolescence.

Previous research has suggested some support for Pammett's view. In comparing the political socialization patterns of legislators in Canada and the United States, Allan Kornberg and his colleagues (1969: 87) came to the conclusion that Canadians "seem to go through the same general process as do Americans, but that for the former the events take place somewhat later in life." Although isolated findings, such as the children's ability to name their chief executives at the early grade levels, support such an hypothesis, the majority of our data do not show that the Canadian children in Belleville acquire their orientations at any later date than their American counterparts in Watertown. Whether in terms of political information and knowledge, willingness to rate authority figures on various characteristics such as benevolence, ability to perceive and rate the levels of government in their federal system, and partisan attachment,[6] the Canadian and American children are very similar in the extent and age at which political orientations develop. If our data are representative they indicate that the patterns of political learning may not be very different for English-Canadians and Americans in the early 1970's, a conclusion which is contrary to Pammett's hypothesis and much of the conventional wisdom about the political socialization process in Canada. Such a conclusion, we feel, points to the significance and need for additional comparative research conducted in both systems at the same point in time.

The Acquisition of Partisan Orientations

In comparing the child's acquisition and development of political orientations in Belleville and Watertown, it is not unreasonable to expect that such a key component of a system's political culture as political party identification might differ considerably in nature and extent. While previous research has usually indicated a high level of partisan identification in American children (Greenstein, 1965: 64–84), it has often been suggested that Canadians do not

---

6   Only a part of the data on which this conclusion is based has been presented in this article. For a fuller treatment of the many possible comparisons see the original thesis text (Landes, 1973).

exhibit such an early attachment to political parties (Pammett, 1971: 140). In assessing these ideas we will analyze both the total level of party identification and the apparent continuity in the transmission of party identification between the parent and child. Table 7 presents a comparison between the levels of party identification for the various grades in Belleville and Watertown, along with similar data from previous research. These results are all based on a question similar to the one we used: "If you could vote, what would you be?"

Table 7
Comparative Party Identification

		Grade				
		4	5	6	7	8
	Sample location		*(% with a partisan preference)*			
(1)	Belleville, Ontario (Dec., 1971)	33	55	63	62	48
(2)	Watertown, New York (Jan., 1972)	20	31	34	42	43
(3)	Kingston, Ontario (1966)*					
	(a) Public Schools	25	27	44	42	46
	(b) Separate Schools	35	29	53	54	54
(4)	National American Sample (1961–1962)*	49	55	57	56	53
(5)	New Haven, Connecticut (1958)*					
	(a) Upper SES	63	66	61	71	49
	(b) Lower SES	63	56	56	67	61

*   The data are taken from the following sources: (1) Kingston, Ontario: Jon H. Pammett, "The Development of Political Orientations in Canadian School Children," *Canadian Journal of Political Science*, 4 (March, 1971), pp. 132–141; (2) National American Sample: Robert D. Hess and Judith V. Torney, *The Development of Political Attitudes in Children* (Chicago: Aldine Publishing Company, 1967); (3) New Haven, Connecticut: Fred I. Greenstein, *Children and Politics* (New Haven, Connecticut: Yale University Press, 1965).

Contrary to our expectations based on previous research, the data for the Canadian children indicate a higher level of partisan identification in all grades than for the American children in Watertown (row 1 *versus* row 2). In grade four 33 percent of the children in Belleville identify with a political party, while only 20 percent of the children in Watertown make such a selection. By grade eight 48 percent of the Canadian compared to 43 percent of the American children express a partisan affiliation. Comparison of these data with previous research also shows some interesting deviations from the expected pattern. Our data (row 1) tends to show, particularly in grades 4 through 6, a higher level of party identification than Pammett found in Kingston (rows 3a and 3b). Such evidence, we feel, should prevent the easy acceptance of the view that the level of party identification is lower in Canadian than in American children.

The American data (row 2) for Watertown also exhibit important differences from previously reported research (rows 4 and 5). Particularly at the younger grade levels, the children in Watertown show a very low level of partisan attachment. For example, only 20 percent of the children in grade four in Watertown identify with a political party, while in the Hess and Torney data (row 4) 49 percent and in the Greenstein study (rows 5a and 5b) 63 percent indicate such an attachment. The levels of identification in grades seven and eight in Watertown (42 and 43 percent, respectively) are still less than the identifications of children in grade four in the Hess and Torney and in the Greenstein study (49 and 63 percent, respectively). In addition our data from Belleville (row 1) are very similar to the American sample of Hess and Torney (row 4). Given these data we feel that it would be unwise to conclude that the development of party identifications among Canadian children are learned less frequently and later in life than in their American counterparts.[7]

A usual corollary of the view that partisan identification is lower in Canadian than American children (an interpretation which our data questions) is the idea that a possible explanation of such a pattern might be the lack of continuity in many Canadian children of the partisan orientations of their parents. Again our data do not seem to support such an inference.

Table 8 presents the results of crosstabulating the child's party preference with his perception of his parent's party affiliation. Because of the small N's for the minor parties in Canada, we include only the results for the major parties

Table 8

Crosstabulation of the Child's Party Preference with
Knowledge of his Parent's Preference

| | American Sample | | |
| | Child's Perception of Parental Preference | | |
Child's Party Preference	Don't Know	Republican	Democrat
Republican	32	61	2
Democrat	20	8	70
Sometimes One and Sometimes Another	50	25	20
Don't Know	81	8	8
Don't Know What These Words Mean	92	2	4

| | Canadian Sample | | |
| | Child's Perception of Parental Preference | | |
Child's Party Preference	Don't Know	Conservative	Liberal
Conservative	18	68	10
Liberal	28	6	62
Sometimes One and Sometimes Another	58	16	15
Don't Know	78	5	7
Don't Know What These Words Mean	89	4	6

7   The nature and extent of partisan identification among Canadian adults has produced a number of conflicting interpretations. For an example of the recent arguments both pro and con regarding the concept of party identification, consult the following sources: Meisel (1975), Jacek (1975), Jenson (1975, 1976), and Sniderman et al. (1974).

in each system. The evidence of parent-child congruence in party identifications is undeniable. For example, of the Canadian children who indicate that
they would vote for the Conservatives, 68 percent say their parents are also
Conservatives. Similarly, 62 percent of the children who select the Liberals
also say their parents are identified with the Liberal party. A corresponding
pattern is also apparent in the American data.

This pattern of parental-child congruence is also seen in the various "don't
know" categories. For example, of the Canadian children who say they would
sometimes vote for one or another party, 58 percent do not know the party
affiliations of their parents. Also, 78 percent of the children who answer "don't
know" for their own voting preference indicate they "don't know" their parents
identification either.

Of course we must stress that these data are based on the child's perception
of his parent's political affiliation. We have no way of knowing whether or not
the child is correct in his information. However, the data in Table 8 would at
least question the view that the apparent transmission of partisan preference
from parent to child is low in Canada. In addition, the level of parent-child
congruence in partisan preference, as perceived by the child, is very similar in
Belleville and Watertown.

Perception of Similarity Between Canadians and Americans

As a final point of comparison the children in Belleville and Watertown
were asked whether or not they thought that Canadians and Americans were
alike or different in most ways (Table 9). About 55 percent of the Canadian
children at all grades indicate that they are similar to the Americans in most

Table 9
Similarity of Canadians and Americans

Grade	I'm not Sure	Belleville, Ontario Alike in Most Ways	Different in Most Ways
4	24	55	22
5	18	58	23
6	18	58	23
7	16	55	28
8	12	58	29

Grade	I'm not Sure	Watertown, New York Alike in Most Ways	Different in Most Ways
4	41	43	16
4	23	60	16
6	28	70	3
7	19	70	11
8	28	65	8

ways. Only 22 percent of the Canadian children in grade four and 29 percent in grade eight feel that there is much difference. For the American children 43 percent in grade four and 65 percent in grade eight feel that they are like Canadians in most ways. In contrast to the Canadian children, the older the American children are, the more they feel they are like the Canadians. While the Canadian children increasingly perceive themselves to be different from the Americans over the grade span, the Americans see themselves as more like the Canadians in the later grades. By grade eight 29 percent of the Canadian children, but only 8 percent of the American children, perceive a difference between themselves.

It is interesting to compare the Canadian data in Table 9 with the earlier study by John C. Johnstone (1969: 22–36) which was conducted among a national sample of adolescents in 1965. In response to whether or not Americans and Canadians were generally the same, Johnstone found that among the English-speaking adolescents 79 percent thought they were alike in most ways and 18 percent thought they were different. These findings are much higher than the ones found in Belleville. For the children in Belleville around 55 percent of all grade levels thought that the Americans and Canadians were alike, while an increasing number of the older children (29 percent by grade eight) perceived a difference. Also, in Belleville anywhere from 12 to 24 percent selected the "I'm not sure" category, while only 3 percent did so in Johnstone's Survey.

In comparing Johnstone's findings with our own, we can speculate on the discrepancies apparent in the results. We would offer as a possible explanation the recent and growing emphasis in the Canadian system on its distinctiveness in relation to its American neighbor. Particularly revealing is the small but steady trend among the older Canadian children to see a greater difference between themselves and the Americans. In contrast to the adolescents surveyed in 1965, the children in Belleville in late 1971 were perhaps expressing a growing awareness of their own Canadian identity.

Conclusion

Using a purposive sample of approximately 600 children in grades 4 through 8 in both Belleville, Ontario and Watertown, New York, we have sought in this article to summarize some of the major findings from the first explicitly comparative study of the political socialization process in Canada and the United States. Several major conclusions seem to be warranted by the data. First, many of the differences we expected to find between the Canadian and American children simply were not evident in our results. On many indicators (for example, the development of partisan preferences) our findings ran counter to those of previous research. Moreover, in several important areas, the similarities in the patterns of political learning are very apparent for the Canadian and American children. A second major finding was that there were in specific areas (i.e. the child's affective response to government, the effects of the political structure on the institutionalization of political authority) important differences in the development of political orientations between the Canadian and American students. In addition to these findings based on the comparisons between the students in Belleville and Watertown, we also sought to relate our findings to previous research, in particular the work of Easton and Dennis for the American system and Jon Pammett for the Canadian system. Here again major discrepancies were apparent between the various data sets (for example, the American child's affective response to government).

Given the nature of our data (i.e. that our sample was limited to one city in both countries), it would perhaps be unwise to assert that the patterns found in these two cities are definitive for all other areas in these two systems. However, such data as presented above at least make us reluctant to accept the conclusions of previous research and thus, they clearly demonstrate the need for and importance of additional comparative research on the political socialization process in Canada and the United States.

REFERENCES

ABRAMSON, Paul R. and Ronald INGLEHART
  1970 "The Development of Systemic Support in Four Western Democracies," *Comparative Political Studies* II (January), 419–442.
ARNOLD, Stephen J. and Douglas J. TIGERT
  1974 "Canadians and Americans: A Comparative Analysis," *International Journal of Comparative Sociology* XV (March-June), 68–83.
BLONDEL, Jean
  1972 *Comparing Political Systems.* New York: Praeger Publishers.
DAHL, Robert A.
  1976 *Democracy in the United States: Promise and Performance*, third edition. Chicago: Rand McNally and Company.
DAWSON, Richard E.
  1973 *Public Opinion and Contemporary Disarray.* New York: Harper and Row.
EASTON, David and Jack DENNIS
  1969 *Children in the Political System: Origins of Political Legitimacy.* New York: McGraw-Hill.
  1965 "The Child's Image of Government," in Roberta Sigel (ed.), *Political Socialization, Annals of the Academy of Political and Social Science* (September), 40–57.
GREENSTEIN, Fred I.
  1965 *Children and Politics.* New Haven: Yale University Press.
HARTZ, Louis
  1955 *The Liberal Tradition in America.* New York: Harcourt, Brace, and World.
HESS, Robert D. and Judith V. TORNEY
  1967 *The Development of Political Attitudes in Children.* Chicago: Aldine Publishing Co.
HOLT, Robert T. and John TURNER (eds.)
  1970 *The Methodology of Comparative Research.* New York: The Free Press.
JACEK, Henry J.
  1975 "Party Loyalty and Electoral Volatility: A Comment on the Study of the Canadian Party System," *Canadian Journal of Political Science* VIII (March), 144–145.
JENSON, Jane
  1976 "Party Strategy and Party Identification: Some Patterns of Partisan Allegiance," *Canadian Journal of Political Science* IX (March), 27–48.
  1975 "Party Loyalty in Canada: The Question of Party Identification," *Canadian Journal of Political Science* VIII (December), 543–553.

JOHNSTONE, John C.
    1969   *Young People's Images of Canadian Society*. Ottawa: Queen's Printer.
KORNBERG, Allan, *et al.*
    1969   "Some Differences in the Political Socialization Patterns of Canadian and American Party Officials: A Preliminary Report," *Canadian Journal of Political Science* II (March), 64–88.
LANDES, Ronald G.
    1973   *Socialization to Political Culture: A Comparative Study of English-Canadian and American Schoolchildren.* Toronto, Ontario: Ph.D. Dissertation, Political Science Department, York University.
LIPSET, Seymour Martin
    1967   *The First New Nation.* New York: Anchor Books.
MAYER, Lawrence C.
    1972   *Comparative Political Inquiry: A Methodological Survey.* Homewood, Illinois: The Dorsey Press.
MEISEL, John
    1975   *Working Papers on Canadian Politics*, second enlarged edition. Montreal: McGill-Queen's University Press.
MILLER, Arthur H.
    1974   "Political Issues and Trust in Government: 1964–1970," *American Political Science Review* LXVIII (September), 951–972.
PAMMETT, Jon H.
    1971   "The Development of Political Orientations in Canadian School Children," *Canadian Journal of Political Science* IV (March), 132–140.
    1967   *Political Orientations in Public and Separate School Children.* Kingston, Ontario: M.A. Thesis, Political Science Department, Queen's University.
PRESTHUS, Robert
    1974   *Elites in the Policy Process.* New York: Cambridge University Press.
    1973   *Elite Accommodation in Canadian Politics.* Toronto: Macmillan of Canada.
PRZEWORSKI, Adam and Henry TEUNE
    1970   *The Logic of Comparative Social Inquiry.* New York: John Wiley Interscience.
SCARROW, Howard
    1969   *Comparative Political Analysis: An Introduction.* New York: Harper and Row.
SNIDERMAN, Paul M., *et al.*
    1974   "Party Loyalty and Electoral Volatility: A Study of the Canadian Party System," *Canadian Journal of Political Science* VII (June), 268–288.
VAN LOON, Richard J. and Michael S. WHITTINGTON
    1976   *The Canadian Political System*, second edition. Toronto: McGraw-Hill Ryerson Limited.
WHITTINGTON, Michael S. and Jon H. PAMMETT
    1976   *Foundations of Political Culture: Political Socialization in Canada.* Toronto: Macmillan of Canada.
ZUREIK, Elia and Robert M. PIKE (eds.)
    1975   *Socialization and Values in Canadian Society.* Volume One: *Political Socialization.* Toronto: McClelland and Stewart.

The Controlled Entry of Canadian Managers to the United States[*]

CARL J. CUNEO

McMaster University, Hamilton, Canada

STUDIES of social mobility have tended to emphasize the influence of individual characteristics alone rather than their relations with broad macro sociological, political and economic forces (cf. Blau and Duncan, 1967; Turritin 1974; Cuneo and Curtis, 1975; but see Clement, 1975). These studies have usually focused on educational and occupational status attainment across several generations as the most "interesting" individual characteristics. By neglecting the relation between such micro-level characteristics and broader macro-level structures and changes, it is not surprising that these studies have not been successful in explaining a very high proportion of the variance in final occupational attainment. While it is difficult to include macro variables in such microlevel models, an attempt at least to take them into account promises to be a good beginning.

There are two theoretical arguments, not conventionally part of the social mobility literature, which are suggestive of the influence of macro structures on mobility. The one argument is that of social closure advocated by Max Weber (1968: 341–348) and Frank Parkin (1974). The other is more complex but essentially suggests that the monopoly capitalist mode of production influences the relative expansion of the new middle class and hence the creation of vacancies at this level and the way they are filled (cf. Becker, 1973a; 1973b; Braverman, 1974; Carchedi, 1975a; 1975b). Because social closure has some of its most interesting applications in the imperialist phase of monopoly capitalism (Amin, 1974), it is theoretically and empirically fruitful to consider the role of macro forces on mobility at the international level.

This paper has three purposes. First, a theoretical framework will be set out within which international mobility at the new middle class level can be studied. Special attention will be paid to managerial personnel. This framework integrates mobility at the individual level, social closure at the group level, and monopoly capitalism at the international macro level. Second, a qualitative summary of the individual reasons for which Canadian-born managers now resident in the United States moved there will be given. This analysis will focus on their perceptions of Canadian and American opportunity

---

[*] Thanks are due to Wallace Clement for use of the data analyzed here. An earlier draft of this paper was critically read by Wallace Clement and Robert Gardner.

structures as reasons for migration. Third, this individual-level analysis will be set within a broader context by considering the relation of these reasons for migration to other individual characteristics and to macro historical changes in the relation between Canada and the United States. This will be a quantitative analysis of factors influencing the avenue of migration to the United States.

Social Closure in International Monopoly Capitalism

Max Weber (1968: 341–343) suggests that competitors for social and economic opportunities often form interest groups that monopolize opportunities for their members and exclude or restrict access by outsiders through social closure. "If the monopolistic interests persist, the time comes when the competitors, or another group whom they can influence (for example, a political community), establish a legal order that limits competition through formal monopolies; from then on, certain persons are available as 'organs' to protect the monopolistic practices, if need be, with force. In such a case, the interest group has developed into a *'legally privileged group'* . . . and the participants have become *'privileged members'* . . . Such closure . . . is an ever-recurring process; it is the source of property . . . and other group monopolies" (Weber, 1968: 342). When these insights are applied to the structure of social class, it is seen that monopolization of social and economic resources by privileged classes can be reinforced by the state through legal sanctions.

The link between social class and Weber's concept of social closure has been made explicit by Parkin. "Strategies of exclusion may be regarded as the predominant mode of closure in all stratification systems. The common element in these strategies is the attempt by a given social group to maintain or enhance its privileges by the process of subordination – i.e. the creation of another group or stratum of ineligibles beneath it" (Parkin, 1974: 4). " . . . techniques of exclusion exert political pressure downwards, as it were, in that group advantages are secured at the expense of collectivities that can successfully be defined as inferior." Thus, " . . . exclusion is a form of closure that stabilizes the stratification order . . ." (Parkin, 1974: 5).

The paradox in this is that closure can be maintained only through openness, albeit a controlled access. A privileged group or class often finds either that it is not completely reproducing itself across several generations, or that to maintain and extend its monopolistic position, it must grant entry to outsiders. The privileged group or class will then set up a set of procedures by which it can judge the suitability of the qualities of the candidates applying for admission to the "inner circles" (Weber, 1968: 344). The criteria used for total exclusion or controlled entry are almost limitless. Weber states: "Usually one group of competitors takes some externally identifiable characteristic of another group of (actual or potential) competitors – race, language, religion, local or social origin, descent, residence, etc. – as a pretext for attempting their exclusion. It does not matter which characteristic is chosen in the individual case: whatever suggests itself most easily is seized upon" (Weber, 1968: 342). Parkin takes this one step further by distinguishing between classes of reproduction and classes of nomination. Classes of reproduction, typical of feudal and aristocratic societies, practice exclusion by judging competitors on the basis of their *collective* traits – such as sex, ethnicity, and class origin. Classes of nomination practice exclusion by judging competitors on the basis of their *individual* characteristics, the most typical being educational credentials. This is more usual in bourgeois societies, although Parkin notes a mixture of both types of classes in such societies (Parkin, 1974: 6–9). Classes of reproduction and classes of nomination both operate in Turner's "sponsored mobility." "In this process the elite or their agents who are best qualified to judge merit *call* those individuals to elite status who have the appropriate qualities" (Turner, 1966: 451).

The writings of Weber, Parkin, and Turner allow us to understand social mobility, not from the perspective of individual characteristics considered in isolation, but in view of the relevance of these characteristics for mobility as determined by privileged groups monopolizing society's social and economic opportunities. Dominant groups and classes affect, both directly and indirectly, the general volume and mode of upward mobility by making decisions designed to protect their privileged positions. The regularization of this pattern over time has the effect of reproducing the social class structure at all levels.

The capitalist or bourgeois class in control of the monopoly mode of production seems to be the most powerful one in advanced western industrial society. The monopoly mode of production is characterized by a few very large corporations, high labour productivity and wages, large investments in technology both at home and abroad, and a transfer of the intellectual control of production from the plant floor to the office. These characteristics have come to the fore as the capitalist class has sought to accumulate and expand its capital resources in the transition from competitive to monopoly capitalism. For our present argument here it is important to note that the effect of this transition has been the creation of a "new middle class" consisting of managers, professionals, technical workers, and sales and clerical personnel. The creation of such a class, its expansion, and the mode of mobility into it are determined by the desire of the capitalist class to historically protect and expand its monopolistic position in society (cf. Becker, 1973a; 1973b; Braverman, 1974; Carchedi, 1975a; 1975b).

The development by the capitalist class of the monopoly mode of production within national frontiers often takes on an international phase in what has been described as "imperialism" (cf. Lenin, 1973; Magdoff, 1969; Mandel, 1975; Poulantzas, 1975: 37–88). This international phase of monopoly capitalism includes the merging of financial and industrial capital, the export of capital, multinational operations of large companies, the formation of international cartels, foreign aid, military ventures, and international political pressures (see especially Magdoff, 1969; Goldstein, 1974). The imperialist power has typically been described as a "centre" or "metropolitan" country and the countries which are subordinate in this international phase of capitalism are often called the "periphery" or "satellite" (cf. Frank, 1969: 3–14;

Galtung, 1971; Sunkel, 1973). Between these two extremes are "semi-peripheral" countries which combine some of the characteristics of both centre and peripheral countries. Galtung goes on to distinguish within each nation a centre which correspond to a dominant class and a periphery which consists of all subordinate classes. The important proposition that emerges out of this literature is that the structure of class in semi-peripheral and peripheral countries is deeply affected by their subordinate relation to the centre nation and its dominant class. Hence, we should expect the volume and mode of social mobility in the semi-peripheral and peripheral countries will be affected by this relationship. Further, it can be argued that mobility in such countries is a reflection of the exclusion policies of their own dominant native class that maintains some independence from the centre nation and of the alliance between the dominant class of the centre nation and the sections of the dominant classes of the semi-peripheral and peripheral countries tied to the centre nation.

These points are clearly illustrated in the way the new middle class is a creation of the monopoly capitalist mode of production and the dominant capitalist class members that give shape to it. The dominant capitalist class in the centre protects its monopolistic position by extending its control not only over the new middle class within its own national frontiers but also over the new middle classes lying outside its frontiers in the semi-peripehral and peripheral countries. The effects of this control will be different in the two cases and this affects social closure in national and international mobility. The new middle class in the centre nation will be distorted by being "over-developed" while this class in the semi-peripheral and peripheral nations will be distorted by being "under-developed." This means specifically that the upper reaches of the managerial stratum of this class will expand in the centre nation at a more rapid rate than, and at the espense of, its counterpart in the semi-peripheral and peripheral countries. The reason for this is that the dominant capitalist class in the centre nation reserves major decision-making powers in its multi-national corporations to its head offices in its national home base. This reduces major managerial decision-making powers in the semi-peripheral and peripheral countries. Closure at the high managerial level will thus be much more restrictive in semi-peripheral and peripheral nations than in centre nations. Opportunity for upward social mobility into high managerial ranks will therefore be greatest in the centre. The dominant class in the centre nation reproduces its exclusionist policies in the semi-peripheral and peripheral countries such that upward mobility into high managerial ranks in these latter nations necessarily entails international migration to the centre nation. The traditional career pattern of upward mobility within national corporations inside political boundaries has partially been replaced by upward mobility within multinational corporations across political boundaries.

This internationalization of class practices will also affect the closure practiced by the indigenous capitalist class in the more independent part of the national class structure in the semi-peripheral and peripheral countries. This indigenous national class structure at the managerial level will also be under-developed to the extent that multinational corporations from the centre nation exercise a presence in such countries which hems in or restricts its full development. Thus, from the perspective of both the international and national segments of social closure in semi-peripheral and peripheral nations, upward mobility to high managerial ranks may be seen by their citizens as not very great. Those inclined toward career development will perceive barriers in both the national and international segments of their countries' class system. By contrast, they may perceive greater opportunities in centre countries. Thus, a significant portion of them will migrate internationally to the centre in order to move upward occupationally.

This theoretical framework sheds light on the relations between Canada and the United States. Most authors consider the United States as the leading imperialist power in the post-World War II period, although it has become customary to view greater inter-imperialist rivalry since the early 1970's between the United States and such other "metropolitan" powers as the European Economic Community and Japan (e.g. cf; Poulantzas, 1975: 42–88; Mandel, 1975). A very high proportion of the Canadian economy is foreign-owned, particularly its resources and manufacturing industries. Out of all foreign investors in Canada, the United States is clearly dominant, especially in foreign direct investment (cf. Levitt, 1970; Gray, 1972). Although much detailed empirical research needs to be done, initial impressions are that major decision-making affecting broad company policies are made, not in the branch plants and subsidiaries in Canada, but in their head offices in the United States. This would seem to reduce the proportion of high-level managerial positions in Canada relative to the United States.[1] Unfortunately, the censuses of the two countries do not allow detailed comparisons that would confirm or deny this proposition. If this proposition is correct, we should expect opportunities for moving into high managerial positions to be much less in Canada than in the United States. Clement (1975: 204) shows a greater influx of lower origin people in Canada into the "comprador elite" (boards of directors of foreign subsidiaries) than the "indigenous elite" (boards of directors of Canadian-controlled corporations). Given the weaker decision-making powers possessed by the comprador elite relative to the indigenous elite as well as the apparent decline between 1951 and 1972 in mobility from lower origins into elite levels in Canada (Clement, 1975: 192), upwardly mobile Canadians may be encouraged to migrate southward to continue their career development in U.S. multinational corporations (cf. Parai, 1969: 88; Thomas, 1973: 306–329).

Two crucial issues arise in the controlled entry of Canadian managers to the United States: the mechanism of exclusion imposed on Canadians by various sections of the U.S. upper class and its agencies and institutions, and the individual and collective characteristics of Canadians on the basis of which exclusion is exercised. There are two main mechanisms of exclusion – political

---

1   This is confounded by the fact that a sizable minority of managerial positions in Canada (about 12% to 16%) are reserved for Americans sent to Canada to manage branch plants (McKie, 1977).

and corporate-occupational. While both of these are interrelated and supportive of one another, they can be analytically separated. The political refers to
the regulations imposed by the U.S. federal state and its upper class representatives on the entry of immigrants at border points. The corporate-occupational
refers to those categories of labour that are in demand by U.S. corporations and
other legal entities. The implementation of this latter mechanism is much more
under the direct control of the U.S. economic elite than the political mechanism
although support is required from the state elite through the Department of
Justice and its Immigration and Naturalization Service. The political and
corporate-occupational mechanisms combine Parkin's classes of reproduction
and classes of nomination discussed above.

Classes of reproduction exist, as previously noted, to the extent that exclusion operates on the basis of collective characteristics. The most prominent
feature of this in U.S. immigration policy is the national origins quota legislated
in 1921 and subsequently modified in 1924, 1929, and 1952 (U.S. Dept. of
Commerce, 1973: 91). The general principle involved in these quotas is the
restriction of immigration from a particular country to the United States on the
basis of its representation in the U.S. population at particular points in time.
The 1965 Act created quotas for the Western Hemisphere (120,000 immigrants)
and the Eastern Hemisphere (170,000 immigrants from all other parts of the
world) (U.S. Dept. of Justice, 1970: 4). The effect of such exclusion policies
based on locality of birth has been to reinforce from 1921 to 1965 the status quo
in the distribution of immigrant groups in the United States, and to give
preference after 1965 to Western Hemisphere immigrants.

Classes of nomination have been applied especially in the occupational
preferences implemented by the Immigration and Naturalization Service after
1965. The 1965 Act set up in the Eastern Hemisphere quota four "family
reunion" preferences (1st, 2nd, 4th, and 5th prefernces), one refugee preference
category (the 7th preference), and two occupational preference categories.
Professional and highly skilled personnel became the 3rd preference, and skilled
and semi-skilled workers became the 6th preference (U.S. Dept. of Justice,
1970: 4). What is particularly noteworthy is that the professional occupational
preference category is operative *even when it is not written into the law* (see Table 1).
This preference category does not *legally* apply to Eastern Hemisphere immigrants outside of the occupational preference categories, and to Western
Hemisphere immigrants. As shown in Table 1, 69% of the Eastern Hemisphere
immigrants in the occupational preference category in 1970 were professionals
in contrast to 14% of the U.S. labour force. This exclusion policy is determined
by law. But even where the law does not apply, anywhere from 24% to 34%
of the immigrants are professional. This range is still considerably above the
comparable 14% professional in the 1970 U.S. labour force. This is part of the
new middle class that expands with the rise of monopoly capitalism, as discussed above. Another sector of this class, to which we give major emphasis in
this paper, are managerial personnel. As seen from Table 1, a higher proportion
of managers are drawn from Canada (7%) than the other three immigrant

Table 1

Professional and managerial immigrants to the U.S., 1970[1]

Occupation	U.S. Labour Force, 1970	All immi-grants	All immi-grants In Occupationally Preferred Categories (3rd + 6th preference)	All Immi-grants not in Occupationally Preferred Categories	All Immi-grants from Canada
Professional, technical and kindred	14%	29%	69%	24%	34%
Managers, adminis-trators and proprietors (ex. farm)	10%	4%	2%	4%	7%
All others	76%	67%	29%	72%	59%

1 Calculated from U.S. Dept. of Commerce (1973: 233) and U.S. Dept. of Justice (1970: 49–51). Immigrants not stating an occupation have been deleted from the calculations.

categories listed. However, this category includes a high proportion of middle and lower managerial levels. Our interest is in the upper part of the managerial category. It is clear from immigration law that this latter category is important in the context of the growing importance of the U.S. multinational corporation. In 1970, subparagraph (L) was added to the U.S. Immigration and Nationality Act: "The 'L' classification is for an alien who immediately prior to entry has been employed abroad for at least 1 year by a corporation or other legal entity in an executive, managerial, or specialized knowledge capacity and who is seeking to enter the United States to continue such service with the same employer or an affiliate" (U.S. Dept. of Justice, 1970: 8). Such persons were now classified as "non-immigrants." This amendment is extremely significant because it indicates that intracompany transfers were no longer considered "normal" immigration. The political border recedes into the background as mobility within the multinational corporation, as determined by the exclusionist policy of the U.S. economic elite, becomes much more important. Much of our paper will be concerned with such intracompany transfers by Canadian managers to the United States.

In the context of this southward migration, two different dominant classes (Canadian and American) operate their own exclusionist policies in such a way that they become integrated. The dominant classes in Canada in the economic sector (both indigenous aud comprador) operate an exclusion policy regarding entry into their own circles. Collective characteristics (such as sex, ethnicity, class origin, and region of birth) are used in classes of reproduction. The dominant classes prefer applicants who are males of British and upper class origin from Ontario and Quebec. Individual characteristics (such as educational qualifications) are used in classes of nomination. Applicants who meet both sets of criteria are more likely to become powerful members of the dominant classes in their own generation. Such applicants are prime candidates for inter- and intracompany transfers to the United States. In this way, the exclusionist policy practiced by dominant classes in Canada is an initial screening device after which a select number of applicants undergo a second screening under the exclusionist policies of dominant classes in the U.S. This mode of migration to the United States is called here *continental sponsorship* because its suggests an integration and co-ordination of the exclusion policies of both the U.S. and Canadian upper classes on the basis of privileged social background. A second mode of entry we shall call the *continental crawl*. This mode applies to Canadians who do not possess the collective or individual characteristics to gain entry into the Canadian upper class and hence experience opportunity barriers in their own country. They thus migrate on their own to the United States either to receive advanced education or to look for a job. After either or both of these moves, they attempt to move up into the upper reaches of the U.S. class structure.

Empirically, four types of migration to the U.S. will be studied in this paper. (i) *Familial migration*, or migration as a child with one's own parents. The parents may experience either continental sponsorship or the continental crawl. However, in this type of migration, our focus is on the children. (ii) *Educational migration*, or migration for the express purpose of receiving advanced education. (iii) *Job migration*, or migration in search of a job without having been previously promised one. Both educational and job migration appear to be empirical sub-types of the continental crawl. Yet it is important to stress that such migration is not totally dependent on the individual efforts of the migrants since they must pass the test of political exclusion enforced by the U.S. Immigration and Naturalization Service. (iv) *Transfer migration*, or migration because of a transfer from one part of a multinational corporation in Canada to another part, usually the head office, in the United States. This is the typical example of continental sponsorship since it involves both the political and corporate-occupational exclusion policies of the U.S. upper class in favour of privileged Canadiaus.

The rest of the paper will deal empirically with the migration of Canadian managers to the United States on the basis of a 1975 survey. After describing characteristics of the sample in the next two sections, we will discuss some avenues of migration and some individual reasons given by the respondents in the survey for their migration to the United States. The last section will deal mainly with the individual and collective characteristics of the respondents affecting the avenue of their migration within the context of historical changes in the relations between Canada and the United States.

Sample and Method

The names, addresses, age, education and province of birth of the 516 Canadian-born residents in the United States listed in Standard and Poor (1975) were collected. Mailed questionnaires were sent out in the autumn of 1975 to all these persons, 58% (297) of whom returned completed questionnaires by the start of the mail strike in the Canada Post Office. The sample is representative by province of birth, but slightly biased toward the younger and more highly educated. Comparisons with Porter (1965: 292) and Clement (1975: 192, 232) reveal that the sample comes from a less privileged class and ethnic background than the Canadian economic elite but from more privileged origins than the Canadian population as a whole.

Almost one-half of the sample (48%) were employed in manufacturing. A further one-quarter (24%) were in finance, the majority of these being in insurance companies. Practically all (93%) of the corporations represented in the sample were American-controlled. Eighty percent of the careers in the sample were concentrated in the four areas of finance (33%), management and administration (20%), sales (16%), and engineering and science (11%). Twenty-six percent of the sample were presidents of corporations and a further 9% were chairmen. Thus 35% occupied very senior corporate positions. The other largest single category are vice-presidents (45%). The remaining 20% of the sample are distributed almost equally among treasurers, general and sales managers, secretaries, vice-chairman, owners, etc. Only 3% of the sample are members of Clement's (1976) U.S. economic elite located at the head of the 194 dominant U.S. corporations.

Avenues of Migration

Respondents were asked whether they migrated to the United States as children with their parents and family, went for education, migrated to look for a job, or were transferred by the corporation which employed them. The largest proportion (41%) were involved in familial migration, followed by job migration (24%), transfer migration (21%), and education migration (14%). Respondents involved in famil al migration indicated why their parents left Canada. The largest proportion (38%) mentioned the experience of unemployment in Canada. Other reasons were: transferred to the United States (11%), returned home to the U.S. after a period of residence in Canada (18%), health reasons (5%), setting up a business in the U.S. (4%), and various other reasons (25%). Looking at respondents who migrated without their parents as a separate subsample, job migration (41%) and transfer migration (36%) accounted for the majority followed by educational migration (24%). It seems that transfer migration is much more significant in the respondents' generation (36%) than in the parental generation (11%). This suggests that continental sponsorship may be increasing over time, although the two generations are not strictly comparable. This issue will be returned to later in a more direct way.

Canadian Barriers, U.S. Opportunities

As suggested above, Canadian managers migrated to the U.S. partly because of their experience of exclusion or barriers in Canada and their expectations of greater opportunities in the United States. About 40% of the sample not migrating with their parents reported having experienced some type of barrier in Canada while 78% stated they migrated because of greater opportunities in the U.S. Social exclusion from the upper levels of Canadian society is strongly related to ethnic and class origins. Thirty-eight per cent of the British in the sample experienced Canadian barriers in contrast to 55% of the non-British. Only about 37% of the upper, upper-middle and middle classes reported barriers in Canada compared to 51% of the working class.

Perceptions of barriers and opportunities differed markedly by type of migration to the U.S. Managers transferred to the U.S. were less likely to perceive barriers in Canada or greater opportunities in the U.S. than individuals migrating on their own for education or work. Only 31% of managers transferred experienced Canadian barriers compared to 47% involved in job migration and 67% in educational migration. Similarly, only 80% of those transferred migrated because of greater U.S. opportunities compared to 90% of the job migrants and 95% of the educational migrants.

It appears that more privileged Canadians receive continental sponsorship while less privileged migrants are more likely to engage in the continental crawl. Thirty-nine per cent of managers with British origins were transferred compared to only 21% of the non-British. The latter are more likely to engage especially in educational migration. About 37% of managers with upper, upper-middle and middle class origins were transferred in contrast to 30% of the working class.

The rest of this section will focus on the respondents' specifications of Canadian barriers and U.S. opportunities as reasons for their migration. These perceptions of the opportunity structures of Canada and the U.S. concern classes of reproduction and nomination in Canada and the United States, the relation of individual traits to corporate organization, and the U.S. (elite) appraisal of Canadians.

Classes of Reproduction and Nomination

The managers in the sample appear to believe that classes of reproduction are more operative in Canada than the U.S. and classes of nomination are more operative in the U.S. than Canada. Thus they felt excluded from the Canadian upper class because of their collective characteristics and felt they had gained entry into the U.S. upper class because of their individual characteristics. The characteristics along this collective-individual dimension that will now be examined qualitatively are ethnic and national origin, family, age, sex, and region.

Ethnic and National Origin. Many managers not of British stock complained of "corporate discrimination against the non-British" in Canada. One respondent argued that "corporate access was very limited in Canada to minorities. CPR, CNR, Sun Life, etc., etc. were closed Anglo-Saxon clubs." At times such exclusivity took the form of feelings of discrimination against specific minorities, as in the case of a Jewish person who migrated on his own to the U.S. in 1936 because of "racial prejudice" in Quebec. Other persons left Quebec for the U.S. because of their "inability to speak French fluently." In contrast, the U.S. was described by respondents as relatively free of such "ethnic encumbrances." The managers saw "less religious prejudice and less 'British Empire' influence" in the U.S. One manager argued that there was a greater "chance of acceptance in the U.S.A. and promotions on my own merits and achievements, rather than on ethnic or social background."

Regarding national origin, some respondents complained of the hold the "British empire" had on Canada resulting in blocked business opportunities. One manager expressed the "desire to be free of the English cult of colonialism" which was concretized by a second manager: "Canadian post-war industry [was] 'slaved' to English technical management misfits – no opportunity for a colonial (Canadian) and so chance for a successful product. (E.g. Can. crown companies – Avro & Canadair)." Other respondents, Canadian-born but of American parents working for U.S. subsidiaries in Canada, complained of anti-Americanism north of the 49th parallel. One manager explained: "I was born of American parents and castigated at school (in Canada) during W. W. I because of it." A second Canadian-born manager of American parentage migrated because of the following bitter experience in Quebec: "*Bitter Canadian anti-Americanism* [this was underlined in red ink by the respondent]. A determination not to endure any more of it." This manager then wrote in the margin of the questionnaire in red ink: "This, really, is the crux of it all!"

Family. Some managers migrated southward because of their perception of greater family capitalism in Canada than in the U.S., although the objective stock-holding evidence on this comparative problem is not clear. One respondent wrote: "My experience and my friends' experience in Canada at that time (1924 to 1950) was that most Canadian firms were family owned with advancement limited by family members. Advancement appeared to be based on 'who you know' instead of what you knew or your contribution to [the] company. In the U.S.A. I have been able to advance to [the] president's position in a firm with multiple plants employing 650. Could I have done that in Canada?"

Sex. Sex discrimination also comes into play, but seems more related to the question of why women do not become high ranking executives than to the type of migration among Canadian managers. This is evident from the fact that only two women found their way into our sample. One women reported "being female" as a barrier in Canada and the other stated: "at the time I started women were not so apt to get a chance in the finance field."

Age. Some managers thought opportunities for advancement were closely related to the emphasis placed on age and seniority. One respondent argued that "Canadian business seemed more restrictive in that opportunities were based more on seniority than ability" while another manager stated that "in the U.S. ability is better recognized vis-a-vis age than in Canada." However, Tepperman (1975: 60–71) argues that the probability of some upward mobility is greater in an age-dependent than an age-independent opportunity structure. Perceptions and experiences do not always blend.

Region. Region of birth can also influence the experience of exclusion since mobility opportunities in Canada are deeply affected by rates and types of expansion in capitalist structures which vary markedly across the country. Only 33% of migrants born in Ontario experienced barriers. These percentages were much higher for all other regious: Atlantic (44%), Quebec (51%), Manitoba and Saskatchewan (41%), Alberta (41%), and British Columbia (47%). These differences are not surprising in view of the fact that Ontario is the centre of capitalist expansion in Canada (Cuneo, 1977). One respondent reported "not enough manufacturing in Western Canada" and another referred to the "lack of opportunity in the Maritime Provinces." The Atlantic is peripheral to the centres of both Canadian and American corporate power. As a result, analogous to the Canadian equation of upward mobility with outward migration to the United States is the Atlantic equation as well of upward mobility with eastward migration to Montreal and Toronto. This is illustrated by one manager who stated as a reason for his migration to the U.S.: "Lack of opportunity here in Nova Scotia, except in banks. Had I remained in Nova Scotia, I would probably have gone into the Bank of Nova Scotia and moved up in that organization. But this would have required moving to Montreal or Toronto."

Corporate Organization and Individual Characteristics

The greater importance of classes of nomination in the U.S. was linked in the minds of the respondents to differences in corporate organization in the two countries. The managers recognized that opportunities for individual career advancement were greater in the United States because of the smaller and more stunted corporate organization in Canada.

Respondents consistently complained about the "lack of opportunity" in Canada in contrast to the U.S. This was dramatically underscored by one manager who stated the reason why so many Canadian businessmen migrate to the U.S.: "I would say for money and potential for speedier advancement based on ability. Personally, I was VP of my company at 34, GM at 39, and president at 41. I don't think I could have moved that rapidly in Canada."

The managers complained of a "lack of economic development," the "lack of venture capital," and the "lack of large Canadian controlled companies" in Canada. The complaint was not over the lack of *any* large Canadian companies but over the *small number* of them. This meant for at least one manager that positions at the top were controlled by "the 'Banking Monopoly' and the 'Professional Monopoly' !" Another respondent traced the problem to market size: "the population of Canada was simply too small to generate adequate financing for the development of the products I was researching." In contrast, in the U.S. "there is greater opportunity through (the) sheer size of U.S.

business." This was quantitatively expressed by one manager: "business opportunities expand as a function of market sizes, x^n, where n is greater than 1, $\therefore$ greater ranges of opportunities in U.S. – unless special circumstances supplies the same thing in Canada." The larger American corporations and their markets are associated with the existence of more venture capital which attracts Canadians who are innovative capitalists, as the following quote illustrates: "5 men and myself started a successful helicopter company using venture capital. 15 years later we had 5200 employees and I was V.P. Engineering. This phenomena of new venturism was not possible in Canada in 1946, and I see no sign of it in 1975."

Many of these characteristics were related to the multinational nature of U.S. companies. As one manager succinctly expressed the situation: "In today's economic world, many of the opportunities for satisfying careers in world wide corporations are found in the U.S. This attracts Canadian businessmen." But the issue is more complicated than this. It is not merely the greater number of multinationals in the U.S. that attracts Canadian businessmen but also the fact that they extend into Canada. Such companies employ Canadians and their career advancement is necessarily linked to southward migration .One manager expressed it this way: "In so many instances the 'ladder' just happens to lead to the U.S." The "just happens" is explained by another manager: "if one works for an American company subsidiary in Canada, it is often necessary to move to the U.S. to have continuing advancement." Thus we see that the eldorado or highly laudatory view of Canadians toward the United States (Cuneo, 1976) is deeply rooted in the corporate dependence of Canada on its southern neighbour.

U.S. (Elite) Appraisal

The continental sponsorship and the continental crawl of Canadians into the American corporate world is dependent, in the final analysis, on the appraisal of their suitability by Americans in general and the U.S. state and economic elites in particular who control their entry. Some comments by the managers in the sample reveal that they were at least vaguely aware of this. One Canadian manager who had been in the U.S. since 1926 stated: "The Canadians that have come to the States have done a good job for their employer, therefore other Canadians can ride their coattails. Let's face it, nowhere in the world can you find very nice people, except in Canada. Canadians as a rule are very highly regarded by Americans." One reason for this was offered by another manager: "Over here (in the U.S.A.) Canadians have a reputation of being good workers." It is revealing that one manager was so blunt in drawing the conclusion that Canadians were colonials in the following manner: "Canadians are highly regarded in the U.S.A. much as Scots are in London."

The above qualitative analysis of reasons for migration to the U.S. gives us concrete indications of the motives of managers but fails to provide a systematic and rigorous determination of the independent influences affecting avenue of migration. It is to such a determination that we now turn.

Factors Influencing Avenues of Migration

In this section a quantitative analysis of several influences on type or avenue of migration will be carried out. These are four collective characteristics under classes of reproduction (ethnicity, whether father was a corporate official, father's education, and father's occupation), one major individual characteristic prominent in classes of nomination (respondent's educational attainment), two ideological perception variables (Canadian barriers and U.S. opportunities), the social link of Canadian managers with the U.S. before migration, and three "time variables" (year of birth, year left Canada for the U.S., and age left Canada). For the sake of this analysis, only the contrast between transfer migration on the one hand and educational and job migration on the other hand will be focused on. Children migrating with their families are not subject to the same set of forces in the same way as adult migrants. Our expectation is that managers with high social origins and educational attainment will more likely be transferred to the U.S. (continental sponsorship) than move on their own in search of education and work (continental crawl). Because the latter have lower social origins, they are more likely to experience greater barriers in Canada and perhaps perceive greater opportunities for themselves in the U.S. We will thus attempt to disentangle the influence of the ideological perceptions of barriers and opportunities on avenues of migration from the collective and individual characteristics, respectively, of social origins and educational attainment. Because controlled entry into the U.S. managerial class is a selective exclusion process, we would expect those Canadians previously having various types of contacts with the U.S. to more likely be transferred. Such contracts allow their appraisal by U.S. multinational corporations. The lack of such contacts probably forces aspiring managers to "try it on their own" in the continental crawl. Finally, the influence of time on avenues of migration is considered in three ways: historical changes in relations between Canada and the United States; the generation or year of birth of the managers; and, the point in their careers when they leave Canada for the United States. Because of the increasing historical presence of the American multinational firm in the Canadian economy and the increasing difficulty of gaining access to the upper reaches of the corporate world through the long crawl from low social origins, it is expected that continental sponsorship through transfers from high Canadian social origins to corporations in the U.S. will increasingly become prevalent throughout the twentieth century. The other two time influences relate more directly to the biography of the individual. Because most executives and managers peak in their careers between 45 and 65 years of age, older persons will more likely be transferred to the United States and at a later point in their careers. Younger persons and those at earlier points in their careers will migrate to the U.S. more in search of education and jobs. These influences will be expressed separately as year of birth and the age that executives and managers left Canada permanently.

The independence of the influences of these factors can only be determined through a multivariate analysis. The results of this analysis appear in Table 2. The dependent variable, avenue of migration, equals 2 if transfer migration and 1 if education or job migration. The correlation coefficients in column 1 measure the degree of association between avenue of migration and the eleven

Table 2

Zero- and partial-order effects of eleven independent variables on avenue of migration ($N=116$)

Independent Variables	Zero-order correlations (1)	Partial-order		Standardized Regression		
		(2) Origins	(3) Origins, Respondent's Education	(4) Origins, Respondent's Education, Ideology	(5) Origins, Respondent's Education, Ideology, Ties	(6) Origins, Respondent's Education, Ideology, Ties, Time
Social Origins						
1. Ethnicity	.15	.13	.13	.08	.01	.02
2. Father Corporate Official	.01	−.07	−.08	−.08	−.05	−.05
3. Father's Education	.20	.18	.16	.16	.10	.08
4. Father's Occupation	.07	.05	.08	.05	.06	.09
Educational Attainment						
5. Respondent's Canadian Education	.18		.16	.17	.09	.06
Ideological Perceptions						
6. Canadian Barriers	−.23			−.21	−.10	−.04
7. U.S. Opportunities	−.04			−.02	.00	.05
Continental Ties						
8. Pre-Migration Ties	.55				.49	.35
Time: History and Careers						
9. Year left Canada	.40					.39
10. Year of Birth	.07					−.26
11. Age left Canada	.49					.11
R		.24	.29	.36	.58	.65
R²		.06	.08	.13	.33	.43

2   The independent variables were coded as follows: Ethnicity: British=1; non-British=0; Father corporate official: yes=1; no=0; Father's education: elementary=1; secondary= 2; university=3; Father's occupational class: working=1; middle=2; capitalist=3; Respondent's Canadian education: university=2; non-university=1; Perception of barriers to succeeding in Canada: yes=2; no=1; Perceived greater opportunity in U.S. as one reason for migrating: mentioned=2; not mentioned=1; Continental ties with the U.S. before migrating is an index from 0 to 3 covering social ties, intra-company business ties, and other bisiness ties; Year left Canada: 1930 or before=1; 1931–40=2; 1941–50= 3; 1951–60=4; 1961 or later=5; Year of birth: 1900 or before=1; 1901–10=2; 1911– 20=3; 1921–30=4; 1931 or later=5; Age left Canada permanently: 20 or younger=1; 21–25=2; 26–30=3; 31 or older=4. A listwise deletion of missing cases is employed (67% valid cases).

variables listed on the left. The independent influences of these eleven variables are measured by the standardized regression of avenue of migration on them shown in columns 2 to 6.

Social Origins. Of the four social origin variables shown in column 1 (ethnicity, father corporate official, father's education, and father's occupation), ethnicity (r = .15) and father's education (r = .20) seem most strongly related to migration. This means that respondents with British ancestry and university-educated fathers have a greater chance of being transferred to the U.S. than those not having British ancestry and fathers with only secondary or elementary schooling. The latter are more likely to go to the United States on their own by way of the continental crawl in search of education or work. The independent influences of these four origin variables are separated from one another in column 2. Ethnicity and father's education still continue to have stronger influences on migration than father being a corporate official or father's occupational class. The negative coefficient associated with father being a corporate official suggests that paternal involvement with the corporate world does not result in children's inheritance of corporate privileges in the form of corporate transfers. This, of course, attests to the difficulty of passing on family inheritance through an organizational form over which at least our sample may not have exclusive control. Also interesting is the weakness of father's occupational class. This finding along with the strength of father's education perhaps suggests, at the managerial level, that the socialization experiences associated with education may be more important in establishing contacts useful for later company preferences in transfers than father's occupation which largely operates outside the sphere the individual child grows up in. The persistence of the ethnic influence is interesting because it suggests that the British are privileged not only in the internal stratification system of Canada, as Porter and others have shown, but also in exits from Canadian society. Conversely, the non-British appear "negatively privileged" not only in terms of the internal Canadian social structure, but also in having to exit from this structure with little continental sponsorship from the corporate world.

Educational Attainment. The independent influence of respondent's Canadian education relative to the four social origin variables is introduced in column 3. Comparing the r = .18 for respondent's education in column 1 with the B = .16 in column 3 suggests that this variable has an influence on migration almost entirely independent of the four social origin variables. Respondents with high education are most likely to be transferred to the U.S. regardless of whether they come from high or low social origins. By comparing columns 2 and 3 it is seen that ethnicity and father's education persist almost at the level of strength they had without controlling for respondent's education. It cannot therefore be said that the effect of privileged social origins is wiped out by the greater importance of educational attainment in the child's generation. Thus, classes of reproduction and classes of nomination are both important influences on type of migration to the U.S.

Ideological Perceptions. The introduction of the two ideological variables relating to perceptions of barriers in Canada and opportunities in the U.S. in column 4 considerably weakens the influence of ethnicity on migration. This is so particularly because the non-British seem to have migrated because of their experience of barriers in Canada ($r = -.22$ between ethnicity and perception of barriers). Also significant in itself is the decrease in the effect of the barriers variable from only $r = -.23$ in column 1 to $B = -.21$ in column 4. This suggests that the experience of barriers in Canada forces migrants out looking for education and jobs and that this influence operates independently of social origins and respondent's education. The perception of greater opportunities in the U.S. has little influence on the type of migration of managers ($r = -.04$; $B = -.02$). This suggests that aspiring managers who leave Canada on their own do so, not primarily because they perceive greater opportunities in the U.S., but because they are "pushed out" by the lack of opportunities in Canada.

Continental Ties. The introduction of pre-migration continental ties with the U.S. in column 5 drastically alters the influence of several other variables on type of migration. As noted previously, managers who set up contacts with the U.S., whether social or business, have a greater chance of subsequently being transferred to the U.S. ($r = .55$ which reduces slightly to $B = .49$). Establishing such ties makes a candidate for transfer known to his U.S. supervisors. The latter appraise the suitability of his qualities and, on the basis of their first-hand assessment, are able to sponsor his move into the U.S. managerial group. The lack of such contacts seriously hinders the chances of transfer to the U.S., as suggested by the moderately large size of this regression coefficient. The fact that this influence on type of migration operates almost independently of the other variables reported in column 5 suggests that, regardless of the qualifications of the candidate established by privileged social background and the "correct" Canadian training, he still must go through a final selection process involving first-hand appraisal before being admitted into the American managerial group. The deterioration of the influences of ethnicity ($B = .01$), father's education ($B = .10$), and Canadian education ($B = .09$) is testimony to the crucial nature of the social selection of Canadian managers enforced by the exclusion policies of the corporate elite of both the U.S. and Canada.

History and Careers. Finally, the three time-related variables (year left Canada, year of birth, and age on leaving Canada permanently) are introduced in column 6. There is practically no change in the influence of year left Canada from column 1 to 6 ($r = .40$; $B = .39$). This suggests that a broad macro-historical process is at work which is difficult to specify operationally but intuitively seems related to the increasing presence of the American multinational corporation in Canada as the twentieth century progresses. There is a drastic change over time, then, in the type of migration to the U.S. Those who left early in the twentieth century were more likely to migrate on their own in search of higher education or a job in the U.S. (continental crawl). Very few such migrants were transferred directly. However, as the twentieth century wore on and as the American multinational corporation in Canada became a route to the highest occupational levels outside Canada, Canadians migrating to the U.S. were more likely to be transferred through continental sponsorship. This suggests an increasing direct control over migration by multinational organizations, an increasing predominance of continental sponsorship mobility, and a decline in the continental crawl. Since sponsorship mobility favours those from more privileged Canadian backgrounds, the data suggest that the route south from Canada to the U.S. is increasingly becoming exclusive and perhaps less open to upward mobility from humble origins. However, the situation is somewhat more complicated than this. Although migrants leaving Canada at a later point in time tend to be more highly educated ($r = .21$) and to have more highly educated fathers ($r = .12$), occupationally they come from lower paternal occupational origins ($r = -.13$) and have non-corporate fathers ($r = -.10$). This perhaps suggests that to be transferred out of Canada, Canadian managers must increasingly either be from higher origins or attain that position from lower origins *before* migrating. Individual migration to the U.S. directly from lower origins is increasingly less possible. For those of humble origins, the continental crawl directly into the U.S. is increasingly being shifted to the struggles of upward mobility *in Canada* followed by continental sponsorship into the U.S. for the successful. For those of humble origin, unencumbered mobility is blocked not only within Canada, as before, but increasingly *out of* Canada as well.

The other two time variables in column 6 relate more to the biography of the individual. They suggest that at the partial-order level, migrants leave Canada through transfers more when they are older while the young are more likely to go to the U.S. searching for education and jobs.

Variance Explained. By conventional standards of survey analysis, we have done fairly well in explaining 43% of the variance in type of migration (see bottom of column 6). This is mainly accounted for by the time and continental links variables. The other variables have weaker independent influences.

Conclusions

A traditional proposition has been that Canada is less of an open society than the United States, and that this difference is embedded in their value structures and historical experiences (cf. Lipset, 1963; 1970; Naegele, 1964). Recent analyses on Canadian-American differences based on samples drawn from diverse subgroups in their populations suggest that this proposition appears invalid (cf. Turritin, 1974; Cuneo and Cutris, 1975; Pineo, 1976). However, the case may be different at the higher managerial level, as argued in this paper. The exclusionist practices of dominant classes in these societies in the context of international monopoly capitalism may weaken the degree of upward mobility into high managerial ranks in Canada in contrast to the United States.

The traditional proposition concerning Canadian-American differences may therefore be correct but for incorrect reasons and applied to inappropriate levels of the class structure. This new proposition, with the weight of the theoretical framework and some evidence provided in this paper, underscores the importance of studying social mobility in its social structural and historical context rather than strictly as an individual phenomenon torn from its broader setting.

As the multinationalization of corporations has increased throughout the first three-quarters of the twentieth century, the direction and type of mobility into high managerial ranks have changed. Mobility into high managerial ranks within national frontiers has been redirected to movements across national frontiers, often within the same corporate organization. The type of mobility has changed from the continental crawl from low origins in the early twentieth century to continental sponsorship from high origins in the latter part of this century. These changes have profound implications for the structure of class and mobility in both Canada and the United States. The class system of each country becomes identified less with political-legal distinctions and more with international corporate integration. This means that appeals for mobility opportunities can no longer be made only in national public forums in state organizations but must seek out international private forums in multinational corporations.

REFERENCES

AMIN, Samir
    1974   *Accumulation on a World Scale*. New York: Monthly Review Press.
BECKER, James F.
    1973a "Class structure and conflict in the managerial phase: I," *Science and Society* XXXVII, 259–277.
    1973b "Class structure and conflict in the managerial phase: II," *Science and Society* XXXVII, 437–453.
BRAVERMAN, Harry
    1974 *Labour and Monopoly Capital*. New York: Monthly Review Press.
CARCHEDI, G.
    1975a "On the economic identification of the new middle class," *Economy and Society* 4 (1), 1–86.
    1975b "Reproduction of social classes at the level of production relations." *Economy and Society* 4 (4), 361–417.
CLEMENT, Wallace
    1975 *The Canadian Corporate Elite*. Toronto: McClelland and Stewart.
    1976 *Continental Capitalism: Corporate Power Relations Between Canada and the United States*. Ph.D. dissertation, Dept. of Sociology, Carleton University, Ottawa, Ontario.
CUNEO, Carl J.
    1976 "The social basis of political continentalism in Canada," *Canadian Review of Sociology and Anthropology* 13 (1), 55–70.
    1977 "A class perspective on regionalism," in Dan Glenday, Hubert Guindon and Allan Turowetz (eds.), *Modernization and the Canadian State*. Toronto: Macmillan.
CUNEO, Carl J. and James E. CURTIS
    1975 "Social ascription in the educational and occupational status attainment of urban Canadians," *Canadian Review of Sociology and Anthropology* 12 (1), 6–24.

FRANK, Andre Gunder
    1969   *Capitalism and Underdevelopment in Latin America*. New York: Monthly Review Press.
GALTUNG, Johann
    1971   "A structural theory of imperialism," *Journal of Peace Research* 8, 77–117.
GOLDSTEIN, Walter
    1974   "The multinational corporation: a challenge to contemporary socialism," pp.
            279–301 in Ralph Miliband and John Saville (eds.), *The Socialist Register* 1974.
            London: Merlin.
GRAY, Herb
    1972   *Foreign Direct Investment in Canada*. Ottawa: Information Canada.
LENIN, V. I.
    1973   *Imperialism, The Highest Stage of Capitalism*. Peking: Foreign Languages Press.
LEVITT, Kari
    1970   *Silent Surrender*. Toronto: Macmillan.
LIPSET, S. M.
    1963   "Value differences, absolute or relative: the English-speaking democracies," Ch. 7
            in *The First New Nation*. New York: Basic.
    1970   "Revolution and counterrevolution: the United States and Canada," Ch. 2 in his
            Revolution and Counterrevolution. Garden City, N.Y.: Doubleday.
MAGDOFF, Harry
    1969   *The Age of Imperialism*. New York: Monthly Review Press.
McKIE, Craig
    1977   "American managers in Canada: a comparative profile." *This Issue*.
MANDEL, Ernest
    1975   *Late Capitalism*. London: NLB.
NAEGELE, Kaspar D.
    1964   "Canadian society: further reflections," pp. 497–522 in Bernard R. Blishen *et al.*
            (eds.), *Canadian Society* (2nd ed.). Toronto: Macmillan.
PARAI, Louis
    1969   *Immigration and Emigration of Professional and Skilled Manpower During the Post-War
            Period*. Ottawa: Queen's Printer.
PINEO, Peter C.
    1976   "Social mobility in Canada: the current picture," *Sociological Focus* 9 (2), 109–
            123.
PARKIN, Frank
    1974   "Strategies of social closure in class formation," pp. 1–18 in Frank Parkin (ed.),
            The Social Analysis of Class Structure. London: Tavistock.
PORTER, John
    1965   *The Vertical Mosaic*. Toronto: University of Toronto Press.
POULANTZAS, Nicos
    1975   *Classes in Contemporary Capitalism*. London: NLB.
STANDARD and POOR
    1975   *Standard and Poor's Register of Corporations, Directors and Executives*, Vol. 2. New York:
            Standard and Poor's Corporation.
SUNKEL, Osvaldo
    1973   "Transnational capitalism and national disintegration in Latin America," *Social
            and Economic Studies* 22 (1), 132–176.
TEPPERMAN, Lorne
    1975   *Social Mobility in Canada*. Toronto: McGraw-Hill.
THOMAS, Brinley
    1973   *Migration and Economic Growth*. Cambridge: Cambridge University Press.
TURNER, Ralph
    1966   "Modes of social ascent through education: sponsored and contest mobility," pp.
            449–458 an Reinhird Bendix and S. M. Lipset (eds.), *Class, Status and Power*.
            New York: Free Press.

TURRITIN, A. H.
    1974   "Social mobility in Canada: a comparision of three provincial studies and some
           methodological questions," *Canadian Review of Sociology and Anthropology*, special VIII
           World Congress of Sociology publication, 163–186.
U.S. Dept. of Commerce
    1973   *Statistical Abstract of the United States 1973*, Washington, D.C.
U.S. Dept. of Justice
    1970   *Report of the Commissioner of Immigration and Naturalization*, Washington, D.C.
WEBER, Max
    1968   *Economy and Society*. New York: Bedminster.

"Equality before the Law" and "Equal Protection of the Law"

A Comparative View

WILLIAM V. MONOPOLI

Boston College Law School, Boston, U.S.A.

CONSIDERATION of the development of equality before the law in the United States and Canada perhaps most productively might begin by giving attention to some salient social and political characteristics of the two nations. Differences between the Canadian and American political systems, and their implications for judicial development of the concept of equality, will be discussed in later sections of this paper. This section will consider why the two nations' treatment of so seemingly fundamental an issue as equality before the law is so different.

It should be noted at the outset that Canadian and American guarantees of equality are similar but not synonymous. Section 1 of the Canadian Bill of Rights identifies specific "human rights and fundamental freedoms" declared to exist "without discrimination by reason of race, national origin, colour, religion or sex." Section 1(b) specifies that one such freedom is "the right of the individual to equality before the law and the protection of the law . . ." In the United States, Section 1 of the Fourteenth Amendment to the Constitution declares that no state [shall] "deny to any person within its jurisdiction the equal protection of the law." Both the Canadian and American guarantees are sufficiently vague so as to require judicial interpretation, and the courts of each country have had to define the key phrases.

In some respects, Canada and the United States are very similar. Both share an English common law heritage. Both are highly urbanized and industrialized; both are representative democracies; both enjoy considerable per capita wealth. And immigration has been essential to the development of both. John Porter suggests that Canadians as often as not compare themselves with Americans. In that way, if Canadians make any judgments about how they have done since Confederation, they are more likely to make them in terms of North American standards, by comparing what they have accomplished with the American experiment (Porter: 1967, 386).

The nature of the political traditions of the two countries clearly is associated with Canadian and American dispositions toward equality guaranteed by law. Canada, in the British tradition and in contrast to the United States, has avoided so-called entrenchment of fundamental freedoms. The Canadian

Bill of Rights, after all, is a legislative enactment which can be repealed entirely or made not to apply to specific legislation. Perhaps illustrative of its status is that discussion of it is often preceded by the caveat that the Bill is "only" or "merely" a law passed by Parliament and not part of the British North America Act.

Despite that, and despite Canadian traditions of Parliamentary supremacy, interpretation of the Bill has been left to the courts. The development of the interpretation of Section 1(b), the specific guarantee of "equality before the law," will be traced later.

For the present, sociological and demographic material will be considered to explain how two apparently similar societies have come to differ so much in developing guarantees of legal equality.

The important historical difference, of course, is that political and legal institutions in the United States emerged from revolution. As a result, liberty and equality were "charter values"; equality of opportunity has been one of the recurring themes of American culture (Porter: *ibid.*, 386). On the other hand, as Robert Presthus has shown, Canada, with roots in counter-revolution and monarchical institutions has been considerably influenced by European forms, with salient consequences for such functional areas as higher education, economic productivity and political participation (Presthus: 1974, 1976). Porter suggests that Canadians judge more in terms of what they have achieved rather than in what they might achieve, and that this social conservatism has been reinforced by the efforts of Canadians to distinguish themselves from Americans. He concludes that the lack of a revolutionary tradition means that the "charter values" that guide the nation are not clear. Lipset's analysis also hold that Canada's anti-revolutionary posture has led to the continuance of British ascriptive and elitist value patterns (Lipset: 1964. 181). Clearly, egalitarian "charter values" are not necessarily a requisite of constitutionally-guaranteed equality before the law. The point, however, is that there is likely to be an association between identifiable national values and the existence of guarantees of equality.

Seymour Lipset notes that Canadian values reflect the fact that Canada has always been more conservative than the United States, "that its early political history from 1776 on involved the defeat of radical reform, and that consequently some of the traditionalist 'Tory' values which declined in the United States continued in Canada" (Lipset: 1971, 478). He attributes the historical prevalence of ascriptive rather than egalitarian attitudes in Canada at least in part to anti-Americanism, or to a desire to maintain separation from the United States. Throughout the nineteenth century, Canada guarded against U.S. expansionism and could not leave its frontier communities unprotected or autonomous. "Frontier egalitarianism and individualism were muted in Canada because they were linked to American values and might conceivably undermine national integrity" (Lipset: 1971, 480). One consequence of the value system which emerged is that Canadians "have always been less intolerant of economic inequality and social stratification" (Lipset: *ibid.*).

The British influence effectively contributed to this conservatism; democratization was likely to have been considered an American influence in Canada in the nineteenth century, and partly for that reason, was a trend to be avoided. "Since the survival of Canada as a separate entity depended on her not being submerged under an American flood, such influences were fought as dangerous to our Canadian ethos" (Underhill: 1961, 15).

Although these attitudes may have to do only indirectly with the development of "equality before the law" in Canada, they suggest why no attempt was made at the national level to provide such a guarantee. In light of the nation's traditional conservatism, it is not surprising that when a Bill of Rights finally was enacted in 1960, it was as an act of Parliament rather than as an amendment to the B.N.A. Act.

That Canada is traditionally identified as having ascriptive and elitist values, while the United States is more often described as being oriented toward egalitarianism and opportunity to achieve, suggests that differences exist along these dimensions in the legal systems of the two nations. These expectations are in fact well-founded. In Canada, lack of a constitutionally-based guarantee of equality before the law has been reinforced by a conservative judiciary and by traditions of Parliamentary supremacy. In the United States, the Constitutional guarantee of equal protection of the law has been extended (largely by a politically active Supreme Court) to substantive areas – education and employment, for example – an outcome probably neither intended nor anticipated by the authors of the Fourteenth Amendment.

Another important dimension along which Canada and the U.S. may be compared is the extent of political integration – the sense of "nation" present in the two societies. This concept might be understood as the extent to which citizens consider themselves members of a national (as opposed to provincial or state or ethnic) body. In societies otherwise as similar in their support for democratic government and institutions as the U.S. and Canada appear to be, the country whose citizens have less sense of belonging to a national entity may be less likely to promote the existence of a national substantive guarantee of equal protection. One reason is that the Canadian lack of a sense of "nation" as described here suggests the presence of a national government that may be unwilling to provide a guarantee of legal equality or equal protection, especially if such a guarantee may be perceived as a divisive measure exceeding the bounds of federal jurisdiction. Another reason is that such a national government may simply be politically unable to institute such a guarantee without exacerbating relations with provincial governments. Although the extent to which citizens identify themselves as "belonging" to a national entity is not easily judged, ther eare ways in which this tendency, or lack of it, can be indicated. One offered for consideration here is the manner in which, and the extent to which, immigrants are assimilated.

In Canada, biculturalism and bilingualism were given legal status in the Act of Confederation. Partially as a result of the arrangement by which the English and French "charter" groups were constitutionally permitted to retain their identities, other ethnic groups have had considerable freedom to retain their own cultural identities (McKenna: 1969, 433–47). In contrast, the federal union created in the United States in 1789 has been described as primarily political and economic, with relatively little direct ethnic import or cultural implications (McKenna: *ibid.*, 440).

One of the signal historical differences between Canada and the United States, then, is the lack in the United States of any force similar to what has become known in Canada as the French fact. Ethnic groups in Canada, again in part as a result of the nature of the Canadian federation, have at least a potential veto against one another.

In eighteenth-century United States, the dominant group in every state apparently descended from approximately the same British ancestry. One result of this seems to have been that the increase in the sources of immigration in the nineteenth and twentieth centuries has not altered the distribution of ethnic power. The Canadian arrangement, however, leaves the national government open to demands by later-arriving large ethnic groups for language and cultural rights similar to those of the English and French (Higham: 1968, 94–5).

Despite the fact that Canada and the United States share roughly similar physical environments and a common cultural heritage, they developed very different patterns of assimilation (McKenna: *op. cit.*, 433). In the Canadian system, it appears that the difference among ethnic groups, rather than the common characteristics of these groups, has been emphasized. The distinction seems to be that between the "mosaic" in which groups retain an identity, and the so-called American "melting pot", in which group identity declines in favor of a national ideal.

Marian McKenna argues that for Americans, the task of defining a national identity has been made easier by the fact that for nearly two centuries, the idea prevailed that all Americans were immigrants. For Canadians, the task has been more difficult, in part because of the necessity that Canadians "reassure themselves that they were not and should not become Americans" (McKenna, *ibid.*). This has been accomplished, as noted earlier, by the disparaging of American values associated with the development of mass democracy. In this respect, anti-Americanism played an important part in Canadian political and legal development.

The theory that groups in the Canadian "mosaic" have "the right to sustained collective individuality" has been described as being an English concept (McKenna: *ibid.*, 436). Consistent with traditional Tory values was Canadian immigration policy, which attempted to keep the tide of immigrants preponderantly British, or at least American and European. Nearly one-half the immigrants to Canada between 1851 and 1950 were from the British Isles; a quarter of the rest were from the United States. In the same period, the U.S. received 12% of all its immigrants from Italy, 13% from Austria-Hungary and the states that succeeded it, 16% from Germany, 10% from Russia and Poland, and one-third from the British Isles (Higham: *op. cit.*, 97). Few, if any other countries, have received their populations from as many sources as the U.S.;

in comparison, until relatively recently, Canada has tended to receive its immigrant population from a few favored ethnic backgrounds.

It might be useful here to define terms that recur in most discussions of immigration. Ethnicity of a group refers to descent from "ancestors who shared a common culture based on national origin, language, religion or race, or a combination of these." Ethnicity is an ascribed quality which can define status and role (Vallee, Schwartz and Darknell: 1971, 599). Assimilation can be understood either in terms of individuals or ethnic groups taking on the ways of a dominant social group, or as a process in which different ethnic groups become increasingly similar to one another.

Immigrants to the U.S. traditionally have been under pressure to become assimilated into the "American way of life." Becoming an American was a recognized goal of immigrants generally. Two major ways to avoid this assimilation – ethnic bloc settlements and continued loyalty to the native language (if it was not English) faded as immigrant families moved into their second and third generations (McKenna: op. cit., 433). Immigrants to Canada generally have not been subjected to the same kinds of pressures.

It seems likely that for the next several generations, those now considered to be the "new Canadians" will have a very significant impact on Canadian institutions. The nature of this impact – specifically, whether second and third-generation assimilation of the descendants of the present immigrants will result in a stronger sense of "nation" – is uncertain. Still, it appears reasonable to suggest that as the new Canadians and their descendants receive Canadian education and gain exposure to an emerging Canadian national identity, what historically has been for the most part a socially and legally conservative nation in the British tradition may become a more egalitarian one.

Frank Jones notes that historically the Canadian government used ethnic origin as a criterion of selection and encouraged the admission of immigrants such as the British and Northern Europeans, who were considered easiest to assimilate. Jones quotes Mackenzie King as having stated that selection was aimed at maintaining proportions among ethnic groups to avoid making "a fundamental alteration in the character of our population" (Jones: 1971, 633). Despite this, the admission of non-British and non-French immigrants has changed the ethnic composition of Canada: those claiming British origin contributed only 28.3% of the population in 1971, compared to 34.1% in 1961, and 44.3% in 1951. Jones does not attempt to assess the consequences of these changes, except to suggest that the reduction of British-origin population may mean a reduction of British domination of the society.

French Canadians, however, generally have doubted that such trends will benefit them, tending to believe instead that non-British groups assimilate to British value and behavior patterns. French immigration itself traditionally has been low; that the French comprise more than 25% of the total population is due almost entirely to natural increase rather than to immigration (Porter: 1967, 391). The contrary position is that the trend toward relinquishing sub-cultural (i.e., ethnic) patterns in favor of conforming to uniform values is not simply assimilation to the British majority, but rather to secular values and customs which emerge from modern industrial societies (Jones: *op. cit.*).

Two important variables may be expected to change the nature of French Canada, and with it, the nature of Canadian federalism. One variable is low immigration from French sources. In 1926, the French constituted only 2.1% of all arriving immigrants, and in 1961, the proportion was about 3.1%. Since 1926, the proportion of French immigrants has exceeded 10% only twice – in 1931 and 1932 – and it has been suggested that in those years the immigrants of French origin were returning to Canada from the United States rather than emigrating from France (Kalbach: 1972, 35). Low immigration rates historically have been offset by a high natural birth rate. In recent times, however, this second variable, birth rate, has declined significantly.

Both Canadian charter groups, then, are declining proportions of population. As has been noted, the essential conservatism of Canada toward the need for or existence of guarantees of legal equality (as manifested by the fact that not until 1960 was a Bill of Rights of any kind enacted) has been associated with an anti-revolutionary tradition and with political institutions designed to preserve the identities of the two major ethnic components of the population. A society in which those two groups lose their pre-eminent positions may be more favorably disposed to movement away from traditional conservatism toward democratic-based notions of guaranteed fundamental freedoms. Another possibility is that such guaranteed freedoms will evolve from Canadian Supreme Court decisions interpreting the Bill of Rights. This appears unlikely, however, for reasons that will be considered later.

Whether there will be a demand in Canada for increased substantive guarantees of equality before the law is also related to the issue of whether there will be a growing, better-educated middle class in Canadian society. Porter argues that Canadian educational systems were seriously inadequate for meeting the demands for the period of large-scale industrial development that followed World War II. At the beginning of that development, 25 years ago, 55% of the men in the labor force had no more than an elementary school education; about one-third had some high school training, and less than 10% had attended university (Porter: 1971, 403). Porter notes that there was only a marginal improvement in educational levels by the time of the 1961 census.

It has been suggested that industrialization and democratization of a society are concomitant social processes. Both may be delayed by a conservative-value orientation, and both may be served by values resulting from revolutionary beginnings (Porter: 1971, 387). The slowness of the trend toward higher education does not bode well for the possibility that an increasingly better-educated population will make what might be characterized as civil-libertarian demands on Canadian government in the near future.

Many of the factors discussed above – a conservative political tradition based on the separation of the two charter ethnic groups, relatively low educational levels, and a need to maintain some separation from perceived American values – appear to be useful in explaining why Canada has not followed the

U.S. in providing constitutionally-based guarantees of equal protection under the law. Other reasons, of course, can be traced to the very different development of the concept in the two nations.

Development of Constitutional Equal Protection in the United States

The debate preceding the adoption of the Fourteenth Amendment does little to suggest that the authors anticipated that the guarantee of "equal protection of the laws" would later be extended to cases involving such diverse issues as sex discrimination and legislative representation. Two characteristics of the development of equal protection theory are salient here: the extension of equal protection beyond racial questions did not begin until 25 or 30 years ago; and the evolution of the equal protection guarantee occurred, at least initially, in the absence of either legislative or executive action.

Guarantees of equal protection of the laws, or equality before the law, are inherently vague. Such pledges in both Canadian and American law leave the most important terms undefined. Left for judicial resolution are the questions of what constitutes equal protection and under what conditions legislation which makes classifications does so in a way which denies equal protection.

Of the post-Civil War amendments, the Fourteenth clearly has had the most profound implications in American society. Although the Thirteenth Amendment abolished slavery and the Fifteenth Amendment extended to blacks the right to vote, those guarantees alone undoubtedly were insufficient to provide blacks with anything resembling the rights and privileges enjoyed by whites in the nineteenth century (Schwartz: 1970, 30).

The Fourteenth Amendment was apparently designed specifically to protect the civil rights of the emancipated blacks against infringements by the states. Two principal effects were intended: one was to eliminate the effect of the *Dred Scott* decision, which in 1857 barred citizenship for blacks; the other was to make it illegal for the states to deny equal civil rights to blacks given citizenship by Section 1 of the amendment, by providing that no state was to "deprive any person of life, liberty, or property without due process of law" or to "deny to any person within its jurisdiction equal protection of the law" (Schwartz: 1971, *ibid.*).

The Fourteenth Amendment was a command to the states, and thus differs significantly from the first ten amendments to the Constitution – the Bill of Rights. Those amendments, guaranteeing such fundamental freedoms as those of religion, speech, and trial by jury – applied only to the federal government. (The exclusion of the states from the limitations of the Bill of Rights was a result of the Supreme Court's decision in *Barron* v. *Baltimore*, 7 U.S. 243 (1833).) The Fourteenth Amendment provided not only for state protection of rights of citizenship – due process and equal protection – but also for national power to guarantee those rights. Section 5 gave Congress "power to enforce, by appropriate legislation" the other provisions. In some measure, the failure of Congress and the executive to lend substantive meaning to the protections of the Four-teenth Amendment probably impelled the Supreme Court to act.

Although by 1875 Congress had enacted five major pieces of civil rights legislation giving blacks a broad range of rights (e.g., to enter contracts and to acquire and convey property), there is little to indicate that these guarantees existed other than on paper. At least two reasons exist for this condition. One is that the federal leadership of a nation that had just survived a civil war had nothing to gain by pressing for substantive guarantees of equality for recently-freed blacks. A second reason is that blacks, as the intended beneficiaries of the amendments and legislation, had neither the organization nor the political influence to press demands that the legislation be enforced.

The Civil War supposedly freed the federal government to turn from nation-state problems to guaranteeing civil rights. In fact – as might be expected at a time of considerable industrial expansion – when the Fourteenth Amendment was first given effect, its impact was almost entirely restricted to economic and property rights. As a result, the Fourteenth Amendment became a "Magna Carta for business" rather than a guarantee of individual liberties. There is some irony in that for nearly a century after its passage, the Fourteenth Amendment was of no assistance in securing equal rights for blacks, while it protected busi-ness from governmental restraints. In that context, the Supreme Court was consistent with the other branches of government in not developing the Amend-ment in ways which would have assisted the intended beneficiaries. (The strength of Section 5 – which gave Congress the power of enforcement – was reduced in the *Civil Rights* cases (109 U.S. 3 (1933)). The Court held that the rights guaranteed by the Fourteenth Amendment were derived only from the states and that the constitutional authority to protect those rights could be found only in the state's police power. Further, the amendment's prohibitions against denying equal protection or due process were ruled as applying only where state, as distinguished from private, action was involved.

The Supreme Court's reluctance to use the Equal Protection Clause to guarantee individual rights is perhaps best demonstrated by *Plessy* v. *Ferguson* (163 U.S. 537 (1896)). In that case, the Court agreed that equality was the objective of the Fourteenth Amendment. In defining its terms, however, the Court decided separation of the races did not constitute inequality. In effect, *Plessy* said that blacks had an equal right to use public highways but that the use of those highways could be racially differentiated. This resulted from the Court's attempt to distinguish between "political" and "social" equality.

More than a half-century later, *Plessy* was criticized as a "compound of bad logic, bad history, bad sociology and bad constitutional law" (Harris: 1960). Of course, it is relatively easy to assail an old decision that appears by twentieth-century standards to enforce inequality. The more important point, however, is that the Court's decision in *Plessy* probably was an accurate reflection of pre-vailing social and political culture. After *Plessy*, Congress even repealed sub-stantial parts of post-Civil War legislation. The Equal Protection Clause, mean-while, was interpreted as protecting business. As late as 1922, a federal court wrote that of the "three fundamental principles which underlie government, and for which government exists, the protection of life, liberty, and property, the chief of these is property." (*Children's Hospital* v. *Atkins*, 284 Fed. 613, 622 [D.C. Cir. 1922]).

The emphasis in the so-called economic due process decisions was upon the protection of property rights against government action. This process began in 1886 when the Supreme Court first ruled that the Fourteenth Amendment was intended to protect corporations as well as "natural persons" (*Santa Clara County* v. *Southern Pacific R.R.* 118 U.S. 394 (1886)). Laissez-faire economic theory was popular late in the nineteenth century, and civil libertarianism was not. As states attempted to legislate controls over industrialization, corporations found – and the courts ratified – the Due Process Clause as a shield against economic and social legislation (Warren: 1970, 223). The Equal Protection Clause also came to be used much more frequently on behalf of property rights than civil rights. Robert Harris, considering 554 decisions in which the Supreme Court ruled on equal protection claims before 1960, found that 426, or 76.9%, involved legislation affecting economic interests (Harris: 1960, 59). State laws allegedly imposing racial discrimination, or acts of Congress designed to eliminate discrimination, were involved in only 14.2%.

Chief Justice Earl Warren found it "remarkable" that the Court "failed to grasp the importance of the nation's commitment to equality and the increasingly desperate plight of the Negro" (Warren: 1970, 225). That may be true, but it seems to overstate the Court's ability to perceive such issues as equality abstractly, apart from the existing political culture. Indeed, within that culture, the Court's decisions must have been expected. Warren noted that there was no substantial public opposition to the decisions which had the effect of denying blacks equality – or at least equality by present standards. He suggested that if the nineteenth-century Court could be faulted, it must be because the justices "failed to comprehend the significance of the Fourteenth Amendment's promise of equality." Left unanswered, however, is the question of how the justices could have understood in 1896 those truths which appeared self-evident to the Chief Justice 60 years later.

There is general agreement that by the early 1930's, the Court had begun to move toward protection of civil liberties and civil rights. By that time, the Court had begun to subject racial discrimination in the selection of trial and grand juries to scrutiny. In *Norris* v. *Alabama* (294 U.S. 587 (1935)), one of the Scottsboro cases which first developed safeguards for criminal defendants, the Court found a "long-continued, unvarying and wholesale exclusion" of blacks from jury service. This exclusion was deemed inconsistent with the equal protection mandate.

The Court's early decisions on jury trials and defendants' rights were related to the emergence of organizations promoting civil rights. But the work of these groups, such as the N.A.A.C.P., was most markedly rewarded in *Brown* v. *Board of Education* (347 U.S. 483 (1954)), which signalled the Court's intent to define the Equal Protection Clause in terms of individual rather than economic rights.

The circumstances in which that landmark school desegregation case was decided explain why the Court returned to the original intention of the authors of the Fourteenth Amendment. Perhaps the most important of those circumstances was that by 1954, blacks had become an emerging political force in the U.S. Blacks as a group had made substantial gains in education and income during the post-World War II period – or at least those gains were substantial by the standard of how blacks had fared at the turn of the century. With that slowly developing economic power came organization – a prerequisite for gaining a share of political power. Earl Warren attributed the success of blacks seeking to use the Equal Protection Clause in the 1950's to the financial resources and the "remarkable legal talent" of such organizations as the N.A.A.C.P.

The contrast between *Brown* and *Plessy* (which was, in effect, overruled by *Brown*) exemplifies how the Equal Protection Clause was judicially declared to mean in 1954 something entirely different from what it meant in 1896. In *Plessy*, the Court denied the assumption that the enforced separation of the races (in that case, separation in railway passenger coaches) "stamps the colored race with a badge of inferiority." The standard used by the Court in judging the legislation was whether it was reasonable, and the Court found that it was. In *Brown*, the Court found the opposite: that segregation did attach a stigma to the discriminated-against race. The case was brought by blacks who sought admission to public schools on a non-discriminatory basis. The Court found that segregation of children in public schools solely on the basis of race deprived the children of the minority group equal educational opportunities and that "separate educational facilities are inherently unequal" under the Equal Protection Clause.

The *Brown* decision accompanied the development of a social movement toward guaranteeing equality before the law. Civil rights legislation – the first in more than 70 years – was enacted in 1957. Other civil rights bills were passed in 1960, 1964, and 1968. The 1957 and 1960 acts were weak and far from comprehensive, but the fact that they were adopted at all was indicative of the willingness of the legislative and executive branches to become involved in what had previously been exclusively an area for judicial action.

Brown also contributed to the demise of the fiction that held that when presented with a constitutional issue, the Court compares the statute to the Constitution and then declares the statute valid or invalid. What is accepted today as judicial lawmaking was implied early in this century by Charles Evans Hughes's remark: "We are under a Constitution, but the Constitution is what the judges say it is."

As we have seen, the Equal Protection Clause developed from being an instrument to protect economic interests from state intervention to being used to guarantee individual rights. It is necessary to consider how the Court accomplished this. The justices' perceptions of the political role of the Court appear to have had a considerable influence on development of equal protection theory. The unspecific language of the Constitution, and particularly of the Fourteenth Amendment, lends itself well to varying interpretations by the

Court. The substantial judicial discretion involved in policy was indicated by Justice Holmes in 1920 (*Missouri* v. *Holland*, 252 U.S. 416 (1920)).

> When we are dealing with words that also are a constituent act, like the Constitution . . ., we must realize that they have called into life a being the development of which could not have been foreseen completely by the most gifted of its begetters. . . . The case before us must be considered in the light of our whole experience, and not merely in light of what was said a hundred years ago.

This kind of approach lends to the Fourteenth Amendment what Justice Fortas called a "life of its own." Since *Brown*, this has included expansion of the equal protection guarantee from race to such diverse substantive areas as reapportionment and sex discrimination. In criminal law, the Court decided in *Griffin* v. *Illinois* (351 U.S. 12 (1956)), the Fourteenth Amendment required that "all people charged with crime must so far as the law is concerned, stand on an equality before the bar of justice in every American court." On that principle, the Court ruled in *Gideon* v. *Wainwright* (372 U.S. 335 (1963)) that the Fourteenth Amendment required the state to furnish counsel to indigent defendants at the defendants' request.

The Court's departure from nineteenth-century concepts of equality is perhaps best illustrated by its decisions on cases alleging discrimination because of sex. As a result of case law developed since *Brown*, when the constitutionality of a state agency policy is challenged on denial of equal protection, it is subject to a "rational basis" test – that is, the Court determines whether there was a rational basis for the distinctions made in the law. A classification based on race, however, is a suspect classification which the Court subjects to "strict scrutiny." This test shifts the burden to the state to demonstrate that the classification is required by a "compelling state interest." In effect, litigants seeking a remedy for sex-based discrimination asked the Court to consider sex a classification which should come under strict scrutiny, as do legislative classifications based on race, alienage or national origin. The Court, in *Frontiero* v. *Richardson* (411 U.S. 677 (1973)), heard this argument in a case where Mrs. Frontiero, a U.S. Air Force lieutenant, had been denied the right to claim her spouse as a dependent in order to obtain fringe benefits. Although she won on other grounds, four justices agreed that sex should be a suspect classification.

The Court's decisions on sex discrimination, following those on race and reapportionment, support the argument that the drive for equality has been part of a pervasive social movement. The process has not been confined to validation of the rights of blacks. The Supreme Court's support of this social movement, and the resulting "strict scrutiny" test for legislation, has raised questions about policies designed to eradicate discrimination. Specifically in question are "affirmative action" programs developed by government agencies and by private institutions and designed to eliminate racial and sex discrimination. The paradox is that to be effective, policies designed to eliminate racial discrimination must take into account both past and current discrimination. Advocates of such programs argue that the Constitution permits the law to be color-conscious for this purpose; opponents argue that the Constitution forbids it.

The significant point is that the question was in one sense initiated by the Court's new construction of the Equal Protection Clause and has been challenged through the judiciary rather than in the legislature. The first major case to go to the Supreme Court on an issue of "reverse discrimination" was *DeFunis* v. *Odegaard* (94 U.S. 1704 (1974)). DeFunis had applied to the state-operated University of Washington Law School. The Law School had received 1,600 applications for 150 places in the first year class; DeFunis, a white, was among those denied admission. He sued, arguing that separate admission standards for whites and minorities discriminated against him because of race, violating the Equal Protection Clause. The case, nonetheless, typifies the kind of question the Court will soon be required to decide.

Just as the decisions expanding the Equal Protection Clause were a product of a broad-based social movement, it might be predicted that as that movement fades, the Court will be reluctant to further extend equal protection. Although it surely may not be said that equality before the law exists universally for Americans, the expansion of the equal protection guarantee has contributed to at least a partial realization of that ideal. The Constitution mandates equality of right as a principle. But as has been pointed out, the specific form, shape and content of equality is not constitutionally-ordered. There is agreement that elements in society other than the courts should determine the practices, so long as the constitutional principle of equality is followed. The judicial task, then, is essentially negative. "The courts . . . properly refuse to prescribe how the constitutional commands shall be carried out except where the legislatures have so completely failed to act that the courts, in effect, must cope with a default situation – a bankruptcy" (Fortas: 1970, 105).

The importance of "entrenched" fundamental freedoms may not be over-estimated in this context. Unlike the Canadian case, in which the Bill of Rights may be suspended or avoided by Parliament, the U.S. system considers the judgments of the Supreme Court final, absent a constitutional amendment. The U.S. Supreme Court has not been concerned with the possibility of veto by another branch of government.

Judicial involvement in the political process has been criticized as undemocratic (Russell: 1975, 576–93). Nonetheless, the Court has acted when the other branches did not, and in acting, the Court extended the equal protection guarantee to groups who otherwise likely would have remained outside the protection of the Fourteenth Amendment.

Development of Equality Before the Law in Canada

Development of equality before the law in Canada may be compared to the evolution of equal protection theory in the United States at least in the sense that the issues raised before the Canadian Supreme Court resemble the kinds of claims raised by litigants seeking to invoke the Fourteenth Amendment's guarantees in the United States. Other similarities may be noted: in both nations claims for equality have been made by (or in behalf of) members of traditionally disadvantaged groups – blacks in the U.S. and Indians in Canada. And, of course, the concepts of equality before the law and equal protection are very similar (Harris: 1960, xiv).

These similarities notwithstanding, the Canadian Supreme Court has not developed Section 1(b) of the Bill of Rights into the kind of substantive guarantee of equality that the U.S. Supreme Court found 75 years after the adoption of the Fourteenth Amendment. Of the many explanations that could be offered for the Canadian Supreme Court's development of other standards of equality, three seem to be especially important.

First, the traditional role of the judiciary has not included broad political policy-making, as has been the case in the U.S. Second, the fact that the Bill of Rights is not entrenched probably has reinforced the judiciary's reluctance to lend to Section 1(b) the strength of a constitutional guarantee of equal protection. Third, the nature of Canadian federalism apparently has contributed to conditions in which the national government has found that it is not in its interests to guarantee substantive equality. All three explanations are related not only to what the Supreme Court has (and has not) done since the passage of the Bill of Rights but also to potential future interpretations of equality before the law in Canada.

It seems appropriate here to distinguish a "substantive" guarantee from a "procedural" one. For the purposes of this paper, a substantive guarantee would be that kind of protection developed by the U.S. Supreme Court in decisions on the Fourteenth Amendment. State classifications based on race, sex or alienage are subject to strict judicial scrutiny; the burden is on the state to demonstrate that the classification is not a denial of equal protection. Any classification of persons must be reasonably relevant to the purposes of good government. And if there is a relevant state interest, that interest must be carried out by the least restrictive means (Tarnopolsky: 1975, 293). A "procedural" guarantee is that described by Mr. Justice Ritchie in *A.G. Canada* v. *Lavell* ([1974] S.C.R. 1349): " . . . (T)he phrase 'equality before the law' . . . is to be treated as meaning equality in the administration or application of the law by the law enforcement authorities and the ordinary courts of the land." The differences in how the concept of equality is dealt with in the United States and Canada are well-illustrated by these definitions.

In several respects, the structure of the Supreme Court of Canada is similar to that of the U.S. Supreme Court. The Canadian Supreme Court is the final court of appeal in a federal system, it is composed of nine justices, and it exercises both original and appellate jurisdiction. With those structural comparisons however, the similarities end. Reflecting the bicultural nature of Canadian society, the Supreme Court Act requires that at least three justices come from Quebec. The Court's position in the political system is relatively more tenuous than that of the American Court; the Court exists by statute rather than by constitutional provision (Fouts: 1969, 258). This means that the Court could be abolished by the Dominion Parliament, although that possibility has been described as inconceivable (Strayer: 1968). Perhaps most important, the Supreme Court did not replace the Judicial Committee of the Privy Council as the final court of appeal until 1949. This undoubtedly has inhibited the Supreme Court from developing a distinctively Canadian jurisprudence, and perhaps has contributed to the Court's reluctance to develop a theory of equal protection.

The concept of judicial review has been essential to the development of the Fourteenth Amendment in the United States. Although the American Constitution makes no specific provision for judicial review, the principle was developed early in the history of the Court. The Canadian experience has been similar, at least to the point that in the Canadian system, the power of the courts to declare Acts of Parliament *ultra vires* has never been seriously challenged (Tarnopolsky: 1975, 93). "Judicial review" may be understood in at least two ways (Schmeiser: 1964, 21). A court may declare legislation invalid on the grounds that the legislature does not have authority to enact a law on a particular subject – i.e., acted *ultra vires*. Judicial review may also describe a court's power to declare legislation invalid if it is in conflict with fundamental (usually constitutional) values. Although the U.S. Supreme Court has reviewed legislation in both senses, its decisions expanding the Equal Protection Clause represent the latter kind of review. (*Brown* is a good example.) The Canadian Supreme Court, however, generally has reviewed legislation in the former sense. It seems reasonable to suggest that determining whether the enacting body was performing within its authority is inherently a more conservative procedure than considering the possible conflict of legislation with fundamental norms. In the United States, then, the power of judicial review has been used by the Supreme Court in taking an active role in public policy formation; in Canada, the judiciary has been reluctant to assume such a role (Russell: September, 1975).

Chief Justice Bora Laskin has identified several differences between judicial review in Canada and the United States (Laskin: 1970, 172) that bear on the question of why equality before the law has not developed in Canada as it has in the United States. The range of inquiry into constitutional law issues has generally been limited in Canada by the ordinary rules of statutory construction. The Canadian Court, unlike its U.S. counterpart, does not consider evidence on the likely effect of a particular ruling. The Canadian Supreme Court does, of course, consider the intent of Parliament, but it generally has not applied any tests similar to the U.S. Supreme Court's requirement that legislative classifications have a rational basis. The Canadian Court has required less; its test has been that of whether an act is within the scope of authority. The result of asking whether a law is within the legislature's authority – and not whether the act accomplishes a *justifiable state objective* – is that the Court has been able to avoid many policy considerations. There is some indication, however, that the Supreme Court may be moving away from the *ultra vires* test on equality before the law, and toward a rational basis test (Tarnopolsky: Winter, 1975). If that tendency is affirmed in future cases, the use of such a rational basis test could lead to a more substantive meaning for "equality before the law."

As Laskin notes, another difference has been that Canadian judicial review has not been concerned with preservation of the doctrine of separation of powers. This appears to be another reason why the Court has not developed a broad policy-making role: it has not been required to. The Court surely has made its influence felt (e.g., in matters of provincial rights against the federal government), but it has been able to do so without pre-empting the role of Parliament.

Perhaps most important in relating differences in American and Canadian judicial review to differences in how equality before the law has been interpreted is Laskin's argument that since the Canadian constitution has no Bill of Rights, Canadian courts never developed the "near-legislative" function involved in the exposition and application of an entrenched Bill of Rights. Laskin contends that had such a responsibility fallen to the judiciary, its discharge could have been expected to influence judges' attitudes in interpreting grants of legislative power.

But would a constitutionally-entrenched Bill of Rights have resulted in the development by the Canadian Supreme Court of a more comprehensive role in policy-making? Although Laskin suggests that it might have, there are persuasive arguments that an entrenched bill would have made no difference. One is that until 1949, the Supreme Court was, after all, an intermediate court of appeal. Such courts generally are not expected to write opinions encompassing any broader a rule of law than that required to resolve the issues in dispute on appeal. Because of the possibility of appeal to the Privy Council, then, it is doubtful that even if the British North America Act had included a Bill of Rights the Supreme Court would have found it appropriate to adopt a role similar to that of the American Court. Donald Fouts contends that one result of the Supreme Court's long subordination to the Privy Council was the curtailment of its authority over the interpretation of Canadian law. Another, more lasting, effect, has been the Supreme Court's adoption of the Privy Council's positivist legal philosophy (Fouts: 1969, 259). Fouts cites Austin's argument that law should be defined simply as the commands of the sovereign:

> The science of jurisprudence . . . is concerned with positive laws, or with laws strictly so-called, as considered without regard to their goodness or badness.

Fouts compares the results of that philosophy with the so-called "mechanical jurisprudence" of decisions of the U.S. Supreme Court in the 1930's which contended that anti-New Deal decisions were dictated by the meaning of the Constitution rather than by political policy considerations. This analysis of the Canadian Court may not be so appropriate now as it may have been a decade ago, but does further explain why the Supreme Court has not developed equality before the law in the manner of the U.S. Court.

Another reason why even the existence of an entrenched Bill of Rights might not have led the Canadian Supreme Court to adopt a "legislative" role is the tradition of the supremacy of Parliament. Even with a constitutional guarantee of fundamental freedoms, it seems unlikely that the Court could have overcome that tradition.

The reasons suggested to explain why the Supreme Court has not followed the U.S. equal protection model – differences in judicial review, entrenchment of fundamental freedoms, and the nature of federalism – are inter-related. As Laskin has pointed out, the possibility of an entrenched Bill of Rights has raised questions about what would happen to the careful balance between federal and provincial powers: "Promulgation of such a bill . . . even if agreement on its language and range [were] reached, would . . . flout the principle of parliamentary supremacy in a way which the mere distribution of legislative power does not" (Laskin: 1970, 174).

The complex nature of Canadian federalism, and its effect on how equality before the law has developed, is well illustrated by the circumstances leading to the enactment of the Bill of Rights in 1960 and the rejection of the proposed Canadian Constitutional Charter in 1971. Not until the post-World War II period was there any serious debate in Canada about a Bill of Rights. The discussion that took place then was inspired by the U.S. Bill of Rights and the Supreme Court's elaboration of its meaning, and by the United Nations' Universal Declaration of Human Rights.

Traditional theory holds that the Dominion Parliament and the provincial legislatures were absolutely supreme in their respective spheres and that there was no restriction on the type of legislation which each may have enacted (Schmeiser: 1964, 10). Judicial declarations that legislation was *ultra vires* resulted from the division of legislative authority rather than from specific limitations on the exercise of authority. It was generally accepted that, aside from the provisions protecting the French language and denominational schools, the legislatures – so long as they kept within the jurisdiction set out in Sections 91 and 92 of the B.N.A. Act – had powers as unlimited as those of the British Parliament, no matter what fundamental rights they infringed (Atkey and Brandt: 1968, 633). Discussions of the appropriateness of a Bill of Rights, then, took place in the context of parliamentary supremacy and division of legislative authority. Both principles were preserved when the Bill of Rights was enacted.

Although the bill was adopted as a statute, the Special Committee on Human Rights and Fundamental Freedoms (1950) concluded that the preferable place for a law protecting those rights would be in the constitution. To have entrenched rights there beyond the reach of the provinces and Parliament, however, would have required an amendment by the British Parliament, and it was argued that that would have amounted to a surrender of sovereignty (Laskin: 1970, 178). The Committee subsequently recommended that the Canadian Parliament adopt a Declaration of Human Rights, limited to its own legislative jurisdiction.

The conditions which have contributed to the absence of a substantive Bill of Rights created by the judiciary were those that led to the adoption of the Bill as a statute rather than as part of the constitution. The result was a Bill that is an "admonitory statute prescribing a rule of construction for federal statutes" (Smiley: 1972, 18). It preserves legislative supremacy for acknowledging the power of Parliament to enact laws explicitly overriding the fundamental freedoms specified. Although some questions remain about the intent of Parliament in enacting the Bill, there is agreement that Prime Minister Diefenbaker had hoped that the courts would use the Bill to invalidate federal legislation inconsistent with the protection of fundamental freedoms (Tarnopolsky: Winter, 1975, 3). In part because that has not happened, debate over the preferability of an entrenched Bill has continued. In 1967, Prime Minister Trudeau proposed that a constitutionally-entrenched Bill of Rights be agreed upon with the provinces, as a prelude to a renewed federal-provincial debate on the Constitution (Trudeau: 1968, 53). This in itself was not surprising: five years before passage of the Bill, Trudeau wrote that Quebec should declare itself "ready to accept the incorporation of human rights in the constitution . . ." (Tarnopolsky: 1975, 10).

As the nature of Canadian federalism contributed to the adoption of the Bill of Rights as a statute rather than as a constitutional amendment, so it has contributed to the failure of subsequent attempts to guarantee fundamental rights. At the first Federal-Provincial Constitutional Conference in February 1968, the federal government proposed a constitutionally-entrenched Charter of Human Rights, binding both the federal and provincial legislatures. According to its supporters in the federal government, such a measure would not only have provided more effective safeguards but would have removed the ambiguities in the division of legislative powers related to human rights (Laskin: 1969, 187–89). Subsequent discussions with the provinces, however, indicated that no agreement on entrenchment as extensive as that advocated by the federal government was possible.

The document that did emerge from the conference in 1971 exemplifies what can result from federal-provincial compromise. The Victoria Charter provided for constitutional entrenchment of certain political, legal, and egalitarian rights. No federal or provincial law was to abrogate "freedom of thought, conscience and religion, freedom of opinion and expression, and freedom of peaceful assembly and association." Omitted, however, were guarantees related to arrest and trial, and equality before the law, even in the form provided in the 1960 Bill.

One of the reasons why "equality before the law" in the Canadian Bill has not developed as it has in the United States is found in Section 2 which provides that every law of Canada be construed and applied so as not to abrogate or infringe any of the specified rights, unless Parliament declares that the law shall operate notwithstanding the Bill. Such a clause of itself may inhibit the judiciary from lending a substantive meaning to equality; invalidating federal legislation as violating one of the Bill's enumerated freedoms could be construed as merely an invitation to Parliament to pass the same legislation a second time, stating that it is to operate, the Bill notwithstanding.

The Victoria Charter would have entrenched some fundamental rights, but it also would have entrenched phrasing similar to that of the *non obstante* clause. Article 2 of the Charter states that no law of Parliament or the provincial legislatures shall abrogate any of the enumerated fundamental freedoms. But Article

3 states that nothing in that part of the Charter "shall be construed as preventing such limitations on the exercise of the fundamental freedoms as are reasonably justifiable in a democratic society in the interests of public safety, order, health or morals, of national security, or of the rights and freedoms of others . . ." The "reasonably justifiable" standard is that applied by the U.S. Supreme Court to legislative classifications. Article 3 of the Charter, however, does not specify which branch of government would determine whether limitations on fundamental freedoms are in fact justifiable. One could assume that the courts would make that determination. But some question could be raised about whether the judiciary might avoid that task, given the presumption of the supremacy of Parliament. On the other hand, the judiciary could interpret Article 3 as giving the courts the authority to decide which limitations are justifiable. Such an interpretation could result in judicial adoption of a legislative function similar to that of the U.S. Supreme Court. Perhaps that possibility alone makes it unlikely that the Canadian Court would accept such an interpretation, given the historical differences between the functions of the two highest courts.

As noted, there generally has been little judicial restraint on legislative policy. In decisions on the B.N.A. Act, the Privy Council generally contended that it was not concerned with the wisdom or justice of legislation, but only with constitutional validity based on jurisdiction. It is incorrect, however, to believe that the separation of powers (e.g., criminal law under federal jurisdiction and property and civil rights under provincial jurisdiction) has left Canadians without remedies on issues of human rights. Most provinces have enacted comprehensive statutes barring racial, sex or religious discrimination. In 1951, Ontario (subsequently followed by the other provinces) adopted fair accommodation and fair employment practices acts modeled on legislation first adopted in North America in New York State (Tarnopolsky: 1975, 68). The provinces acted independently in the 1960's to consolidate anti-discrimination statutes into Human Rights Codes to be administered by commissions. The problem with such commissions, however, is that some victims are reluctant to initiate action. A greater problem is that commissions make their decisions on a case-by-case basis that has little effect on society (or on victims of discrimination) at large. This contrasts with the situation in the United States, in which the work of commissions has been paralleled by the role of the judiciary in prescribing broad-based remedies.

At this point, it seems appropriate to consider how the differences between the Canadian and American systems have affected judicial development of equality before the law in Canada. The specific question is, How has the Supreme Court interpreted Section 1(b) of the Civil Rights Bill, and is that interpretation likely to change?

The first section of the Bill acknowledges the existence of specific "fundamental freedoms" in Canada and declares that those rights "shall continue to exist without discrimination by reason of race, national origin, colour, religion, or sex." Among the fundamental freedoms specified are those of the individual's right to life, liberty and security, religion, speech, and the press – and, in

Section 1(b), "the right of the individual to equality before the law and protection of the law."

In the first decade after the adoption of the Bill, Section 1(b) was given a limited meaning by the judiciary (Tarnopolsky: 1975, 14). This may have been because of the courts' doubt as to what Section 1(b) really meant as well as doubt about the Section's intended effect. There may have been misunderstanding among potential litigants about the potential availability of Section 1(b). Walter Tarnopolsky points out that within two or three years of the Bill's enactment, "the lower courts seemed reluctant to face its implications, and the trend was to ignore or explain away its existence" (Tarnopolsky: 1975, 14). He also notes that although the Supreme Court neither dismissed nor rejected the applicability of the Bill, it did not declare any federal legislation or administrative act to be invalid.

There seems to be general agreement that the first important case under 1(b) was *R. v. Gonzales*, (1962) 32 D.L.R. 2d 290, decided by the British Columbia Court of Appeal. The defendant, an Indian, was convicted under Section 94(a) of the Indian Act for being in possession of an intoxicant off a reserve. The court dismissed the defendant's appeal. Writing for a unanimous court, Mr. Justice Tysoe interpreted Section 1(b) as meaning that Canadians have a fundamental right "to stand on an equal footing with every other person to whom a particular law relates or extends [and] be on the same level in such respects . . ." (32 D.L.R. 2d 297). Tysoe held that the word "before" in "equality before the law" meant "in the presence of." He reasoned that the clause had nothing to do with the application of the law equally, but only to the position occupied by persons to whom a particular law extended.

The opinion in this first major case on Section 1(b) clearly shows how the Bill of Rights – a statute which might appear on first reading to be an expansive, egalitarian document – can be severely limited by the courts. Tysoe's opinion may be criticized on the basis that his definition of "equality" ratifies substantive inequality – e.g., laws applying to blacks or women or Catholics could be interpreted as not coming under the protection of the Bill of Rights if those laws applied equally to members within the groups. Nonetheless, given Canadian traditions of judicial review and parliamentary supremacy discussed earlier, it is difficult to see how a provincial court of appeal sitting two years after the adoption of the Bill could have ruled differently.

The second major decision on the Bill was *R. v. Drybones*, [1970] S.C.R. 282. In that case, Joseph Drybones, an Indian, was convicted of intoxication off a reserve, a violation of Section 94(b) of the Indian Act. The point raised successfully on Drybones's behalf was that his conviction denied him equality before the law because of race. The key was the difference in treatment between Indians and other Canadians committing the same act. In the majority opinion, this difference constituted inequality before the law, based on a purely racial classification.

In a 6–3 decision, the Supreme Court held that Section 94 was rendered inoperative by the Bill of Rights. The important fact, wrote Mr. Justice

Ritchie for the majority, was that in the (federal) jurisdiction in which the case arose, "it is not an offence for anyone except an Indian to be intoxicated otherwise than in a public place." The majority ruled that when an Act of Parliament conflicted with the Bill, the Bill had overriding force; the Court in effect said that the Bill was more than a canon of interpretation. The *Drybones* decision noted that Parliament had placed on the judiciary the responsibility for enforcing the Bill's standards. It might have added that the judiciary also had been left with responsibility for creating those standards.

Although *Drybones* cannot easily be distinguished from *Gonzales*, one difference is between the courts that decided the cases. One may assume that the responsibilities of the Supreme Court are different from those of a provincial court of appeal. It might be suggested that if the Supreme Court had *not* ruled as it did in *Drybones*, a question could be raised about whether there was *any* situation at all in which the Bill could be applied to render a portion of a statute invalid. In *Drybones*, criminal legislation purporting to regulate the behavior of Indians off a reserve punished Indians while not punishing other Canadians for the same behavior. (Of course, it is highly unlikely that the case could have arisen at all on these or similar grounds if Drybones had been charged with public intoxication under a statute which applied equally to Canadians at large rather than to Indians only.)

Ten years after the adoption of the Bill, then, *Drybones* presented a situation in which the Bill invalidated part of a statute. But one case does not make a trend, and the Supreme Court's subsequent decisions indicate a retreat from even the narrow beginning of a substantive interpretation of equality made in *Drybones*. *Curr v. The Queen*, [1972] S.C.R. 889, challenged a provision of the Criminal Code which made it an offence to refuse to supply a breath sample to a police officer and which made such a refusal admissible in a charge of impaired driving. The Court unanimously agreed that those provisions did not contradict the Bill of Rights.

Although the case focused on the due process clause of Section 1(a), the majority opinion also discussed the circumstances in which the Bill is to be applied. Mr. Justice Laskin's opinion, in which four of his colleagues concurred, was that federal legislation which does not offend Section 1 of the Bill (the stricture that the enumerated fundamental freedoms are to exist without discrimination) may still contradict the Bill if it violates any of the enumerated clauses (a) through (f) of Section 1: "The absence of such discrimination [based on race, national origin, color, religion or sex] still leaves open the question of whether [a particular provision] can be construed and applied without abrogating ...the rights of the individual listed in ... Section 1(b)" ([1972] S.C.R. 889, 896–7).

A related question arises on the issue of whether federal law enacted before the Bill can be found to contradict the Bill. In *Drybones*, Ritchie indicated that the meaning to be given the Bill was that which was recognized in Canada before the Bill's enactment (Tarnopolsky: 1975, 145). But in *Curr*, Laskin wrote that the Bill "did not freeze the federal statute book as of its effective date"

[1972] S.C.R., 893). Tarnopolsky interprets these opinions to mean that legislation, whether enacted before or after the Bill, can be rendered inoperative if the legislation can only be construed as being inconsistent with the Bill of Rights (Tarnopolsky: 1975, 145).

Laskin's interpretation of Section 1(b) in *Curr* is perhaps more liberal than the Court intended. Tarnopolsky notes, somewhat optimistically, that because four justices concurred in Laskin's decision, Laskin's summation "must be taken as the most authoritative statement of the Supreme Court . . . up to and including 1972." Two years later, however, in *Lavell*, the court departed from Laskin's view in *Curr*. Although four justices ostensibly concurred with Laskin in *Curr*, Laskin's comments on "equality before the law" may, after all, have been *dicta* not bearing on the decision in the instant case, which concerned the due process clause.

"Equality before the law" was the principal issue in *Lavell*. Mrs. Lavell, an Indian, married a non-Indian. In doing so, she surrendered status as an Indian under Section 12(1)(n) of the Indian Act which states that "a woman who marries a person who is not an Indian" is not entitled to be registered as an Indian. Mrs. Lavell claimed to have been denied equality before the law by reason of sex. It must be noted that *Lavell* was essentially a dispute among Indians – specifically between Indian men and women. Nineteen Indian organizations made representations to the Court in behalf of the appellant or respondent. Indian men probably saw the issue as relating to the preservation of the Indian race. Indian culture presumably would have been challenged if Indian women (1) were allowed to retain their status as Indians despite marriage to non-Indians, and (2) were permitted to raise as Indians the children of such marriages. For Indian women, the question was one of equality with Indian men, who were not denied Indian status for the same act.

Drybones suggested that the Court might be willing to adopt a substantive interpretation of equality before the law. In *Lavell*, the Court specifically avoided such an interpretation. Giving a narrow construction to the effect of "equality," a majority of the Court decided that the treatment of Indian women under Section 12(1)(b) was not analogous to criminal punishment as had been the situation in *Drybones*. Ritchie, for the majority, wrote that conditions like those created by 12(1)(b) "can be changed only by plain statutory language expressly enacted for the purpose." The Bill of Rights, then, was limited by a decision which said that a statute cannot be invalidated because of discrimination, unless that discrimination involves denial of a guaranteed right or freedom, and unless, concomitantly, the discrimination results in a punishment. This is considerably more conservative a view than that which the Court seemed to have taken in *Drybones*.

Lavell is made more confusing by Ritchie's inclusion of Dicey's definition of equality before the law. Ritchie undertood Dicey to mean that equality before the law means "equality in the administration or application of the law by the law enforcement authorities in the ordinary courts of the land." (This is quite similar to the language used by the British Columbia Court of Appeal in

Gonzales.) It has been argued that Ritchie's interpretation of Dicey is incorrect, and that Dicey's concept of equality was meant to exclude the idea that officials or others were exempt from the duty of obedience to the law (Tarnopolsky: 1975, 145). Even if Ritchie's interpretation were correct, however, one could argue that it is no longer appropriate. In defining equality, Ritchie specifically rejected "any egalitarian concept exemplified by the Fourteenth Amendment" of the U.S. Constitution. Ritchie's definition separates Section 1(b) of the Bill from the non-discrimination clause in Section 1. But, as Tarnopolsky points out, that ignores not only the juxtaposition of the two clauses but also twentieth-century egalitarian concepts.

Laskin, dissenting, wrote that the majority decision compounded "racial inequality even beyond the point that the *Drybones* case found unacceptable." Following what he had written in *Curr*, Laskin contended that each of the enumerated clauses should be read as if the prohibited forms of discrimination were recited as part of them.

The Court in *Lavell*, then, reached a decision contrary to what one might have assumed would have been dictated by *Drybones*. Although it is difficult to state with assurance the principle of law for which *Lavell* stands, it is possible that in a future decision, the Supreme Court will overlook Ritchie's interpretation of Dicey much as Ritchie overlooked Laskin's definition of Sections 1 and 2 of the Bill of Rights in *Curr*.

The Supreme Court's next major decision on equality was in *R. v. Burnshine*, [1974] 4 W.W.R. 49, involving the Prisons and Reformatories Act under which a court in British Columbia may sentence anyone under age 22 who is convicted of a criminal offence punishable by three months or more imprisonment, for an indeterminate period of up to three years. Burnshine, who was 17 years old, had been charged with an offence for which the maximum punishment prescribed by the Criminal Code was six months. Under Section 150 of the Prisons and Reformatories Act, he was sentenced to a term of three months definite and two years less one day indeterminate. The British Columbia Court of Appeal held that Section 150 was inoperative because it contravened Section 1(b) of the Bill of Rights. The Crown's appeal to the Supreme Court was only on the issue of the effect of the Bill on Section 150. Burnshine's argument was that Section 150 contravened Section 1(b) of the Bill by denying him equality before the law in authorizing a greater term of imprisonment than he would have been subject to had he been older or female or had he committed the offence in almost any other province.

The Supreme Court ruled against Burnshine, finding no contradiction between Section 1(b) and the challenged section of the Prisons and Reformatories Act. If *Lavell* is considered a retreat from *Drybones*, *Burnshine* may be a retreat from *Lavell*. Mr. Justice Martland, for the majority, concluded that the Bill of Rights only "declared and continued existing rights and freedoms" (S.C.R. [1974] 4 W.W.R., 58). In the majority view, then, the Bill of Rights added nothing to Canadian fundamental freedoms as they existed in 1960. However, as Tarnopolsky notes, Martland assessed Section 150 not just by

1960 standards but in light of whether the provision contravened "equality before the law" because it could not be justified rationally. Tarnopolsky contends that Martland, in effect, applied the "reasonable classification" test – the test of whether the challenged section was rationally related to a legitimate legislative objective (Tarnopolsky: Winter, 1975, 13).

Tarnopolsky's point is that the Supreme Court cannot avoid using a rational basis test for the "equality before the law" clause. He argues that that standard, rather than Martland's comments about the Bill, is the *ratio* of *Burnshine*. This would be significant because if the Court were prepared to use such a standard– similar to that used by the U.S. Supreme Court – the possibility for a more substantive interpretation of equality would exist. This could result if the Court assesses the *reasonableness* of value judgments made by Parliament rather than restrict its determination to an *ultra vires* test. Some have suggested that this role is inevitably required by the Bill of Rights (Weiler: 1974, 224).

Still, there is little indication that the Court is willing to take this step. *Curr*, *Lavell*, and *Burnshine* are narrow interpretations of the meaning of the Bill; and despite Tarnopolsky's contention, it seems difficult to construe Martland's application of what seemed to be a rational basis test as the *ratio* of *Burnshine*, especially considering Martland's comments about the Bill's limitations. It seems possible that in raising what Tarnopolsky assumed was the rational basis standard, Martland was only responding to the arguments raised in behalf of Burnshine.

If it may be said that a trend has developed regarding interpretation of equality before the law in Canada, that trend has not paralleled development of equal protection theory in the United States. With the exception of *Drybones*, which apparently was decided on a narrow principle of law, the Supreme Court has declined to lend a substantive meaning to Section 1(b). On the one hand, it might be pointed out that the Bill is relatively recent and that the U.S. Supreme Court did not interpret the Fourteenth Amendment substantively until 70 years after it was adopted. If the Canadian Supreme Court in future decisions adopts a rational basis standard for legislative classifications, the Bill conceivably could be used to invalidate acts of Parliament contrary to its terms. On the other hand, such an interpretation would be incompatible with the traditional role of the judiciary in Canada and with the nature of Canadian federalism.

REFERENCES

ATKEY, Ronald G. and Gregory BRANDT
    1968   *Constitutional Law*. London: University of Western Ontario, p. 633.
BONNET, J.
    1972   *Population of the United States*. Washington, 1972.
FORTAS, Abe
    1970   "The Amendment and Equality Under Law," in B. Schwartz, ed., *The Fourteenth Amendment*. New York: N.Y.U., p. 100.
FOUTS, Donald
    1969   "Policy-Making in the Supreme Court of Canada," in Glendon Schubert and David Danielski, eds., *Comparative Judicial Behavior*. London: Oxford, p. 258.

HARRIS, Robert
    1960   *The Quest for Equality*. Baton Rouge: Louisiana State University Press.
HIGHAM, John
    1968   "Immigration," in *The Comparative Approach to American History*. New York: Basic Books, pp. 94–95.
JONES, Frank E.
    1971   "Some Social Consequences of Immigration for Canada," in Bernard Blishen,ed., *Canadian Society*. Toronto: Macmillan, p. 633.
KALBACH, Warren and Wayne McVEY
    1971   *The Demographic Bases of Canadian Society*. Toronto: McGraw-Hill.
LASKIN, Bora
    1970   "Constitutionalism in Canada," in B. Schwartz, ed., *The Fourteenth Amendment*. New York: N.Y.U., p. 172.
    1969   *Canadian Constitutional Law*, 3d edition. Toronto: Carswell, pp. 187–189.
LIPSET, Seymour
    1971   "Value Differences, Absolute or Relative: The English-Speaking Democracies," in Bernard Blishen, ed., *Canadian Society*. Toronto: Macmillan, p. 478.
    1964   "Canada and the United States: A Comparative View," *Canadian Review of Sociology and Anthropology* 1 (November), p. 181.
McKENNA, Marian C.
    1969   "The Melting Pot: Comparative Observations in the United States and Canada," *Sociology and Social Research* (July), pp. 433–447.
PETERSON, William
    1971   "The Ideological Background to Canada's Immigration," in Bernard Blishen, ed., *Canadian Society*. Toronto: Macmillan, p. 54.
PORTER, John
    1967   "The Human Community" in J. M. S. Careless and R. C. Craig, eds., *The Canadians: 1867–1967*. Toronto: Macmillan, p. 386.
PRESTHUS, Robert
    1974   *Elites in the Policy Process*. New York and London: Cambridge University Press.
    1976   "Evolution and Canadian Political Culture: The Politics of Accommodation," Bicentennial Conference on Revolution and Evolution, Canadian Studies Center, Duke University.
RUSSELL, Peter H.
    1975   "The Political Role of the Supreme Court of Canada in its First Century," *Canadian Bar Review*, pp. 576–593.
SCHMEISER, Donald
    1964   *Civil Liberties in Canada*. London: Oxford, p. 21.
SCHWARTZ, Bernard
    1970   "The Amendment in Operation: A Historical Overview," in B. Schwartz, ed., *The Fourteenth Amendment*. New York: N.Y.U., p. 30.
S.C.R. [1972] at 896–897.
S.C.R. [1972] at 893.
SMILEY, Donald
    1972   *Canada in Question*. Toronto: McGraw-Hill-Ryerson, p. 18.
STRAYER, B. L.
    1968   *Judicial Review of Legislation in Canada*. Toronto: University of Toronto.
TARNOPOLSKY, Walter S.
    1975   "The Canadian Bill of Rights and The Supreme Court Decisions in *Lavel* and *Burnshine*: A Retreat from Drybones to Dicey?", *Ottawa Law Review*, 7(Winter), p. 13.
    1975   *The Canadian Bill of Rights*. Toronto: McClelland and Stewart, p. 293.
TRUDEAU, Pierre E.
    1968   *Federalism and the French Canadians*. Toronto: Macmillan, p. 53.
UNDERHILL, Frank
    1961   *In Search of Canadian Liberalism*. Toronto: Macmillan, p. 12.

VALLEE, Frank, Mildred SCHWARTZ, and Frank DARKNELL
    1971   "Ethnic Assimilation and Differentiation in Canada," in Bernard Blishen, ed.,
        Canadian Society. Toronto: Macmillan, p. 599.
WARREN, Earl
    1970   "Fourteenth Amendment: Retrospect and Prospect," in Bernard Schwartz, ed.,
        The Fourteenth Amendment. New York: New York University Press., p. 223.
WEILER, Paul
    1974   *In the Last Resort*. Toronto: Carswell, Methuen, p. 224.

The Interplay of Institutionalization and the Assignment of Tasks in Parliamentary and Congressional Systems

*The House of Commons and the House of Representatives**

COLIN CAMPBELL,

York University, Toronto, Canada

LATE IN 1975, Canada's Liberal Government was piloting a bill through Parliament which had serious ramifications for two U.S. publications, *Time* and *Reader's Digest*. The legislation, which eventually was enacted early in 1975, stripped business firms of the right to deduct from taxes the costs of advertisements in the Canadian editions of the two magazines. The bill thus buttressed the growing number of barriers to American economic and cultural influence on Canada by forcing *Time* Canada out of business and making *Reader's Digest* meet a number of stringent Canadian ownership and content requirements.

For students of Parliament, however, a much more interesting and consequential episode was being reported in the back pages of Canadian newspapers (e.g., the Toronto *Globe and Mail* [December 10, 1975]). In terse columns, we read about another move in Canada's attempt to stave off incursions of American mores. This move concerned the very nature of the Parliamentary system. The strengthening of committees in the House of Commons, a process which had been urged by many in the mid and late 60's as a way of improving Parliament's surveillance of legislation, had received yet another setback. Four Liberal M.P.s on the Broadcasting Committee who opposed the "Time-Digest" bill, one of whom had served on the committee for eight years and was its chairman during the previous Parliament, found their names missing from a revised list of committee members. The Government had chosen to spare itself the embarrassment of these M.P.s' opposition to the bill during committee

---

* My thanks to James Markou and John D. Lorenzo for their help in preparing the data upon which this article is based.

review; the hope that relatively autonomous specialist committees could coexist with party discipline in the House of Commons proved once again to be an elusive goal.

Despite such disappointing episodes, the House of Commons has changed vastly in the last 20 years, if only from the standpoint of its work load and the resources which it has at its command. This article will focus on these changes and contrast them to developments in the U.S. House of Representatives. I will attempt to ascertain whether there is any sense in which the House of Commons has "Congressionalized," or if it has developed instead strictly along Parliamentary lines. My focus centers then on how the House of Commons has institutionalized. Directly related to this focus is a consideration of what difference the type of institutionalization that the House of Commons has followed makes for M.P.s as compared to Congressmen. Do the varieties of institutionalization in the House of Commons and the House of Representatives relate to the types of M.P.s and Congressmen who perform specialized tasks, especially on committees?

Robert Presthus interviewed a number of M.P.s and Congressmen in his study of political elites in Canada and the United States (Presthus, 1974: esp. 469–479). Since Cabinet Ministers participate in committee work only when they testify on behalf of the Government, I excluded these respondents from my analysis. Thus, the analysis will compare the responses of 142 M.P.s and 100 Congressmen to identical interview questions which were asked, respectively, in 1968 and 1971.

Institutionalization

Institutionalization is an important dimension of organizational modernization. Modernization connotes "adaptation," "transformation," or "adjustment" (Huntington, 1969: 1; Kornberg et al., 1973: 475; Campbell, 1971: 23–31, 37–39). An organization modernizes when it enhances its capacity to accommodate rapid change within its environment. There is no discrete point at which an organization becomes institutionalized (Sisson, 1973: 19). It is, however, "on the road" once it can be differentiated from other political organizations (Huntington, 1969: 20–22). Eventually it makes a difference that this organization accommodated a configuration of "political claimants and/or demands" (Sisson, 1973: 19).

Canada's and the United States' policy arenas share the distinction, which is peculiar to advanced liberal democracies, of being polyarchies. The nations have attained that level of development whereby political views are publicly contested and the citizenry is entitled to participate, at least at the electoral level, in the policy process (Dahl, 1971: 4; Blondel, 1969: 319).

In polyarchies, no one political organization has the luxury of sustaining its specialized activity by forcing its membership and that of other organizations into adhering to uniformly centralized patterns of authority. The organizations, in other words, compete in the political marketplace for influence. Their ability to do this depends heavily on the extent to which they are institutionalized.

A major conceptual hurdle stands in the way of a valid comparison of institutionalization and the assumption of tasks in the House of Commons and the House of Representatives. This obstacle is, ironically, the growing degree to which legislative scholars employ the U.S. Congress as the archetype of the legislative body (Loewenberg, 1972: 6). Using Congress as a model these scholars have developed two extremely specialized criteria for evaluation. These criteria set up most of the world's legislatures for failure. One criterion assumes that legislatures by definition *control* lawmaking, that is, they formulate the laws of the land (Gerlich, 1973: 98; Sisson, 1973: 25; Wahlke and Eulau, 1959: 3). The other criterion assumes that legislators must be chosen in free and competitive elections if there is to be a direct link between them and the people (Gerlich, 1973: 98; Polsby, 1975: 260). Admittedly, these criteria are excellent, in that they, if met, provide a powerful instrument for popular control of governmental policy. Democratic ideals notwithstanding, however, the House of Commons only partially fulfills the criteria in that it clearly does not control lawmaking in Canada.

For the purpose of accurate analysis, then, this article strives to take into account the facts, not simply the ideal. Thus, I substitute a dynamic view of the legislative process for the relatively rigid "lawmaking" view (Blondel, 1973: 14–15). Has the process of institutionalization in the House of Commons strengthened its review and modification of, and, ultimately, *influence* on bills? Are patterns of recruitment developing whereby the assignment of tasks within the Commons is beginning to reflect Parliamentary career routes which are distinct from partisan ones?

My emphasis on the dynamic concept, influence, rather than the static one, control, stems from a recent suggestion by Nelson W. Polsby (1975: 260, 277–78). As a result of his legislative studies, Polsby concludes that advanced liberal democracies have two types of legislatures. One he calls the "arena." Arenas are "formalized settings for the interplay of significant political forces in the life of the political system"; here legislators, recruited for predominantly partisan reasons, play out their roles in terms of their personal social status, political power or wealth. How these legislators *influence* lawmaking, depends to a very large extent upon how well connected they are to political forces outside Parliament, including party organizations. Polsby says that the British Parliament is a good example of an arena.

The other type of legislature he calls "transformative." Here legislators are recruited much less under partisan control and so they more often enjoy power bases in their constituencies. These independent bases assure such legislators of comparatively long-term careers because they are less vulnerable to shifts in public support from their party to others. They, therefore, have time to build empires around particular legislative specialties. To this end, they try to secure such powerful positions as committee chairmanships, positions from which they can mold legislative outcomes. Polsby calls the U.S. House of Representatives an archetypical transformative legislature.

Here I adopt Polsby's typology of legislatures in order to compare the House of Commons and the House of Representatives. I emphasize the view, that the differences between the legislatures derive from two distinct forms of institutionalization one Parliamentary, the other Congressional. Following Polsby's typology, I expect in addition that there will be very clear differences in the types of members, Parliamentary and Congressional, who assume certain tasks. The roles in question are as follows:

1. expert party leadership roles, that is, Parliamentary Secretary and shadow cabinet positions (M.P.s only);

2. expert committee leadership roles, that is, chairmanships or vice-chairmanships of committees and sub-committees;

3. committee memberships in four legislative fields: (a) procedure, (b) business and finance, (c) socio-economic resources, and (d) social welfare.

My reading of Polsby suggests the following hypotheses with respect to the main relations between M.P.s and Congressmen's backgrounds, and attitudes, and their positions in the respective legislatures:

1. Congressmen's districts, whether they are urban and contain primary, secondary and/or tertiary industry, will have a much greater impact on their legislative speciality than constituency characteristics will have on M.P.'s assignments.

2. High status background characteristics will relate much more strongly to M.P.s' leadership and committee roles than the same characteristics will relate to Congressmen's positions (Franks, 1971: 472).

3. Although length of tenure influences Congressmen's attaining expert leadership positions it will play a relatively minor part in explaining M.P.s' obtaining expert leadership roles.

4. Much weight is given in Congress to the individual committee preferences of members (Achen and Stolarek, 1974). I expect, therefore, that Congressmen's political liberalism and views of government intervention in the economy will relate more strongly to their committee assignments than will be the case with M.P.s. Further, I expect that political efficacy will be higher among Congressmen and M.P.s who belong to the expert leadership of the respective houses.

5. Responsiveness to subgroups and interests will relate more in the Congressional sample than in the Parliamentary sample to the assignment of tasks. Specifically, Congressmen who are open to lobbyists will tend to serve on socio-economic resource and social welfare committees because, presumably, these bodies establish clientele relationships with particular publics.

The Parameters of Institutionalization in the House of Commons and the House of Representatives

To many the golden age of legislatures in advanced democracies has passed.

This decline, scholars maintain, follows directly from shifts of the center of gravity of these systems from their legislatures to party organizations (Jewell, 1973: 205–11). The principal beneficiaries of these shifts in power have been the executive branches. The rapid expansion of mass media since W.W. II has exacerbated this problem. Personal appeals by prime ministers and chief executives through the media have eclipsed the role of the individual legislator as the representative of the people back home. The process not only has eroded the legislator's personal power but that of his institution as well (Polsby, 1971: 5). As a result of this erosion, the British House of Commons, for example, no longer exerts control over the policy process (Crick, 1970: 33–54). Even the formerly recalcitrant French Parliament has largely succumbed to executive centralization during the current Fifth Republic (Goguel, 1971: 93; Williams, 1971: 101).

Students of Canada's House of Commons generally agree that it does not draft and decide policies (Hoffman, 1971: 150; Farrell, 1969: 144; Franks, 1971: 461–76; Byers, 1972: 234–50; March, 1974). They say, instead, that the Canadian House surveys legislation mainly by criticizing, scrutinizing and publicizing it (Byers, 1972). Some scholars do not even grant the House this much influence. Allan Kornberg (1970: 15) says that the House might well be "a screen behind which the elites who exercise real power are able to operate."

Despite the general decline of power in legislatures, the U.S. Congress still makes law, although its domain is mainly limited to domestic affairs (Davidson, 1970: 134–42; Campbell and Reese, 1977: 17–32). Polsby says that a series of "historical accidents" in the late nineteenth century temporarily sent U.S. political parties into disarray, freeing Congress to institutionalize and, thereby, obtain relative autonomy (1971: 5). Congress has operated, to a large extent, independently of national parties ever since.

The U.S. House of Representatives and Senate have employed different strategies to facilitate lawmaking functions. The House has emphasized the mastery of technical details of legislation carried out in specialized committees while the Senate has evolved into a forum from which its members make appeals to broad national constituencies based on public issues (Polsby, 1971: 6–7). These strategies are not alien to other legislatures. In recent years, for example, the British Parliament has, with only very limited success, tried to strengthen specialization in its committee system (Mackintosh, 1971: 33–65); while the German and French legislatures have tried to improve the quality and public impact of their policy discussions and debates (Hennis, 1971: 65–79; Goguel, 1971: 81–95; Williams, 1971: 97–109).

It is the House of Commons' attempts at the former process, the effort to employ the model of the House of Representatives and to strengthen its legislative review through expert committees, which suggests the relevance of a comparison of institutionalization in the Canadian and U.S. lower houses. I will examine the two houses' organizational characteristics with reference to three aspects of institutionalization: (1) boundaries, the extent to which the legislatures are differentiated from other institutions within their respective political systems; (2) their organizational complexity; and (3) the degree to which they use universalistic, rather than particularistic, criteria for internal decision-making (Polsby, 1968: 145).

Boundaries

In Polsby's terms "boundary" means identity and exclusivity. Is it difficult to become a member of an institution? Do the members share privileges which identify them as belonging to the organization? How then do the House of Commons and the House of Representatives differ in terms of boundaries?

First, the House of Representatives is clearly the more difficult to become a member of. Turnover, which until 1867 remained around 50 per cent each election, has declined steadily since then to the point where it averaged around 20 per cent from 1949 to 1965 (Polsby, 1968: 146-17). Considering that, per person, Congressmen represent approximately 5.8 as many people as M.P.s do (based on 1973 estimates of populations, and 435 seats in the House of Representatives v. 264 in the House of Commons), we see that aspirants to Congress face much greater scarcity in the supply of seats than prospective M.P.s do.

Those who do get into Congress are assured a relatively long tenure. By 1963, Congressmen were serving an average of 5.65 terms (Polsby, 1968: 146). Freshman M.P.s have faced an attrition rate of 40 per cent or more in 16 of the 28 elections from 1872 to 1972 (March, 1974: 41). This fluidity of membership in the House of Commons does not provide a good base for power. In other words, the relatively insecure careers of M.P.s create a situation where even the Parliamentary leadership often is inexperienced. Whereas the Speaker of the House of Representatives usually has served at least 20 years and Congressional chairmen normally are the most senior members of their committees, in Canada tenure plays little or no part in the assignment of these posts (on the latter point, see Table 5 which follows).

Although M.P.s exhibit relatively unstable careers, they work in an environment which has a very distinct tradition and provides abundant amenities. One should keep in mind what an unbounded legislature is like before concluding that the House of Commons is poorly delineated from its environment. The Commons enjoys more status than for example some U.S. legislatures where visitors and lobbyists come and go freely, visiting members who have their offices right in the chamber; where non-members are requested to be seated when votes are taken on the floor. The Commons is steeped in Parliamentary pomp and ritual. Visitors have to be checked by security and, unless they have arranged for special status, they must prove that they are on their way to visit the office of a particular M.P., by appointment, to pass the guards. The actual Commons chamber is an "inner sanctum" in which only M.P.s and certain essential staff are permitted. Visitors may sit in the galleries only.

In addition, M.P.s are accorded a number of privileges. Members receive substantial salaries ($24,000) and a tax-free expense allowance ($10,600). They are entitled to two permanent secretaries (one senior [salary up to $14,000] one junior [up to $10,000]) in Ottawa plus $11,500 for an office in their constituency. They are also entitled to generous travel, postal and telephone subsidies.

In comparison with their Congressional counterparts then, M.P.s have proportionate privileges, especially considering the fact that they represent about one-sixth as many people, in everything but professional level staff. Most M.P.s' senior aides are Girl Fridays who must combine the talents of an executive secretary, an administrative assistant, a research assistant, a case worker and a legislative aid. The Canadian legislator's situation contrasts sharply with the average Congressman who will have several professionals in his Washington office performing these different tasks. A similar dearth of professional help for Commons committees compounds the M.P.s' lack of expert assistance. The committees currently may draw upon the Committees Branch for legal counsel and the Parliamentary Library for research assistance. For the most part, however, these committees receive only part-time help from the two sources. Congressional committees, of course, have very large permanent staffs, including full-time counsels for both the majority and minority party members.

Organizational Complexity

The general abundance of resources in the House of Commons, yet, apparent inability of M.P.s to translate these into specialized services points up the principal way in which the Commons differs from the House of Representatives in terms of institutionalization. That is, the Commons lacks organizational complexity.

Organizational complexity concerns the division of labor. Emile Durkheim said that the division of labor within an organization varies in direct proportion with the volume and density of the society within which it exists (Durkheim, 1964 [trans.]: 262). If an organization becomes more complex it is because its society has become regularly denser and generally more voluminous.

Table 1 reflects the degree to which the growth of the Canadian Federal Government has at least kept abreast of the rate of expansion in the U.S. Federal Government. In 1951, Canada spent almost three billion dollars, or 6.33 per cent of the close to 46 billion paid out by the U.S.; by 1973, Canada spent around 16 billion or 6.55 per cent of the U.S. budget. Canada would require a greater percentage of the U.S. figure if it were not for the circumstances of the federal system. This system has led to extensive provincial jurisdiction over funds collected by the Federal Government, particularly in Quebec (Smiley, 1976: 114–58).

One might argue, in view of the fact that the Canadian Federal Government spends much less than the U.S. and is excluded from several programs which are the responsibility of the provinces, that there has not developed a high enough volume and density of governmental activity to warrant a clearer division of labor in the Commons. Nonetheless, even in the mid-1960's, discussions of reforms of the Commons sprung from the belief that "big govern-

Table 1
Total Expenditures (in 1000's of $'s)

Fiscal year Ending	Canada			U.S.A.		
	Fed. Gov't.	Parliament	H. of Commons	Fed. Gov't.	Congress	H. of Rep.
1951	2,901,000 [100]	4,711 (.162) [100]	2,758 (.095) [100]	45,797,000 [100]	69,990 (.153) [100]	21,575 (.047) [100]
52	3,733,000 [123]	6,157 (.164) [131]	3,613 (.096) [138]	67,769,000 [148]	73,805 (.109) [105]	22,822 (.033) [106]
53	4,337,000 [150]	5,600 (.129) [119]	3,872 (.089) [148]	76,769,000 [168]	76,874 (.100) [110]	24,066 (.031) [112]
54	4,351,000 [150]	6,855 (.158) [146]	3,309 (.076) [111]	70,890,000 [155]	70,008 (.098) [100]	24,989 (.035) [116]
55	4,275,000 [147]	6,821 (.160) [145]	4,165 (.097) [150]	68,509,000 [150]	70,696 (.103) [101]	27,425 (.039) [127]
56	4,331,270 [149]	7,177 (.166) [152]	4,509 (.104) [150]	70,460,000 [154]	92,809 (.131) [133]	31,123 (.044) [144]
57	4,849,035 [167]	6,846 (.141) [146]	4,192 (.086) [152]	76,741,000 [168]	117,404 (.152) [168]	35,499 (.046) [165]
58	5,087,000 [175]	7,627 (.150) [162]	4,201 (.083) [152]	82,575,000 [180]	104,845 (.127) [150]	37,827 (.046) [175]
59	5,364,039 [185]	7,669 (.150) [162]	4,716 (.088) [172]	92,104,000 [201]	123,297 (.133) [176]	39,338 (.042) [182]
60	5,702,860 [197]	8,507 (.149) [181]	4,743 (.083) [172]	92,223,000 [201]	128,797 (.140) [184]	42,398 (.046) [197]
61	5,958,100 [205]	8,438 (.141) [179]	5,208 (.087) [189]	97,795,000 [214]	129,470 (.132) [185]	42,492 (.043) [197]

62	5,520,640 [225]	8,108 (.147) [172]	5,158 (.079) [187]	106,813,000 [233]	135,432 (.126) [194]	47,857 (.045) [222]
63	6,520,640 [227]	12,913 (.198) [274]	4,881 (.074) [177]	111,311,000 [243]	146,477 (.131) [209]	48,151 (.043) [223]
64	6,570,325 [237]	14,215 (.216) [302]	8,618 (.125) [315]	118,584,000 [259]	168,293 (.141) [241]	50,131 (.042) [232]
65	6,872,400 [249]	14,712 (.214) [312]	9,501 (.132) [395]	118,430,000 [258]	210,301 (.177) [300]	53,778 (.046) [249]
66	7,218,270 [267]	17,836 (.247) [379]	9,322 (.121) [337]	134,652,000 [294]	189,993 (.141) [272]	66,415 (.049) [308]
67	7,734,790 [303]	18,306 (.237) [389]	11,136 (.127) [404]	158,254,000 [346]	214,464 (.135) [306]	77,676 (.049) [360]
68	8,797,680 [338]	18,587 (.211) [395]	11,832 (.120) [429]	178,833,000 [390]	275,699 (.153) [394]	80,369 (.044) [372]
69	9,824,000 [371]	22,989 (.234) [488]	11,693 (.109) [424]	184,548,000 [403]	298,678 (.162) [427]	85,039 (.046) [396]
70	11,931,280 [411]	27,236 (.228) [578]	14,396 (.121) [522]	196,588,000 [429]	344,734 (.175) [493]	104,814 (.053) [486]
71	13,182,140 [454]	32,597 (.247) [692]	20,814 (.158) [755]	211,425,000 [461]	413,104 (.195) [590]	110,526 (.052) [512]
72	14,840,900 [511]	32,548 (.219) [691]	25,318 (.171) [918]	231,876,000 [506]	518,000 (.223) [740]	136,769 (.059) [634]
73	16,155,000 [557]	41,752 (.258) [886]	25,451 (.158) [928]	246,526,000 [538]	538,000 (.218) [769]	146,925 (.060) [681]

% of total Federal Budget in parentheses, ( ).
% of 1951 expenditures in brackets, [ ].
Figures are from the U.S. Legislative Branch Appropriations Acts, 1951–73, and the Canadian Department of Finance, *Public Accounts*, 1951–73.

ment" and executive hegemony were key factors in the decline of legislative surveillance (Hockin, 1966: 331; Page, 1967: 28).

As a result of the growing amount of criticism of the Commons, the Governments of Lester B. Pearson (1963–8) and Pierre Elliott Trudeau (1968–present) greatly increased the resources of the House and reformed its committees. With respect to the growth of resources, the Commons has enjoyed two large increments since 1951. After Pearson's 1963–4 budget it has consistently claimed over .10 per cent of the entire federal budget; since 1971 it has required at least .15 per cent of total federal expenditures. The magnitude of this gain is highlighted by the fact that the House of Representatives has needed only between .03 and .06 per cent of the U.S. budget from 1951 to 1973, even though the expenditures of the entire Congressional Branch in the U.S. (the Senate, the House, the Library of Congress, etc.) have required almost as large a portion of the U.S. budget as all of Parliament has of the Canadian budget (e.g., Congress spent .22 per cent as opposed to Parliament's .26 per cent in 1973).

What explains this affluence of the House of Commons? Two possible reasons come to mind. First, the relative inactivity of the Canadian Senate adds to the legislative and constituency work of M.P.s. Second, certain fixed costs must be met by any legislature, thus the diseconomies of scale might inflate the funds which are necessary to keep the Commons running. One such fixed cost would be the salaries of M.P.s. Table 2 shows that expenditures for these salaries had increased by 1973 to 503 per cent of their 1951 level. Yet, the Commons has permitted expenditures for staff and operations which exceed the normal inflation of fixed costs. In 1973, monies expended for staff were 1175 per cent of the 1951 figure; funds for operations were 3260 per cent of the base year. The period of astronomical increases in these two salient categories occurred in Trudeau's first three budgets. During that period, the Commons clearly experienced an increase in the density of its resources which was independent of ineconomies of scale.

Have committee reforms allowed M.P.s to exploit their expanding resources by developing specialties? Many have considered committees as an essential component of the reform of the House of Commons. Thus, during the 60's several changes evolved: (1) their number was reduced to allow greater specialization among M.P.s (in 1972, there were 1.6 committee positions per M.P. as opposed to 2.4 before 1965); (2) their terms of reference were revised so as to correspond more closely to the division of labor among governmental departments; and (3) their powers were enhanced in that (a) all bills would be automatically sent to the appropriate committee, rather than Committee of the Whole, after second reading, (b) they would review all relevant governmental estimates, and (c) they would be able to conduct special inquiries into policy questions if these studies were approved by the entire House (Franks, 1971: 46; Jackson and Atkinson, 1974: 122–3).

The actual fruits of these developments have been disappointing. First, as I have already noted, committees still do not have permanent specialized assistance. Second, M.P.s have not been able to exploit the greater opportun-

Table 2

Commons expenditures for staff and operations have grown much more rapidly than those
for M.P.'s Salaries and Allowances (1951–73). Figures in 1,000 of $'s.

Fiscal Year Ending	Total	Members' Salaries/ Allowances	Staff	Operations
1951	2,758 (100)	1,840 (100)	659 (100)	259 (100)
52	3,613 (131)	2,521 (138)	784 (120)	308 (119)
53	3,872 (140)	2,736 (148)	834 (127)	302 (117)
54	3,309 (120)	2,042 (111)	830 (126)	437 (169)
55	4,165 (151)	2,760 (150)	896 (136)	509 (197)
56	4,509 (163)	2,760 (150)	923 (141)	826 (319)
57	4,192 (152)	2,760 (150)	1,021 (155)	411 (157)
58	4,201 (152)	2,741 (149)	995 (151)	465 (180)
59	4,716 (172)	2,778 (151)	1,166 (177)	772 (298)
60	4,743 (172)	2,760 (151)	1,173 (179)	810 (313)
61	5,208 (189)	2,723 (148)	1,480 (225)	1,005 (388)
62	5,158 (187)	2,778 (151)	1,456 (221)	924 (356)
63	4,881 (177)	2,791 (152)	1,428 (217)	662 (256)
64	8,618 (315)	5,437 (296)	1,903 (289)	1,278 (493)
65	9,501 (395)	5,422 (295)	1,862 (283)	2,211 (854)
66	9,322 (337)	5,225 (284)	2,462 (374)	1,635 (631)
67	11,136 (404)	5,556 (302)	3,163 (480)	2,417 (933)
68	11,832 (429)	5,556 (302)	3,479 (528)	2,797 (1079)
69	11,693 (424)	5,667 (308)	3,776 (573)	2,250 (889)
70	14,396 (522)	5,980 (326)	5,114 (777)	3,302 (1274)
71	20,814 (755)	7,382 (401)	4,571 (694)	8,861 (3421)
72	25,318 (918)	10,153 (551)	5,939 (901)	9,226 (3562)
73	25,451 (923)	9,263 (503)	7,745 (1175)	8,443 (3260)

% of 1951 figure in parentheses, ( ).
Source: *Public Accounts*, 1951–73.

ities for developing their own expertise which resulted from the reforms. This second point emerges from an analysis of the data on Table 3 which compares substitutions of committee members in similar lengths of time during the 29th (Jan. 4, 1973–May 8, 1974) and 30th (Sept. 30, 1974–Oct. 30, 1975) Parliaments.

Roman March, in his recent book, provides evidence of the immense flux in committee membership in the mid-60's (1974: 116–117). If anything, the membership of particular committees has been less stable since the subsequent reforms than before. Except for a few committees, the Liberals and Conservatives, on the average, substitute several members of their rosters each committee meeting. The fact that, during the thirtieth Parliament, on nine of 17 committees, 40 per cent or more of the initial members no longer were on the roster by the last meeting reflects the cumulative impact of these substitutions.

I had expected that the practice of sending "taxi squads" of party faithful into committees which are considering controversial bills, i.e., the practice followed in the "Time-Digest" episode, would have inflated the number of substitutions during the twenty-ninth Parliament in which the Liberals lacked a majority on all committees. The figures, in fact, reveal only a modest drop in the number of substitutions in the thirtieth Parliament from 4.43 to 3.83 per meeting. Apparently, party disregard for continuity in the membership of committees transcends partisan necessity. Indeed, M.P.s themselves might often beg off certain committees.

In terms of developing specialities then, the committee reforms have been mainly cosmetic. Certainly, committees have not provided a panacea for improving legislative surveillance in the Commons. The few committees which have distinguished themselves in recent years, Finance and Economic Affairs, External Affairs and National Defense, and Transportation and Communication, have done so through special studies of policy proposals rather than through thoroughgoing and continuous review of actual legislation (Franks, 1971: 471–2; Jackson and Atkinson, 1974: 127).

Universalistic Criteria

Polsby asserts that a highly institutionalized legislature makes internal decisions based on universalistic rather than particularistic criteria (Polsby, 1968: 160–4). The term "universalistic criteria" refers to methods, such as precedents and impersonal codes, which are applied consistently on the basis of such standards as seniority or even merit. These criteria replace discretionary methods for conducting internal business. Discretionary methods subject the assignment of tasks and resources to strong influences from favoritism and nepotism. Since, under the discretionary system, party leaders usually are vested with control over internal decisions, favoritism connotes a party dominance of the assignment of tasks and resources.

The principal partisan component of committee assignments in the House of Representatives centers on two critical aspects of the process, the placement

Table 3

Committee membership was extremely fluid during the 29th Parliament (Jan. 4, 1973-May 8, 1974) and the 30th Parliament (Sept. 30, 1974-Oct. 30, 1975)

Committee	# of members on committee 29th Parl.	30th Parl.	# of days committee met 29th Parl.	30th Parl.	Initial members not listed on Final roster/Total initial members 29th Parl.	30th Parl.	Total 29th Parl.	30th Parl.	Liberals 29th Parl.	30th Parl.	P.C.s 29th Parl.	30th Parl.	N.D.P. 29th Parl.	30th Parl.	S.C. 29th Parl.	30th Parl.
1. Health, welfare and social services	19	20	33	29	.63	.65	5.3	4.5	1.70	1.50	3.00	2.60	.67	.38	.00	.00
2. Labour, Man power and Immigration	19	20	23	21	.53	.30	4.8	4.2	1.60	2.20	2.40	1.90	.78	.08	.00	.00
3. Indian Affairs and Northern Development	19	20	51	30	.42	.40	3.7	3.8	.94	1.20	2.60	2.40	1.80	.10	.00	.00
4. Justice and Legal Affairs	19	20	40	32	.42	.30	3.5	3.4	1.10	1.90	2.00	1.50	.33	.25	.00	.00
5. National Resources and Public Works	19	20	43	35	.58	.40	4.6	4.5	1.80	2.20	2.30	1.90	.44	.31	.00	.00
6. Fisheries and Forrestry	19	20	31	44	.26	.30	2.8	3.3	.65	1.70	1.60	1.60	.50	.09	.00	.00
7. Privileges and Elections	19	20	32	37	.53	.85	6.8	3.4	2.40	1.90	3.20	1.40	.44	.16	.00	.00
8. Broadcasting, Films, and Assistant to the Arts	19	20	44	23	.37	.65	4.3	4.7	1.50	2.70	2.30	2.00	.43	.00	.00	.00
9. Agriculture	30	30	30	62	.27	.20	2.6	3.7	.43	1.50	2.10	2.10	.00	.08	.00	.00
10. Miscellaneous Estimates	19	20	73	41	.79	.50	11.3	4.1	3.70	2.90	6.00	3.60	1.50	.02	.00	.00
11. External Affairs and National Defense	19	20	45	31	.40	.37	2.4	4.6	.69	2.30	1.40	2.30	.33	.00	.00	.00
12. Procedure and Organization	12	16	20	10	.50	.38	2.1	4.6	.20	2.90	1.40	1.50	.45	.10	.00	.00
13. Veterans' Affairs	19	20	12	20	.11	.15	1.6	2.0	.90	.95	.50	1.00	.17	.00	.00	.00
14. Regional Development	19	20	20	9	.58	.60	4.9	3.6	2.40	1.60	2.00	1.60	.30	.33	.00	.00
15. Public Accounts	19	20	23	46	.53	.45	2.0	1.2	.43	.35	1.00	.80	.43	.00	.00	.00
16. Finance, Trade and Economic Affairs	19	20	61	63	.63	.50	4.7	4.3	1.30	2.70	2.30	1.20	1.10	.27	.00	.00
17. Transportation and Communication	19	20	37	26	.68	.45	8.0	5.2	3.30	2.60	3.80	2.60	.84	.00	.00	.00
Average	19.24	20.35	36.35	32.88	.49	.44	4.43	3.83	1.47	2.25	2.35	1.82	.13	.13	.00	.00

Source: *Proceedings* of the respective committees.

of new members in vacancies and the allocation of seats on prestigious committees to incumbents who wish to "trade up." At these two points, party leadership can wield considerable influence by awarding desirable committee positions in recognition of the strong prospect or record of "compliant behavior"
on the part of Congressmen (Westefield, 1974: 1594). Nonetheless, two universalistic practices greatly mitigate partisan influence on committees, thereby,
leaving open the possibility of maverick behavior. First, the seniority rule
assures that the longest tenured member of a committee usually is its chairman
(Polsby, *et al.*, 1969: 787–807). Second, committee positions in essence become
the property rights of individual Congressmen. Thus, vacancies occur almost
exclusively when members leave Congress or relinquish their assignment for a
"better" one (Westefield, 1974: 1603). Trades are rarely made during the life
of a Congress (2 years).

These last two conditions under which committee assignments are made
in the House of Representatives are practically absent in the House of Commons.
There is, in fact, evidence of an inverse relation between tenure in the Commons
and whether an M.P. is a committee chairman (Table 5, below). Further, the
turnover rates of committee membership reflect dramatic fluidity, even during
sessions. So long as there is an absence of universalistic criteria for the holding
of committee positions and the granting of chairmanships, other reforms likely
will not contribute significantly to the development of specialized legislative
surveillance by these bodies. Although the House of Commons, in terms of the
density of resources, might be institutionalizing, it clearly is not fitting into the
Congression mold.

M.P.s and Congressmen: Characteristics, Attitudes and Assignments

The Variables

Table 4 summarizes the comparative data for the dependent and independent variables in this analysis. The dependent variables are: (1) expert party
leadership roles; (2) expert committee leadership roles; (3) membership on
procedural committees (private bills, standing orders, privileges and elections);
(4) membership on business and finance committees (public accounts, finance,
budget, industry and commerce); (5) membership on socio-economic resource
committees (agriculture, transportation, natural resources, tourism, labor and
mining); and (6) membership on social welfare committees (municipal affairs,
education, social security and health).

Assignments among the interviewed M.P.s and Congressmen cluster differently in some important respects. Only M.P.s have the opportunity to serve as
a Parliamentary Secretary to a Cabinet Minister or as an opposition party
shadow cabinet minister. Sixteen per cent of our M.P.s serve in these capacities.
Congressmen hold appreciably more business and financial, and social welfare
committee positions than the M.P.s (the respective Cramer's V.s are .19
[p < .01] and .16 [p < .05]); while M.P.s serve more frequently than

Table 4

Comparison of Interview Responses of M.P.s and Congressmen

Variable	Range	Average (Mean)		Cramer's V
		M.P.s	Congressmen	
Constituency/District				
Urban	0-1	.56	.60	.04
Primary Industry	0-1	.80	.53	.28[a]
Secondary Industry	0-1	.41	.43	.02
Tertiary Industry	0-1	.56	.48	.08
Background				
Age	1-3	1.88	2.20	.21[b]
Father's SES	0-1	.16	.21	.07
Father's Education	1-3	1.36	1.57	.22[a]
Respondent's SES	0-1	.54	.84	.31[a]
Respondent's Education	1-3	2.27	2.62	.25[a]
Lawyer	0-1	.30	.57	.26[a]
Went to private university	0-1	.10	.58	.50[a]
Went to school out of province/state	0-1	.25	.41	.17[b]
Belongs to Business Organization	0-1	.51	.44	.07
Belongs to Public Service Organization	0-1	.34	.44	.10
# of Social Clubs	0,1,2+	.69	.68	.08
# of Elite Clubs	0,1,2+	.57	.73	.15[c]
Tenure	1-2	1.66	2.22	.35[a]
Attitudes				
Political Liberalism				
Denied that democracy depends on free enterprise	0-1	.36	.17	.21[b]
Thinks labor unions do "a lot of good"	0-1	.68	.64	.05
Thinks atheists and communists should have the right to speak	0-1	.87	.77	.12
Government Intervention				
Denied that the government which governs the least governs the best	0-1	.67	.42	.25[a]
Thinks economic security for all is a goal worth striving for	0-1	.97	.16	.82[a]
Thinks the government should spend money to create jobs	0-1	.77	.70	.07
Thinks medicare is necessary	0-1	.78	.66	.12
Political Efficacy				
Denies that a small group runs things	0-1	.30	.59	.29[a]
Thinks anyone has a chance to have his say	0-1	.77	.83	.07
Denies that you "can't fight city hall"	0-1	.68	.73	.05
Views of Lobbyists				
You can rely on interest groups	1-3	1.84	1.88	.12
Frequently in contact with interest groups	1-3	2.12	2.69	.37[a]
Seeks help from interest groups	0-3	1.75	1.21	.40[a]
Roles in House of Commons/Representatives				
Expert Committee Leadership	0-1	.12	.14	.03
Expert Party Leadership	0-1	.15	*	*
Procedural Committee	0-1	.16	.13	.04
Business/Finance Committee	0-1	.25	.43	.19[b]
Socio-Economic Resource Committee	0-1	.42	.15	.29[a]
Social Welfare Committee	0-1	.06	.15	.16[c]

a   Significant at .001 level,   b   significant at .01 level,   c   significant at .05 level.
*   Computation would be meaningless.
Source: Robert Presthus' interviews of M.P.'s and Congressmen, 1964, 1971.

Congressmen on socio-economic resource committees (Cramer's V, .29 [p < .001]). The M.P.s and Congressmen have about an equal chance of holding committee leadership positions (12 and 14 per cent, respectively).

The independent variables fall into four categories. These are: (1) constituency/district characteristics; (2) social and political background; (3) attitudes toward political liberalism and government intervention, and political efficacy; and (4) attitudes toward lobbyists. With respect to constituency/district backgrounds, Congressmen tend only slightly more than M.P.s to come from urban or suburban communities (60 v. 56 per cent). Also, roughly the same proportion of Congressmen and M.P.s say that there is some secondary or tertiary industry in their area. Large differences appear, however, under the primary industry category. The M.P.s ascribe much more of this type of economic activity to their constituencies than Congressmen do to their districts (Cramer's V = .28 [p < .001]). These two findings correspond to actual differences between the Canadian and U.S. economies (Brewis, 1969: 29–42; Clement, 1975: 44–96).

With respect to differences between social and political backgrounds, M.P.s are much younger than Congressmen (Cramer's V = .21 [p < .01], with three groupings). Thirty-nine per cent of the M.P.s are 44 years or younger (group 1), 35 per cent are 45–54 (group 2), and 27 per cent are 55 or older (group 3). The respective proportions for Congressmen are 19, 42 and 39 per cent. By practically every criterion, Congressmen belong to higher echelons of the socio-economic elite than do the M.P.s. Specifically, both they and their fathers are (were) better educated (graduate or professional work = a score of 3, college education = 2, no college = 1) and the Congressmen more frequently are (were) business executives, lawyers, graduates of private colleges and universities, and members of exclusive social clubs (all differences being significant at the p < .001 level). There are more Congressmen, also, who went out of state for some of their education than M.P.s who went out of province for schooling (.17, p < .01). Congressmen tend more than M.P.s to join public service and elite social clubs, especially the latter (Cramer's V = .15).

The Congressmen, as we might expect in view of the discussion above about boundaries, have served much longer in the House of Representatives than the M.P.s have in the House of Commons. Only 21 per cent of the Congressmen have been in office four or less years, 36 per cent have been in for five to nine years and fully 43 per cent have been in for ten years or more. The comparable proportions for M.P.s are 54, 24 and 21 per cent.

With respect to political attitudes, I first attempted to find out if M.P.s and Congressmen differ in their views of democracy. Presthus employed three standard political liberalism items to tap this attitudinal dimension. These items ascertain whether the respondent believes that: (1) democracy depends on free enterprise; (2) labor unions do "a lot of good work"; and (3) atheists and communists should have the right to express their views publicly. The results show that only on the first item do the two types of legislators differ significantly (Cramer's $V = .21$, $p < .01$). Thirty-six per cent of the M.P.s, as opposed to 17 per cent of the Congressmen, disagree or strongly disagree with the assertion that free enterprise is essential to democracy. This finding might reflect the extent to which Canadians have learned to live with much more government involvement in "essential" sectors such as medical insurance, transportation and energy than Americans are used to having.

The above observation about the M.P.s' view of democracy relates to the next cluster of attitudinal variables. Presthus asked M.P.s and Congressmen about their views of government intervention generally and in providing, specifically, economic security for all, jobs and medical care. Large majorities of M.P.s and Congressmen favor government involvement in providing jobs and medicare. Some hesitancy among the Congressmen, however, is reflected in the fact that only 42 per cent, as opposed to 67 per cent of the M.P.s, disagreed or strongly disagreed with the proposition that "the government which governs the least governs the best" (Cramer's $V = .25$, $p < .001$). Quite remarkably, 97 per cent of the M.P.s, as compared to only 16 per cent of the Congressmen, agreed or strongly agreed that economic security for all is a legitimate governmental goal.

I employed three standard items for the measurement of political efficacy. Overwhelming majorities of M.P.s and Congressmen believe that anyone has a chance to speak out on policy and that a person can "fight city hall." Yet, the M.P.s, when confronted with the statement that "most decisions in business and government are made by a small group which pretty well runs things" disagreed or strongly disagreed with the statement much less than Congressmen (the respective proportions were 30 and 59 per cent, Cramer's $V = .29$, $p < .001$). The apparent belief among M.P.s that an elite "inner circle" of decision-makers runs things might derive from Cabinet dominance of Canada's Parliament.

Finally, with respect to M.P.s' and Congressmen's views of lobbyists, I used three of Presthus' questions which concerned interactions with sub-groups and interests. Presthus asked the legislators: (1) whether they could rely on interest groups; (2) how often they are in touch with groups; and (3) whether they actually seek help from lobbyists in (a) writing speeches, (b) collecting information, (c) finding out about constituents' attitudes and (d) massing public support for bills. Under item (1), respondents received a score of three if they said that they can rely on lobbyists all of the time, two if they depend on them "most of the time," and one if they seldom or never rely on them. Under item (2), the legislators were assessed with three points if they were frequently in touch with lobbyists, two points if they were occasionally in contact with them and one point if they were seldom or rarely in touch with lobbyists. Under item (3), respondents obtained a point each time they said that they sought help from the lobbyists for one of the four possible reasons. Since only a small number of legislators checked off all four reasons, I decided, for purposes of statistical validity, to allow a maximum score of three.

M.P.s and Congressmen believe that they can rely on lobbyists to almost identical degrees (the means for the groups are, respectively, 1.84 and 1.88). Yet, Congressmen report much more frequent contact with lobbyists (Cramer's V = .37, p < .001; means: 2.69 [Congressmen], 2.12 [M.P.s]).Surprisingly, the M.P.s scored much higher than Congressmen in terms of seeking help from lobbyists (Cramer's V = .40, p < .001; means: 1.75 [M.P.s], 1.21 [Congressmen]). This last finding appears to be anomalous, given Congressmen's greater contact with lobbyists, until one reflects that Congressmen, with their professional staff and research aids, might need help from lobbyists much less than lobbyists need help from them (Zeigler and Baer, 1969: 36–7, 155–7, 198–9; Dexter, 1969: 80; Presthus, 1974: 257). The M.P.s, apparently, are in a less enviable position.

Principal Correlates of Positions

Table 5 summarizes the results of several cross-tabulations of constituency/ district, social and political background, political attitude, and views of lobbyists variables with M.P.s' and Congressmen's leadership and committee positions. The cross-tabulations test a number of theoretical expectations which I outlined in a previous section.

I expected Congressmen's district characteristics to relate strongly to their committee assignments and M.P.s' constituency variables to relate only slightly to their committee positions. The relations between Congressmen's district characteristics and their committee assignments are not as strong as I had expected. Given the relatively rigorous recruitment process to committee positions in the House of Representatives, it seemed reasonable that Congressmen from urban, and secondary or tertiary industrial areas would sit mainly on business and finance, and social welfare committees. Congressmen from areas with primary industries, on the other hand, would gravitate to socio-economic resource committees. This last expectation is the only one which finds strong support in the actual analysis (Cramer's V = .34, p < .01, gamma = .89). Yet, although the Cramer's V.s generally are weak, the gammas of relationships between district characteristics and committee assignments are higher for the Congressional sample than for the Parliamentary one. Congressional members of socio-economic resource committees frequently come from non-urban areas (urban, gamma = –.45); Congressmen on social welfare committees often represent urban areas in which there is some primary industry (gammas: urban, .34; primary, .32). A glance at the comparable M.P. data reveals that the two strongest relations between constituency characteristics and M.P.s' committee assignments occur under the social welfare category. M.P.s from areas with primary industry and those from areas without large tertiary sectors tend more than others to serve on social welfare committees (gammas: primary, .30; tertiary, –.81 [Cramer's V, p < .001]). The tendency of Congressmen and M.P.s from primary industrial areas to serve on social welfare committees might result from the depressed state of primary industry in areas such as Appalachia and the Maritimes.

The various relations between constituency/district characteristics and the legislators' leadership roles are stronger than I had expected. M.P.s from areas with secondary industry have a very good chance of becoming either Parliamentary Secretaries or shadow cabinet ministers (Cramer's V, .20 [p < .05]; gamma, .50); M.P.s from urban areas have good prospects of obtaining these party offices (gamma, .40). Also, M.P.s from ridings without much secondary industry are fairly successful at winning committee chairmanships (secondary, gamma = −.57). Among the M.P.s, then, constituency characteristics can have a fairly large impact on the types of leadership positions that the legislators gain.

Although Congressmen cannot be Parliamentary Secretaries or members of a shadow cabinet, they can seek committee chairmanships which usually are granted on the basis of seniority. It is practically an axiom of American politics that most seniority is held by Congressmen from rural seats which tend to re-elect the same person for several consecutive terms. The relations between Congressmen's districts and their committee leadership positions reinforce this observation. Although their districts are not as rural as expected (urban, gamma = −.23) and their areas do have some secondary industry (gamma = .32), committee chairmen represent disproportionately areas which do have substantial amounts of primary industry and lack significant tertiary sectors (gammas = .43 and −.45, respectively).

With respect to the relations between the legislators' social backgrounds and positions in the respective Houses, I believed that M.P.s with elite backgrounds would tend to cluster in business and finance committees and gravitate toward leadership positions. I based this expectation on Polsby's assertion that a person's ties outside a Parliamentary legislature are a much greater influence on the tasks he performs than in a Congressional legislature. Despite the fact that several Cramer's V.s between M.P.s' backgrounds and assignments are statistically significant, the patterns of the relations seem somewhat random. It makes sense that older M.P.s often serve on procedural committees (Cramer's V = .24, p < .01). Senior legislators often are sought after to give direction on matters concerning the rules-of-the-game. Yet, the socio-economic correlates of the other types of committee membership clearly run contrary to my expectations. Most remarkably, M.P.s with the least education tend to serve on business and financial committees; M.P.s who do not belong to public service clubs often sit on socio-economic resource committees; and M.P.s who belong to elite social clubs frequently hold positions on social welfare committees (Cramer's V.s for all three relations: p < .05). Indeed, a look at the various gammas adds to the incongruity of the results. Despite what could be expected, only one elite characteristic relates at all positively to M.P.s' service on business and finance committees (went to school out of province, gamma = .13). M.P.s who serve on socio-economic resource or social welfare committees, thus do not have less elite characteristics than members of business and finance committees. Further, committee leaders do not have exceptionally elite backgrounds.

The obvious explanation for these apparent heterogeneous findings is that the cream has been skimmed off the top of this sample. As noted earlier, I ex-

cluded Cabinet Ministers from this sample because they do not serve on committees. There is ample evidence that Cabinet Ministers have much more elite
backgrounds than other M.P.s (Kornberg, *et al.*, 1973: 19–28).

The backgrounds of expert party leaders reflect the degree to which top
talent in Parliament is siphoned off to an executive career route. The various
gammas indicate that potential Cabinet Ministers, on both sides of the Commons, share a number of elite characteristics. Polsby's assertion that socio-
economic position has a great impact on one's standing in Parliamentary systems,
thus finds some support in these results.

The various relations between Congressmen's backgrounds and their
positions in the House of Representatives are stronger than expected. For
instance, the Cramer's V.s reveal that those who went out of state for part of
their schooling and those whose fathers were highly educated very often find
themselves on procedural committees ($p < .05$, for both relations). In addition,
there is strong evidence that Congressmen who did not go out of state for part
of their education frequently receive assignments on socio-economic resource
and social welfare committees (the gammas for "went to school out of state"
and the two types of committee positions are both −.53). Educational background, then, plays a very important part in the types of committee assignments
that Congressmen receive.

Congressmen who obtain committee leadership positions share, in clear
contrast to M.P.s, relatively elite socio-economic backgrounds. This is particularly reflected in the extent to which they are (were) executives, highly
educated and lawyers (the respective gammas are .47, .50 and .52). The
committee leaders also differ from their colleagues in that they very often
belong to public service (gamma = .45) and elite clubs (gamma = .28); yet,
they limit their memberships to social clubs (Cramer's V = .26, $p < .05$).

These various findings about Congressmen's backgrounds and assignments
run counter to Polsby's hypothesis that socio-economic standing plays a relatively minor role in the distribution of tasks in a Congressional legislature. In
the House of Representatives, socio-economic background can have an impact
on the types of positions a member receives. The fact that this is particularly so
in the case of Congressmen who have stayed in their committees long enough
to become chairmen perhaps provides an answer to why Congress is a much
stronger legislature than the House of Commons. The "cream" in Congress
stay there and eventually rise to the top; the elite in the House of Commons
ascend to Cabinet posts and, thus, straddle two careers, the legislative and the
executive.

With respect to the political background variable, tenure, I assumed,
obviously, that it would have a particularly strong affect on whether Congressmen are committee leaders; I did not believe that it would bear much on
M.P.s' positions. My reasoning for the latter prediction was based on the
expectation that, in the absence in the Commons of a seniority system such as
Congress', tenure would play a relatively minor role in the allocation of leadership positions. The relationship between tenure and Congressional committee

leadership posts reflects the operation of the seniority system (tenure, Cramer's $V = .26$, $p < .05$). Further, there is little indication that tenure affects the subject matters of the committees to which Congressmen are assigned. The M.P. data, however, present a strikingly different picture. First, there is some evidence of an inverse relation between tenure and committee leadership positions (gamma $= -.39$). Second, the longer M.P.s have served in the House the more often they hold Parliamentary Secretary or shadow cabinet positions (Cramer's $V = .39$, $p < .001$). Third, fairly short-tenured M.P.s frequently sit on socio-economic resource committees (Cramer's $V = .27$, $p < .01$) and long-tenured M.P.s often serve on social welfare committees (gamma $= .55$).

With respect to the relation between M.P.s' and Congressmen's political attitudes and their legislative positions, I noted earlier that the body of literature indicates that personal preference plays a large role in committee assignments among Congressmen. Thus, I believed that there would be fairly strong relations between Congressmen's attitudes toward political liberalism and government intervention and the committees upon which they sit. For instance, I expected political liberals and supporters of government intervention to serve disproportionately on social welfare committees. The actual results of analysis present far from clear patterns. Regarding political liberalism, the following relations stand out:

1. Members of business and financial committees reveal fairly tolerant attitudes toward labor unions (gamma $= .31$), and atheists and Communists (.22);

2. Congressmen who sit on social welfare committees generally think that democracy does not depend on free enterprise (gamma $= .66$), but they often have reservations about trade unions (gamma $= -.26$). Regarding government intervention, the following patterns emerged:

1. Members of procedural committees reveal agreement with all aspects of government intervention except medicare (gamma, $= -.29$);

2. Congressmen on business and finance committees share rather lukewarm positions with respect to the welfare state, except that they support medicare (gamma $= .33$);

3. Socio-economic resource committeemen are very often negative about the size of government (gamma $= -.54$) and the goal of economic security for all (gamma $= -1.00$);

4. Members of social welfare committees gave rather mixed responses, that is, they showed reservations about the size of government and proposals for medicare, but they supported government provision of economic security and jobs.

Many of the relations between Congressmen's views of political liberalism and government intervention, and their committee assignments appear then to be almost random.

In addition, the above relations are not dramatically stronger than those between M.P.s' liberalism and support of government intervention, and the positions that they hold. Still, M.P.s' attitudes towards liberalism and government intervention are no more homogeneous under specific committee assignments than was the case with Congressmen's attitudes as related to committee work. First, with respect to political liberalism: (1) procedural committeemen are ambivalent; (2) members of business and financial committees, unlike their Congressional counterparts, reveal some intolerance, particularly of atheists and Communists (gamma = –.44); and (3) socio-economic resource committeemen, unlike those holding similar positions in Congress, indicate that they are political liberals. Second, regarding support of government intervention and committee assignments, huge discrepancies appear between M.P.s' views of various aspects of the welfare state. For instance, most members of social welfare committees indicate dislike of big government (gamma = –1.00), yet, they subscribe to the proposition that economic security for all is a goal worth striving for (gamma = 1.00). Again, the findings are surprising in that many of the relations between the attitudes and committee assignments are: (1) fairly strong for *both* Congressmen *and* M.P.s; and (2) very heterogeneous under particular committee headings.

The relations between legislators' views of political liberalism and government intervention, and leadership in the respective Houses are stronger than expected. Congressmen with committee leadership positions reveal fairly strong reservations about unions (gamma = –.33), and the freedom of speech of atheists and Communists (gamma = –.35). Committee leaders in the House of Commons register consistent hesitancy about political liberalism, especially regarding the rights of atheists and Communists (gamma = –.54). Commons committee leaders, also, show distaste for big government (gamma = –.32) and the suggestion that economic security for all should be provided by the state (Cramer's V = .28, p < .01). Some party leaders show signs of being political liberals (e.g., labor unions, gamma = .40) and interventionist in their approach to government (e.g., economic security, gamma = 1.00).

It is striking that both Congressmen and M.P.s who are committee leaders registered negative responses under the liberalism and government intervention items. Clearly, their district/constituency characteristics and their socio-economic backgrounds differ much more. My findings perhaps point toward attitudinal traits which mark one as a leader in both houses. It is possible that those who ply a cautious course in relation to democracy and intervention win the confidence of their colleagues.

My hypothesis that leaders in the House of Commons and House of Representatives would share strong beliefs in political efficacy finds little support in my findings. Indeed, few notable relations emerged from the analysis. For instance, Congressional committee leaders often do not believe that everyone has a chance to have his say about important issues (gamma = –.38). The items themselves might be to blame for the relatively meagre results of this section of the analysis. Thoughts about whether a small group "runs things," the little guy can have his say, and one can fight city hall might not loom very large in the minds of legislators with leadership positions.

With respect to the relation between M.P.s' and Congressmen's views of lobbyists, and leadership and committee positions, a number of expected results appeared. First, committee leaders in the two Houses report stronger links with lobbyists than do non-leaders (frequency of contact: M.P.s, gamma = .42 [Cramer's V, p < .05]; Congressmen, gamma = .37; "seeks help from interest groups": M.P.s, gamma = .20; Congressmen, gamma = .44 [Cramer's V, p < .05]). Second, because socio-economic resource and social welfare committees often deal with particularistic publics in a clientele relationship, I hypothesized that, especially in Congress, members of these two types of committees would report higher amounts of interaction with lobbyists. The results of the analysis lend support to my assumptions from two standpoints: (1) the magnitude of the Cramer's V.s and gammas suggests that legislators' committee assignments relate more to the amount of their interaction with groups in the House of Representatives than in the House of Commons; and (2) Congressmen on procedural, and business and financial committees claim less personal contact with lobbyists than members of socio-economic resource and social welfare committees. In addition to the latter observation, we find that Congressmen on social welfare committees appear to give groups good marks for reliability (gamma = .41); and Congressmen on socio-economic resource committees seek help from lobbyists most consistently (gamma = .38).

Conclusion

The findings of this article have indicated that the House of Commons, judgements to the contrary notwithstanding, has eschewed the Congressional model for institutionalization. The Commons has avoided the model despite large increments in its resources and reforms of its committee system. Its leadership simply has not chosen to increase organizational complexity by providing committees with funds for specialized assistance and transforming committee assignments into vehicles for M.P.s' development of expertise. So long as they continue to follow this course, fears that the House of Commons has "Congressionalized" are farfetched.

What may be said in favor of the peculiar Parliamentary way in which the House of Commons has institutionalized? First, despite the fact that these features probably cannot be attributed to institutional differences, M.P.s have less elite backgrounds than Congressmen and are better disposed to the welfare state. Second, and this feature might reflect the differences in institutionalization, M.P.s, although subject to less pressure from lobbyists than Congressmen, register a relatively strong tendency to seek help from representatives of subgroups and interests. M.P.s' substantial allowances and privileges probably give them sufficient resources to take an active role in this type of brokerage. Their direct requests for help from lobbyists might be preferable, in terms of democratic accountability, to the situation in Congress. There members are so inundated by lobbyists that they must use professional staff to screen and digest requests and representations. Given the fact that M.P.s serve only one-sixth as many people as Congressmen, Canada can probably afford to have its legislators soliciting the opinions and help of groups personally. The danger exists, however, that M.P.s do not have the time or assistance necessary to determine which, if any, of the publics concerned with a problem have legitimate cases.

Judging from the characteristics and attitudes of M.P.s and Congressmen who assume certain positions in their respective legislatures, I concluded that the two ways in which the bodies have institutionalized have had considerable impact on career routes within the Houses. This is true both with respect to expert leadership positions and committee assignments. First, the backgrounds and attitudes of leaders in the two Houses reveal that Congressmen from districts with primary industry, relatively elite backgrounds and long tenure, reservations about political liberalism and government intervention, and strong ties with lobbyists all tend to be committee leaders. Expert party leaders (Parliamentary Secretaries and shadow cabinet ministers) in the Commons are similar to the Congressional committee leaders at least insofar as they have relatively elite socio-economic characteristics as compared to their colleagues. M.P.s who are committee leaders differ from their Congressional counterparts in that their socio-economic backgrounds are relatively modest and they have fairly short tenure. In the Commons, then, it often is the comparatively low status and inexperienced members who take on committee chairmanships.

Second, the relations between the legislators' backgrounds and attitudes, and their committee assignments provide mixed, but somewhat supportive, findings with respect to my hypotheses. The division of committee assignments in Congress reflects, as expected, fairly strong relations to the nature of Congressmen's districts and to their attitudes about lobbyists. On the other hand, the relations between the assignments and Congressmen's social backgrounds are stronger than expected; and those between the division of positions and attitudes toward political liberalism and government intervention are surprisingly heterogeneous. Although I found evidence that some socio-economic characteristics of M.P.s relate strongly to their committee positions, the relations do not support specific hypotheses. For instance, I did not find that M.P.s with the best socio-economic credentials find themselves on business and finance committees more often than their less elite colleagues.

This articles has attempted to delineate exactly how the House of Commons and the House of Representatives have institutionalized and what impact this has on the assignment of tasks in the two legislatures. Ample evidence has indicated that the two houses and their members are on two distinct developmental tracks. The most consequential finding for students of Parliament is that, as a result of the continued lack of specialization in the Commons and the orientation of top talent toward expert party leadership positions, the reforms of the last ten years have not introduced so much as an apparent danger of "Congressionalization." Yet, there are some respects in which M.P.s prove themselves to be very acceptable "representatives" of Canadians.

Still, the Commons does not provide adequate surveillance of legislation. I could argue for further reforms, such as full-time professional staff for committees and greater security of tenure for committee members. Despite my

Congressionalizing instincts, I will resist the temptation to indulge in an exhortation for stronger committees. I urge, instead, more thorough studies of M.P.s' roles in party caucuses and the increasingly important functions of party research offices. How could the M.P. make fuller use of the resources already at his disposal by gaining more decisive influence over these two party-dominated instruments for legislative review? The goal of strengthening committee should not be discarded. For the time being, however, it is in a "holding pattern."

REFERENCES

ACHEN, Christopher H., and John SOLAREK
  1974 "The resolution of Congressional committee assignment contests." A paper presented at the annual meeting of the American Political Science Association, Chicago, August 31.
BLONDEL, J.
  1969 *An Introduction to Comparative Government.* New York: Praeger.
  1973 *Comparative Legislatures.* Englewood Cliffs: Prentice-Hall.
BREWIS, T. N.
  1969 *Regional Economic Policies in Canada.* Toronto: Macmillan.
BYERS, R. B.
  1972 "Perceptions of Parliamentary surveillance of the Executive," *Canadian Journal of Political Science* V (June), 234–250.
CAMPBELL, Colin
  1971 "Current models of the political system," *Comparative Political Studies* IV (April), 21–40.
CAMPBELL, Colin, and Thomas REESE
  1977 "The energy crisis and tax policy in Canada and the United States: Federal-provincial diplomacy v. Congressional lawmaking," *Social Science Journal* XIV (January), 17–32.
CLEMENT, Wallace
  1975 *The Canadian Corporate Elite.* Toronto: McClelland and Stewart.
CRICK, Bernard
  1970 "Parliament in the British political system," pp. 33–54 in Allan Kornberg and Lloyd D. Musolf (eds.), *Legislatures in Developmental Perspective.* Durham: Duke University Press.
DAHL, Robert A.
  1971 *Polyarchy.* New Haven: Yale University Press.
DAVIDSON, Roger H.
  1970 "Congress in the American political system," pp. 129–78 in Allan Kornberg and Lloyd D. Musolf (eds.), *Legislatures in Developmental Perspective.* Durham: Duke University Press.
DEXTER, Lewis Anthony
  1969 *How Organizations are Represented in Washington.* New York: Bobbs-Merrill.
DURKHEIM, Emile
  1964 (trans. by George SIMPSON), *The Division of Labor in Society.* New York: Free Press.
FARRELL, R. Barry
  1969 *The Making of Canadian Foreign Policy.* Scarborough: Prentice-Hall.
FRANKS, C. E. S.
  1971 "The dilemma of the standing committees of the Canadian House of Commons," *Canadian Journal of Political Science* IV (December), 461–76.

GERLICH, Peter
    1973   "The institutionalization of European Parliaments," pp. 94–111 in Allan Kornberg
            (ed.), *Legislatures in Comparative Perspective*. New York: McKay.
GOGUEL, François
    1971   "Parliament under the Fifth Republic," pp. 81–96 in Gerhard Loewenberg (ed.),
            Modern Parliaments. Chicago: Atherton.
HENNIS, Wilhelm
    1971   "Reform of the Bundestag," pp. 65–80 in Gerhard Loewenberg (ed.), *Modern
            Parliaments*. Chicago: Atherton.
HOCKIN, Thomas
    1966   "Reforming Canada's Parliament," The University of Toronto Law Journal XVI,
            326–345.
HOFFMAN, David
    1971   "Liaison officers and ombudsman," pp. 146–62, Thomas A. Hockin (ed.), *Apex of
            Power*. Scarborough: Prentice-Hall.
HUNTINGTON, Samuel P.
    1969   *Political Order in Changing Societies*. New Haven: Yale University Press.
JACKSON, Robert J., and Michael M. ATKINSON
    1974   *The Canadian Legislative System*. Toronto: Macmillan.
JEWELL, Malcolm E.
    1973   "Linkages between legislative parties and external parties," pp. 203–234 in Allan
            Kornberg (ed.), *Legislatures in Comparative Perspective*. New York: McKay.
KORNBERG, Allan, and Lloyd D. MUSOLF
    1970   "On legislatures in developmental perspective," pp. 3–32 in Kornberg and Musolf
            (eds.), *Legislatures in Developmental Perspective*. Durham: Duke University Press.
KORNBERG, Allan, *et al.*
    1973   "Legislatures and the modernization of societies," *Comparative Political Studies* V
            (January), 471–91.
LOEWENBERG, Gerhard
    1972   "Comparative legislative research," pp. 3–22, in Samuel C. Patterson and John C.
            Wahlke (eds.), *Comparative Legislative Behavior*. New York: Wiley.
MACKINTOSH, John P.
    1971   "Reform of the House of Commons," pp. 33–64, in Gerhard Loewenberg (ed.),
            Modern Parliaments. Chicago: Atherton.
MARCH, Roman R.
    1974   *Thr Myth of Parliament*. Scarborough: Prentice-Hall.
PAGE, Donald
    1967   "Streamlining the procedures of the Canadian House of Commons, 1963–1966,"
            Canadian Journal of Economics and Political Science XXXIII (February), 27–49.
POLSBY, Nelson W.
    1968   "The Institutionalization of the U.S. House of Representatives," *American Political
            Science Review* LXII (March), 144–68.
    1971   "Strengthening Congress in national policymaking," pp. 3–13, in Polsby (ed.),
            Congressional Behavior. New York: Random House.
    1975   "Legislatures," pp. 260, 277–78 in Fred I. Greenstein and Polsby (eds.), *The
            Handbook of Political Science* V. Reading, Mass.: Addison-Wesley.
POLSBY, Nelson W., *et al.*
    1969   "The Growth of the seniority system in the U.S. House of Representatives,"
            American Political Science Review LXIII (September), 787–807.
PRESTHUS, Robert
    1974   *Elites in the Policy Process*. New York: Cambridge University Press.
SMILEY, D. V.
    1976   *Canada in Question*. Toronto: McGraw-Hill.
SISSON, Richard
    1973   "Comparative legislative institutionalization," pp. 17–38 in Allan Kornberg (ed.),
            Legislatures in Comparative Perspective. New York: McKay.

WAHLKE, John, and Heinz EULAU (eds.)
  1959 *Legislative Behavior*. Glencoe, Ill.: Free Press.
WESTEFIELD, Louis P.
  1974 "Majority party leadership and the committee system in the House of Represent-
        atives," *American Political Science Review* LXVIII (December), 1593–1604.
WILLIAMS, Philip
  1971 "Parliament under the Fifth French Republic," pp. 97–110 in Gerhard Loewen-
        berg (ed.), *Modern Parliaments*. Chicago: Atherton.
ZEIGLER, Harmon, and Michael BAER
  1969 *Lobbying*. Belmont: Wadsworth.

Attitudes Toward Science:
Canadian and American Scientists

H. T. WILSON

York University, Toronto, Canada

Introduction

THOUGH STUDIES which address the impact of modern science on the economies and political systems of the advanced societies are increasingly commonplace nowadays (Nieburg, 1966; Habermas, 1968; Shroyer, 1970; Haberer, 1969; Greenberg, 1967; Nelson, 1968; Jungk, 1958; Calder, 1968), less numerous (and less well-known) are efforts to discover the impact of present business, industrial, and governmental policies and practices on the character and direction of scientific activity. This is even more the case where these efforts include attempts to discover through questionnaires and interviews the attitudes and values of scientists themselves. While science policy has been an item of great concern to the Canadian government and to some private bodies in Canada over the past decade, there has been almost no systematic attempt to integrate the perceptions of scientists and technologists on matters involving responsibility, commitment, and performance and productivity into "science policy" research.

What follows does not, on its own, purport to be a remedy for this situation, though it is part of a larger concern with improving the quality of the instruments used to solicit the attitudes and values of the scientific community in Canada. It seeks to relate the perceptions of a sample of Canadian scientists controlled for several factors to a burgeoning body of knowledge directly relevant to the role of science in society, economy, polity and culture. It focusses on the *perceptions* of 130 Canadian and American natural scientists on issues arising out of the interpenetration of science, technology, politics, bureaucracy, culture, and professional and intellectual activity. It attempts to discover scientists' views on the way science policy is presently formulated, as well as the impact of political, economic, and cultural concerns on the way science is actually done.

Though aware of the controversy among social researchers regarding the degree to which actions of a particular kind may be presumed to follow from the discovery of the actor's attitudes and perceptions (Warner and de Fleur, 1969), we have assumed here only that attitudes are a cue to *generalized* action patterns for respondents, but not that these action patterns necessarily tend to reinforce existing attitudes rather than challenging them. Indeed, on several counts it was clear that a large number of those responding had changed their views on significant matters as a result of their perception that a particular situation had changed. They had revised their attitudes toward governmental policy-making bodies, for example, as a result of experiences which had challenged an existing view or stereotype. This point suggests the distinct possibility that, contrary to some respondent's claims regarding the *lack* of applicability of scientific standards to daily life, scientific training and career commitment may favour greater openness in the form of willingness to modify or revise existing attitudes on the basis of new evidence (Moore, 1965; Popper, 1963; Ziman, 1968).

The original objective of the study was to make a *comparison* between the responses of Canadian and American scientists its central feature. It was the relatively light response rate to the questionnaire from scientists in the United States which forced the desired comparison to become a peripheral rather than a central feature of the study. Though less systematically drawn than the Canadian sample, it was hoped that significant differences in perception and attitude on the matters being considered would emerge as a remainder from the obvious similarities and common ground that all scientists, particularly in the West, probably share. Admittedly two or three questions were formulated in such a way as to be directed in the main to Canadian respondents, but these were well into the questionnaire and did not affect the American response rate.

American scientists most often demurred because of prior commitments and high work-load. A number drew attention (along with Canadians who chose not to respond) to the open-ended character of the questionnaire, which endeavoured to cover a good deal of ground as a preliminary survey must, and therefore had little choice but to ask scientists to elaborate on the reasons for their choices. They appreciated the dilemma of the writer, but felt that a competent job of responding would demand more concentrated time than they could reasonably afford to give it. A few Americans choosing not to respond alluded to the number of times over the past few years they had been asked to fill in various types of questionnaires or participate in interviews, giving the writer the distinct impression that they, in contrast to the Canadian sample, had been consistently and continually researched (and often in their opinion over-researched) during the past decade.

The remainder of the study summarizes responses under headings very similar to those used to break up the questionnaire sent to respondents: occupational choice and self-image; science and the nation; and power and influence. It occasionally cites individual responses where they are thought to highlight a particular issue, without assuming that such responses would necessarily be acceptable to all, or even most, of those responding. In most cases, however, it was clear to the writer that selected statements giving reasons for particular choices did constitute an elaboration which in fact reflected the stated (but undeveloped) views of a majority of the sample responding. Comparisons with American respondents are made only where significant differences in attitude and outlook were discovered.

Occupational Choice, Self-Image, and Status

The first choice of over half those responding in the Canadian sample was "early and continuing interest and curiosity" as the primary reason motivating their choice of a scientific career, followed by "aptitude" and "pursuit of truth." The same order held generally for the American sample as well. "Early and continuing interest and curiosity" was hardly mentioned at all as second choice, while "aptitude" and "pursuit of truth" appeared far more often. "Example of teacher" was mentioned equally often as second choice. The most consistent third choices were "pursuit of truth", "aptitude", "status and prestige" and "parental expectation and encouragement". The fact that remuneration was mentioned only four times, twice as second choice and twice as fourth choice, is probably far less an indication of any downplaying of its importance by respondents than it is evidence of the fact that the sheer performance requirements and long training period required of any aspirant to a scientific career tends to self-select that relatively tiny minority of individuals who combine interest, aptitude, commitment and high satisfaction and enjoyment.

Remuneration and job security, along with status and prestige, tended to appear consistently as "additional factors" which had become significant motivators only *after* respondents had entered into their respective careers and acquired reputations as researchers and trainers of graduate students. Other factors mentioned, albeit rarely, as initial motivators in the Canadian sample included "challenge", "career independence", "enjoyment and satisfaction", "opportunity to secure financial assistance", "physical limitations", and "betterment of society". Societal improvement was cited more frequently, along with status and prestige and remuneration, as a later motivator. The same was true of "satisfaction", particularly satisfaction received from teaching, training and helping future scientists, associating with professional colleagues, and receiving awards, honourary degrees, and various other perquisites and privileges. "International recognition" was cited only twice in the Canadian sample as a reinforcing motivator. "Success" itself was mentioned by many respondents as a major motivator for them once into their careers. Only one cited university and administrative service as a motivator displacing "special aptitude" and "encouragement from university professors".

Asked to rank-order those areas and activities which secured occupational prestige and recognition for them, the Canadian sample overwhelmingly chose "basic research" as their first-choice, followed by "teaching" and "directing and supervising graduate students". Second and third choice differences were clear but not overwhelming, with "directing and supervising graduate students" ranked second more often than "teaching" was ranked third. The same held true for the American sample, save for the fact that "directing and supervising gradate students" was ranked second over "teaching" by a few more respondents. American respondents, however, ranked "applied research" consistently lower than Canadians, when they ranked it at all, suggesting the possibility that a more extensive and complex division of functions in science may serve to reinforce the dichotomy between basic and applied research. Neither sample ranked "development" higher than fourth, and the choices in both samples were evenly distributed from fourth through eighth choice. Americans were more prone to rank "department service" and "professional associations" higher than were Canadian scientists, while Canadians tended to rank "university service" higher than the American sample did.

A most interesting difference manifested itself in the respective methods of rank-ordering. While the Canadian sample gave a specific number when ranking all, most or some of the activities listed, some American respondents clustered their activity preferences around two rank-order sets. Many broke down their activities in a manner supportive of Gouldner's dichotomy between "locals" and "cosmopolitans" (Gouldner, 1959), qualifying their rank-ordering only by indicating the overall priority of the latter orientation. Thus *both* "basic research" and "university service" would be rated first, *both* "directing and supervising graduate students" and "professional associations", "national organizations" and "international developments" second and so on. A few simply clustered all "cosmopolitan" activities first and all, most or some "locals" second, third, fourth, etc.

Asked to classify themselves by reference to those titles which best described how they thought of themselves as scientists, over half the Canadian sample cited "researcher" first, followed by "teacher" and "trainer of future scientists" as their second and third choices. "Academic" was the second most popular first choice after "researcher", followed by "teacher". "Academic" and "researcher" were frequently cited as second and third choices and "trainer of future scientists" as a second choice. While some ranked "professional" in the top two choices, the rest ranked it somewhat lower. Only one respondent in each sample made "university (or organizational) person" or "administrator" their first choice, while most ranked it below their third choice, either fifth or sixth. This clustering not only evidences the research and training orientation of university scientists engaged in predominantly basic research, but suggests that scientists, though salaried employees in the university, are far more likely to maintain a clear picture of their own collegial reference group outside the university than most other academics do.

A very similar breakdown held for the American sample, save for the fact that "teacher" and "trainer of future scientists" were equally popular as second choices, while "academic" stood slightly ahead of "teacher" as a third choice. None of the American respondents picked "academic" or "teacher" as their first choice, and only one did so for "training of future scientists", in contrast to the Canadian sample. Americans also tended to give the label of "professional" a lower rating with a cluster of respondents placing it fifth or sixth in their respective rank-order schemes. "University (or organizational) person" was distributed fairly evenly from third choice to seventh, while one third of the Americans picked "administrator" as their seventh choice (out of seven).

Such ranking and classifying questions often lead respondents to confuse present self-classification – how they actually perceive themselves – with the way they ideally would like to perceive themselves, or be perceived by others. However, considerable consistency between present and ideal perceptions was suggested by answers to a question which asked respondents to rank the following three activities in order of preference: "participate in a pioneering research project," "head up a government commission or council", or "be science advisor to the prime minister (or president)". Only three persons in the Canadian sample cited something other than "participate in a pioneering research project" – all in three cases "be science advisor . . ." – as their first choice, and all American respondents made it their first choice. Several persons in each sample either listed the other two options far below second and third positions (e.g. 99th) or gave only their first choice. Some of those citing only "participate in a pioneering research project" stated that the other activities were not of any interest to them at all, while others qualified the activity to read "head up" rather than "participate".

Second choice in the Canadian sample only slightly favoured "be science advisor . . " over "head up a government commission or council", in clear contrast to American respondents, who overwhelmingly favoured it for second choice. The far higher percentage of second choices for "head up a government commission or council" among Canadian respondents may attest to the more central role of government bodies in Canadian scientific activity, particularly in the area of the allocation of funds for basic research to scientists in government laboratories and in the universities (OECD, 1973; Science Council Report No. 18, September, 1972; Science Council Special Study, No. 21, December, 1971). The "split" between the available second choice options in the Canadian sample, and the clear preference for "be science advisor . . ." among American respondents, may also suggest a difference in how this latter activity is perceived in each case. Canadians appear to construe *both* options in more honourific terms than the Americans, whose preference for "be science advisor" seems more a reflection of the commitment to wedding expertise with authority in politics than anything else. Many Americans implied by their remarks that heading up a "government commission or council" would be a sheer waste of their time and energies.

On the issue of prestige and status hierarchies in science, respondents in both samples overwhelmingly believed them to exist, though a few Canadian respondents stated they thought this probably or perhaps was the case. Only one Canadian respondent believed prestige and status hierarchies to be nonexistent in the scientific community in his country, while no Americans held such a view. Significant differences between the two samples manifested themselves, however, when respondents were asked whether they thought such hierarchies existed in their "area of special interest". Approximately 30% of the Canadian sample said No, while no Americans believed this to be the case. In almost every instance, Canadian respondents answering No were in applied scientific research and development areas rather than in basic research. Of those Canadians answering Yes, one suggested that science as a whole was clearly stratified on the basis of university affiliation, while another suggested that his discovery that subsequent grants were far easier to get after one had received his first grant constituted evidence for the existence of such hierarchies. Another cited the small size of the scientific community, and the fact that "most members know one another personally" as the reason for such hierarchies in Canadian science (Porter, 1965, pp. 431–34, 495, 507–11; Senate Special Committee on Science Policy, Volume I, 1970, pp. 193–225).

Asked "what factors do you believe are most relevant to membership in prestige hierarchies" in science and in their area of special interest respectively, a large majority of Canadian respondents gave different versions of meritocratic criteria as their answer (Jencks and Riesman, 1968, part I), particularly for the second part. Examples included: "quality of research and publication", "competence", "intellectual stature", "amount published", "production and development of new ideas", and "creative productivity", while a few cited "originality", "national or international reputation", and "capacity for responsible judgement". Those forwarding less meritocratic criteria as key factors cited: "field of study", "Ph.D. thesis adviser", "graduate school attended", "university affiliation", "post-doctoral experience", "administrative ability", and "activity in professional societies". Only a few cited blatantly non-meritocratic criteria like "political savvy", "personality", "personal contacts" and "ability to communicate".

The difference in this latter case between the two samples was that the Americans tended to restrict such factors to membership in prestige hierarchies in science as a whole in their country, while Canadians were only slightly more likely to do so. In neither sample did any respondent perceive subfields and subdisciplines to be stratified on a less meritocratic basis than science as a whole. An interesting possibility, suggested to some extent by the fact that respondents were asked to *state* (rather than select) those factors they thought significant in each case, is that some respondents may have construed status and prestige to be a basis for stratification *different by definition* from one based on meritocratic or performance criteria in science as a whole and in their respective areas of interest. For them, a concern with status or prestige hierarchies might well have led them to emphasize those blatantly non-meritocratic features which did *not* coincide with actual performance and productivity. Several Canadian respondents were plainly unhappy with any allusion whatsoever to status and prestige where differential capacity to command funds and personnel was concerned. "University affiliation" served as a bone of contention for some respondents in both samples, even though a few admitted that quality work may and often does result from such an affiliation. It appeared more a concern about the way some able (or very able) persons could realize far higher levels of scientific *success* than other equally capable individuals, coupled with a belief that the heavy concentration of scientists and research programmers in a very few universities may be hurting rather than helping basic research.

Science and the Nation

The series of questions addressed to responsibility, national interests and the role of unique cultural, political and economic factors began by asking whether respondents believed science to have "a general social function or role" and/or "a specific social responsibility". Almost everyone in both samples gave a positive answer to both parts of the question, though several noted that science's social function did not serve to distinguish it from other occupations and professions in society. To have a social function was not, then, to have specific requirements placed upon science from the outside; it was something essentially given in the very existence and institutional status of science as an ongoing collective enterprise. What this view of social function or role also implied was that science, though itself arguably a social system of sorts (Merton, 1957; Storer, 1966; Kuhn, 1969; Ziman, 1968) was now a central factor comprising the complex structure of interdependent institutions and activities which characterize all the advanced societies (Habermas, 1968; Wilson, 1976 (a) (b)).

The issue of "social responsibility" was encountered initially by most respondents as non-controversial, though several were concerned to point out that only individual scientists, not science as an institution, could be held "responsible". At the same time hardly anyone in either sample was willing to state that science (or scientists) lacked a *specific* social responsibility. For example, only two respondents asked what the writer had in mind by "specific"; the rest appeared to assume the existence of such a responsibility but did not elaborate. This is probably less an indication that those responding have a clear idea of what their social responsibility is, than it is their view of it as something closely related to science's social function or role, that is, something which emerges almost automatically out of science's commitment to the pursuit of knowledge and truth. In neither case, then, would we be likely to be correct in assuming that respondents accept external definitions of either general social function or specific social responsibility where *basic* research is involved.

Responses from the small number of *applied* scientists in the Canadian and American samples constitute exceptions to this, since their employment and assessment is clearly dependent upon the performance of a specific outcome-related function. The question of social responsibility here is more difficult to ferret out. Most of those presently engaged in applied research made it clear to the writer that they were involved in this work because of their commitment to a broad-based notion of human betterment which comprehended ecological and environmental problems, and was consequently more sensitive to the need to temper successful development and exploitation with long-range and "total-system" concerns. A few appeared determined to work in applied rather than basic science because of their belief that the research they were engaged in, whether in forestry, fisheries, northern development or mineral resources, was of central significance to society and urgently needed doing.

Asked whether "national interests" should influence scientific work, most respondents engaged in basic research contrasted their work to applied science and development, stating that national interests should influence only these latter activities and not their own. However, approximately 35% of Canadians engaged in basic research believed that even their scientific work should "to a small extent" be influenced by national interests. Others distinguished "applied research" from "development", stating that the first should be influenced "to some extent" by national concerns, while the second was more obviously an activity where such interests should play an influential role. A few wanted the writer to specify more clearly what he had in mind when he used the term "national interests", and stressed the need for politicians to formulate carefully national goals rather than falling prey to short-run "vote-getting" issues. No respondents in the Canadian sample believed that either applied research or development should be uninfluenced by national interests.

The American sample differed greatly from the Canadian in that respondents overwhelmingly believed, almost all without qualification, that basic research should be influenced by national interests. It appeared that these respondents perceived there to be a far more direct relation between science, technology and national policy than Canadian scientists, even to the point of seeing their efforts as a central component of a national system organized to utilize the discoveries of basic research in as efficient a fashion as possible. This view probably reflects the status of the United States, not only as a world centre for scientific research of all types, but as a nation whose vast intellectual and material resources, coupled with a tradition of science, have allowed it to organize, systematize, and fund the set of inter-related individual and collective activities which are necessary for the existence of a national system. This is not to suggest that Americans have a more application-oriented view of basic research than do Canadians; on the contrary. It suggests instead that Americans have the organizational and administrative machinery, especially in industry, to take better advantage of the products of basic research than is the case in Canada, where a subsidiary economy subject to rationalization truncates this application and development process where it does not frustrate it altogether. (Science Council Reports No. 15, October, 1971; No. 22, December 1971; Wilson, 1975; Lithwick, 1969).

On the question whether there are "certain unique (e.g. nationally or culturally specific) factors that affect scientific work in your country", the vast majority of Canadian respondents believed there were. Some wanted to distinguish basic research from applied research and development here, pointing out that unique or unusual factors affected only the latter two activities and not the first. For example, a few mentioned "geographical concerns", "historical developments" in Canadian science, and the emphasis on applied research in the areas of northern development, agriculture and forestry. Only one respondent made reference to Francophone scientists in Canada, stating that the system for funding through the National Research Council made it slightly easier for them to get support. While the question was certainly not set up in a way geared to elicit responses directed to linguistic and cultural issues of this kind, the writer was quite surprised that Canadian respondents, who with a very few exceptions were Anglophone, made no reference whatsoever to these issues in their answers.

The next question sought to determine more specifically what these unique factors were, and presented a list where respondents could "specify and rank order" those items they thought appropriate, followed by a request that they "explain briefly" the reasons for their first and second choices. A number of respondents felt the question too involved and declined to answer, but most expressed at least three choices and went on to explain their preferences thereafter. Canadians cited "attitudes to basic research" and "the role of government bodies" four times more often than any other factors for their first choice. "Attitudes to basic research" was also the most popular second choice, followed by "the role of industry and business". "Attitudes toward applied research" and "the role of government bodies" were the most frequently cited third choices, with "the role of industry and business" chosen fourth most often. Of those factors which remained, "patterns of teaching and training" was cited as the fifth most popular choice, suggesting the often-noted workmanlike attitude of scientists trained in basic research at Canadian institutions of higher learning.

Under the section requesting a brief explanation for their choices, several Canadians spoke of the crucial formative role of the National Research Council, and two of the Medical Research Council, as reasons for citing "the role of government bodies" and "attitudes toward basic research" as their first two choices. Some lamented the "loss of confidence" in basic research reflected in declining financial support and a decidedly short-run "technological" orientation to Canadian scientific activity by government. One even alluded to the "destruction" of the NRC which, important though it has been, now must try to cope with an "anti-science" attitude in government and in the media. Several suggested that too much had indeed been expected of basic research, with the not unexpected swing back to an overly "results-oriented" short-term view of science by government and the public. Solutions were expected to flow almost automatically from scientific discoveries and, when they did not, criticism was not long in coming (Wilson, 1968).

On the other hand, a few Canadian respondents pointed out the lack of relevance of the "national system" model operative south of the border enroute to stating the need for Canada to establish research configurations in areas it could do best. The result of Canada's attempt to replicate the breadth of specialities and subspecialities found in the United States was bound to be disappointing. The real point of comparison for a few, and a not very heartening one at that, was Canada's status and prowess by comparison to "Great Britain and other European countries", *not* the United States. To expect the level of systemic organization in either government or industry and business which would increase substantially the likelihood of basic research discoveries being *made* relevant to development objectives through applied science was to pretend that the scientific infrastructures of Canada and the United States were only quantitatively, rather than qualitatively, different. It suggested the need to reconsider the mediating role of *applied* science between basic research and development in Canada, in contrast to the United States (Bunge, 1966; Lithwick, 1969).

The relative popularity of the related choices of "the role of industry and business", and "attitudes toward applied research" was explained in a number of fairly extensive comments addressed, not surprisingly, to Canada's subsidiary status in a largely continental economy, at least in those areas where there exists a sizeable investment in in-house research and development activities. Part of the dilemma respecting recent efforts to fund basic research in Canada was seen by several to be related to the "immature" attitude of government, the media, and the public toward the non-linear relation between science and technology, coupled with the absence of a tradition of science. Lacking an industrial or commercial infrastructure able or willing to entertain the sort of risks requisite to independent economic development (Grasley, 1975; Wilson, 1975), it is absurd to turn away from basic research on the grounds that its alleged promise remains unfulfilled. The idea that clear outcomes would be forthcoming from "investing" in basic research, it turns out, is no less an illusion because of the increasingly rationalized character of the growth sector of the Canadian economy than it is an indication of a failure to take seriously the long-term economic and political consequences of the socialization processes that generate and perpetuate conservative attitudes toward risk-taking in Canada (Porter, 1965; Clements, 1973; Wilson, 1975).

American respondents also overwhelmingly alluded in their remarks to the overly short-term attitude of legislators and the public. Like the Canadian sample they focussed on "the role of government bodies" and "attitudes toward basic research". In clear contrast was the lack of any significant concern with either applied research or industrial and business interests. This may point to the difference between perceived "slack" in the American system and the "either-or" character of expenditure where the far more pre-eminent role of government bodies and public financing of basic research is concerned. Nevertheless, American respondents did allude to the lack of confidence frequently exhibited regarding basic research, as well as their own dismay about the expectations of government bodies (NSF, NIH) who fund it. A few blamed this state of affairs in part on the tendency of scientists, as well as politicians, to attempt to "sell" basic research on the promise of later useful applications. Only two thought the public feared the possible (or probable) "evil uses" to which scientific discoveries might be put.

A more pointed question asked Canadian respondents in particular what effect they thought Canada's "economic dependence" in various areas of business and industry had had on basic research, applied research, development, teaching and training, and configurations of research specialities, and asked them to explain briefly their answers. There was a fairly even distribution of answers across the four categories of "very great effect", "considerable effect", "slight effect" and "no discernible effect" for basic research, and the largest number believed that Canada's economic dependence had had a "considerable effect" on basic research. This is surprising in light of the presumption, shared by scientists as well as non-scientists, that basic research is "culture-free", at least by comparison with other kinds of scientific work. The argument for the neutrality or objectivity of science is usually made most resoundingly where basic research is involved.

To be sure, a somewhat higher percentage of those responding chose "very great effect" when contemplating the impact of economic dependence on applied research and development than was the case for basic research, but this was probably, with few exceptions, based on Canada's subsidiary position in both the resource-extractive and the manufacturing sectors. It is of some interest to note, however, that respondents were roughly equally divided on the question of whether economic dependence had had either a very great or a considerable effect on applied research and development. The same distribution and the same percentages held for the effect of economic dependence on "configurations of research specialities" that held for applied research and development. Dependence was thought to have had for the most part a "slight effect" on teaching and training. Only 10% of the sample believed that economic dependence had had "no discernible eflect" on all forms of scientific work cited except for basic research. That approximately 20% believed economic dependence had had no discernible effect on *basic* research suggests that this activity is still seen by many to be less dependent on economy, polity and culture than more application-oriented work or work.

The brief explanations which followed drew attention to what for some constituted the "double dilemma" of Canadian science. First, Canadian firms and Canadian subsidiaries do "relatively little" *applied* research, in the first case because these firms are often in relatively stable areas where technology is not changing, and is not therefore such a key factor, and in the second because most R and D is carried on in the home rather than the host countries, particularly where a rationalized model is operative (Science Council Background Study No. 22, December, 1971; Science Council Special Study No. 21, December, 1971). Second, there was the fact that comparatively little *basic* research is done outside the universities in Canada, particularly in industry, which led government to try to compensate for this through government laboratories and public funding. Now, however, there is a clear "disenchantment" with basic research on the part of government agencies, elected representatives, and the public. What was most intriguing about these answers was the extent to which respondents perceived there to be a clear relationship between the paucity of applied research in Canada and problems connected with the quantity and quality of *basic* research in this country.

This was borne out by the number of respondents who believed there was a relatively fixed amount of funding available for *either* basic or applied research in Canada. They pointed out that this monopoly situation is problematic precisely because the relation between basic and applied research is presently zero-sum, with the result that a preference for one means a decline in available funds for the other. Though admittedly not just one granting agency was involved, respondents believed the situation to be sufficiently monopolistic as to seriously threaten basic research, particularly given recent developments which had led government and the public to question its need in favour of a short-run technological orientation to science. Several respondents stated more emphatically that they believed government's preference for such an orientation to be *technologically*, as well as scientifically, nonsensical, one which reflected an all too-typical response pattern from non-scientists in positions of authority and public responsibility.

Power and Influence

Self-perceived power and influence as an occupational or professional group, and as "producers" of significant knowledge, was expected to contribute importantly to the study. Respondents were asked a number of questions, some specifically directed to ongoing relations with government, industry, business, and the universities, others which attempted to assess more general perceptions regarding the scientist's political role, and the applicability of scientific criteria and standards to other societal and political activities and functions. This section tends to confirm the consequences for basic research in particular of what many respondents referred to as a more generalized "dependence syndrome" or "subsidiary mentality" exemplified in, but not exhausted by, the absence of an independent R and D thrust in key areas of the Canadian economy.

To the question, "How much influence do you think scientists presently have on the following: national science policy, policies affecting science indirectly, funding of universities, policies toward industry and business, national economic and technological developments, and foreign affairs", the large majority of Canadian respondents cited "negligible" for all categories except foreign affairs where "none to speak of" was cited most often. Approximately twice as many respondents believed scientists had "considerable" influence over matters relating to the funding of universities and national economic and technological developments as was the case for both "national science policy" and "policies affecting science indirectly". American respondents, in contrast, were evenly divided between "considerable" and "negligible" in their perception of the extent of scientific influence in the formulation of national science policy and policies which affected science indirectly. The division favoured "considerable" where university funding was concerned, but quickly shifted back to "negligible" for "policies toward industry and business" and "national economic and technological developments". Americans believed the influence of scientists to be "negligible" rather than "none to speak of" in the area of foreign affairs.

Respondents were also asked to explain briefly wherever they thought the type of influence was either insufficient or excessive. An overwhelming majority of Canadians wanted scientists to have a considerable rather than a negligible influence in the formulation of national science policy and policies affecting science indirectly, while a few wanted the scientific input to be "very much", particularly where national science policy was concerned. This did not necessarily mean that respondents refused to separate science and politics. It suggested rather that scientific *influence* needed to be *increased* in situations where politicians and bureaucrats, neither of them working scientists, were formulating policies in these areas. None of those responding, for example, sought to eliminate the political or administrative role and substitute working scientists for these individuals and groups. Many were restating their fear of the consequences of a short-term application-oriented science policy like that presently supported by key politicians, administrators, journalists and elements of the general public concerned about value for dollars spent on basic research.

It was the scientific input in the form of *advice*, then, which was seen to be lacking at both the federal and provincial levels of government. A few respondents even argued that Canada really has no science policy *per se* at all, but rather policies which pertain to science in the absence of an ongoing advisory and consultative relationship which should be built-in to the structure of governments. Several also wanted to distinguish their preference from the relatively random "in-house" advice secured by policy makers and bureaucrats from scientists working in government. They wanted to point out how unrepresentative of working scientists these individuals usually were, and how unlikely it would be for their opinions to be *either* representative or politically independent. One respondent summarized the situation in the following way.

> "I may be wrong, but it seems to me that we do not have in Canada an independent (non-government) scientific body whose advice is solicited by government when questions relating to science and science policy are being considered. We do have the N.R.C. Grants Committees who meet and advise on who should receive support, and how much. But these committees (so far as I know) have no role in advising on priorities: what kind of research should be financed and to what extent."

It is important to note here that several Canadian respondents who thought the influence of scientists in matters relating to science policy insufficient stressed the *responsibility* of scientists rather than the desire for heightened influence for its own sake. One even went so far as to state that:

> "Scientists clearly have a responsibility to the public to be more political in the sense of proposing responsible use of scientific developments and in exploring the need for more scientific activity."

Another believed that scientists had a "special" responsibility in *all* areas connected with science, applied science, and science-based technology, which required them to consider entering private business as entrepreneurs. Only by penetrating the "board set" in Canada could they come to have a significant influence over "policies toward industry and business".

One respondent wanted to distinguish aspects of the present dilemma for basic research in the following way. It was not just that too little basic science was being done because of the increasing influence of a linear and mechanical productivity model in the face of economic trends and the governmental and public response to these trends. In addition was the fact that "a lot of bad science" was being done "because not enough scientists were involved in peer review". He too believed Canada lacked a science policy, as opposed to policies which relate directly or indirectly to science made independent of *working* scientists. Another noted that past presentations of "national science policy groups" have had little or no effect on government policy, and cited the recent experience of the Medical Research Council's budget as illustrative of this.

Several respondents discussed the issue of scientific influence where the funding of universities was concerned. Here there was near-unanimous agreement that the importance of the universities to basic research in Canada was so great that scientists should have at least "considerable" and ideally "very much" influence in this area. While a greater number believed the scientific input to be "considerable" here than in any other area, none believed it to be "very much", and approximately twice as many thought it to be '"negligible". Only two Canadians thought the scientific influence was less than negligible. A few noted the fact that a regional bias is prominent in the funding of universities, and cited this bias as in part responsible for the present pattern of *political* decision-making, with its deleterious effects on the development of basic research in Canada. Though university scientists involved in basic research have been trying "desperately" to influence science policy "at several levels", there appear to be a number of "political" reasons influencing present practices and preferences, not just the short-term application-oriented approach already cited.

An extremely interesting observation was made by two respondents discussing the tendency toward "musical portfolios" in the federal government. They pointed out that such a practice had especially serious consequences where the Ministry of State for Science and Technology portfolio was involved. While probably true that the complexities of *all* ministries take longer to master than present appointment priorities take account of, the already existing bias in favour of political and short-run considerations was heightened by the minister's lack of acquaintance with the technical aspects of activities carried on within his ministry. Another suggested further that revolving portfolios have as one consequence the increased influence of those at the top of the administrative structures manned by career civil servants in the various ministries, and cited this as a serious problem.

As noted, Americans, on the whole, perceived their role in influencing American science policy, either directly or indirectly, to be "considerable", and this also held for the funding of universities. Most declined to elaborate on their choices or made vague references to how in all or most cases the influence was insufficient and should be increased. A few, however, did elaborate, some noting that the scientist in the United States is in the main misrepresented by either the technologist or by the university politician. Another claimed that American scientists in general are "the most underused segment of the intelligent population", while a third wanted to distinguish carefully between responsibilities which all individuals as citizens have and should share equally, and those more occupationally specific responsibilities which issue from particular types of training and work. In the latter case scientists "are better informed than most citizens about the potentialities of scientific exploitation and the consequences". He spoke for others, both in the United States and Canada, when he suggested that "the best solution is for scientists to do a better job of educating their fellow citizens, thereby exerting strong indirect influence". The absence of detailed explanations in the American sample no doubt underscores the fact that a large majority of those responding felt that the influence of scientists on policies affecting science directly and indirectly and on the funding of universities was satisfactory.

Another set of questions sought to relate the issue of funding to the role of scientists in determining priorities and allocating available public monies. Every respondent engaged in basic research believed that there was a need for increased funding in this area, though many qualified this by saying that the issue was not simply a question of increased funding, but related to a different allocation of existing or contemplated monies, however large or small. They tied this point to their earlier criticisms of politicians and administrators, with their lack of concern about the need for ongoing consultations with working scientists. With the exception of approximately 15% of the Canadian sample who "don't know", all those responding believed increased funding was required in both applied research and development as well.

Asked to elaborate, a number reiterated that in both basic and applied research funding is insufficient. Several basic researchers accepted the need for increased funding in applied science and development, noting that the support of such activities in Canadian-owned industries and businesses was "almost non-existent". They distinguished Canadian owned industries from subsidiaries, pointing out that the dilemma of R and D in the latter case was different, being both built into this sort of dependence and further aggravated by trends toward centralization of R and D in the home countries (rationalization). A few again stated their criticism of government and public disenchantment with basic research, saying that application-oriented problem-solving continues to depend on theoretical work in science. Some also restated the unfavourable comparison of Canada with other small and medium-sized countries across a wide range of R and D efforts.

One suggested that "the science situation is getting below the critical point" if we are to sustain a "socially, culturally, and economically independent nation", while another cited inflation and the failure of funding to keep pace with it as factors explaining the underpayment of postdoctoral fellows and the shrinking of research groups. Some compared Canada to other countries experiencing similar or greater rates of inflation and argued that the unwillingness to fund basic research in particular could not be entirely explained by this development. It was at least as much a consequence of declining governmental confidence in the ability of basic research to "deliver the goods".

On the need for more funding in *applied* research and development, a few qualified their assessment by drawing attention to "poor administration" of funds, and the lack of "maturity" required "in knowing how to make proper investment in R and D." This was ascribed to the fact that Canada is "virtually devoid" of people who can perform this function combining good judgement with adequate advice from working scientists. The failure or refusal to establish such an ongoing consultative scheme was seen by some to reflect scientific dependency and "colonialism" in both basic and applied areas. Perhaps the most critical statement came from a respondent who sought to relate the problem of research funding to scientific training':

> "Canada is an intellectual backwater in its attitude towards science endeavour. We spend large sums of money in training bright young Canadians in the sciences and then do not fund science sufficiently to allow them to enjoy an appropriate position upon completion of the training. (If a position is available at all). We are so condescending to other technical areas of the world that we seem to accept second rate as the norm and fund accordingly. Actually, we have the resources and the talents to become first-rate in a number of priority areas."

The Canadian sample split on the question whether public funding necessitated "government supervision" in order to guarantee that research funds were spent wisely, with a few more answering "Yes" than "No". Asked what role "professional scientists" should play in this supervision slightly more than half indicated "the pre-eminent role", while the rest cited "a considerable role". Not surprisingly, none of those responding cited the remaining choices of "little or no role" or "some subordinate role", though several stated that they were referring here to basic research and not to applied research or development. The small number of respondents in applied work for the most part cited "Yes" and "a considerable role" rather than the more radical position. A number qualified their "yes" answers with phrases like "a loose control" or "to some extent". The American sample did not differ in any significant way from the Canadian.

To the question: "How much autonomy from governmental supervision and control should scientists have in determining the use of public funds for scientific work?", well over half of those responding cited "predominant autonomy (requiring only consultation with non-scientists)", while the rest with one exception split evenly between "partial autonomy, but subject to veto" and "total autonomy" – choices on either side of "predominant autonomy". Only one chose "little or no autonomy (only advisory role)" but cited the need for a clear government policy and consultation. A number choosing "total autonomy", and two choosing "predominant autonomy", referenced their choice to *basic* research, while a few focussing on applied research opted for "partial autonomy, but subject to veto".

Twenty percent of those who cited the professional scientists' proper role in the supervision of public funds as either "considerable" or "pre-eminent" believed he should have less than predominant (i.e. partial) autonomy in determining their use. Half of these again distinguished basic from applied research when they made their choices, suggesting that where basic research was concerned a dominant peer review system should be in operation once the overall amount had been set. Others distinguished the sort of advisory role which might be proper when either applied work for government and industry or overall priorities for society were being set from allocations once priorities had been decided. Thus it was possible for respondents to support even "the pre-eminent role" and "total autonomy", and not be requesting an unreasonable amount of professional control.

The theme which came through time and time again was the need to let working scientists in basic research do what they can do better than anyone else: allocate funds once the overall priorities had been established. Apart from the desire for funding to keep pace with inflation, the large majority of respondents were most anxious that what was available to them be wisely spent, and this demanded ongoing consultation with working scientists and collegial review.

A final question asked respondents whether and under what circumstances scientists should speak out on matters of public interest. The following breakdown was given, distinguishing matters: "directly affecting science", "indirectly affecting science", "about which there is great public concern regardless of its relation to science", and "where there is neither public concern nor a relation to science". They were also asked to elaborate on the reasons for their choices where appropriate. Not surprisingly, every respondent in both the Canadian and the American samples answered "yes" to the question when addressed to matters "directly affecting science", some stressing the *responsibility* as well as the necessity of scientists doing this. The same pattern held for matters "indirectly affecting science", save for the fact that three Canadians "didn't know" and two Americans answered "no" and "perhaps". An overwhelmingly majority in both samples also answered "yes" to the question when it referred to matters "about which there is great public concern regardless of its relation to science", though two each in the two samples answered "no" and a few "didn't know". The same held for matters "when there is neither public concern nor a relation to science", except that there were a few more "no" and "don't know" choices in each sample.

Respondents were careful, however, to separate the first two matters from the latter two, stating that while the scientist might (or ought) speak out on matters either directly or indirectly affecting science as a *scientist*, involvement in the latter two types of issues required him to step out of his professional or intellectual role and speak as a citizen or voter. Several stressed that concern about such matters was the scientists' right and obligation as a citizen and that he should speak out if he felt he was competent or had something to contribute. Only a combined total of four in both samples believed that neither scientists nor anyone else should speak out on matters "where there is neither public concern regardless of its relation to science". Two believed that speaking out on matters of the latter two kinds was "optional" for the scientist. What is interesting is the extent to which most respondents saw citizenship as both a right and a responsibility, and argued for the use of the same general standards of competence and thoughtfulness in citizenship (though not the specific procedures of course) that ideally obtain in scientific activity. Citizenship for most was not seen as an opportunity either to be silent or to state one's biases and passions in an unthoughtful fashion.

A few contrasted the idea of scientists trying to speak "with one voice" on the first two kinds of matters, with the scientist as citizen speaking as *an individual,* and were fearful of the ease with which influential members of the scientific community are assumed by the public and their elected representatives to be speaking for or representing that community. Some wanted to distinguish situations of mild public concern in the latter two categories with over-riding moral issues where continuous involvement at a higher pitch was required, for example, sterilization of the allegedly "unfit". Others wanted speaking out on matters not relating to science either directly or indirectly to be reserved for "exceptional circumstances or events", and were concerned that scientists "do their homework". Many Canadians emphasized that the scientist should be particularly concerned "with making the public aware of developments as opposed to selling his point of view". A combination of such concerns among respondents was evident in allusions to the "ecological or environmental movements", where scientists all too often attempted to use their membership in the scientific community to give additional weight to political views and positions which were scientifically dubious and unsound or poorly thought out. American respondents drew attention to the same concerns in approximately the same percentages in their sample.

Conclusion

A preliminary study of this sort is likely to be unsatisfying to readers anxious to discover in depth views and positions in specific areas of concern. Wide-ranging questions covering aspects of three general areas of interest were formulated in open-ended fashion not only to give respondents ample opportunity to explain and/or qualify their choices, but often so that they could state these choices, thereby giving the writer an option to imposing arbitrary categories on respondents which might not be their own. Obviously, it is a matter of balance how far one carries one's commitment to either extreme. Questionnaires cannot be so open-ended that they provide no structure at all to those responding; at the same time, the dangers of overorganization must be clear, particularly in a pilot study. While some respondents, as well as the large number of those choosing not to respond, resented the relative lack of structure, correctly realizing the greater amount of time required in order to be thoughtful, most who responded appreciated the rationale for such an exercise and were extremely helpful.

Although there are a considerable number of points on which we might focus in an effort to summarize, points where the two samples agreed substantially or manifested significant differences of view or unique concerns, I want to conclude by speaking in the main about the Canadian responses. Apart from the far higher response rate from Canadians, there are clearly public issues of considerable moment presently relating to science policy, particularly basic research, in Canada, which do not obtain in the United States. Canada appears to be at a most critical juncture in the development of its science policy, critical because political and bureaucratic decisions about priorities, directions, and points of emphasis, are today so closely bound up with the overall problem of dependence and its more specific economic manifestations. This latter concern makes it more difficult for basic researchers in Canada to get a hearing than is the case elsewhere (e.g. the United States) where economies are also experiencing inflation and resulting austerity.

The over-riding judgement of these scientists seems to be that the increasing "lack of confidence" in basic research in favour of short-run applications-oriented solutions is fundamentally mistaken. Even a substantial number of those engaged in *applied* research and development in Canada pointed this out. It creates a subsidiary mentality among the scientific community and favours a "zero-sum" atmosphere in relations between basic and applied scientists, since funding is by government in both cases. The reason it creates a subsidiary mentality in basic research must be clear enough: such a de-emphasis makes Canada more dependent on basic research done elsewhere. Respondents frequently alluded to Canada's failure to "pull its weight" in this regard, making unflattering comparisons with European countries of small to medium size rather than with the United States.

The major suggestion for reversing this trend, where reversal is justified for many respondents by its long-term *practical and technical* superiority to present policies, is ongoing consultation. As noted, the desire to be permitted to act responsibly on these matters by being *consulted* by government as working scientists was contrasted to effective collegial *control* over allocation to different areas once government had acted. Scientists in Canada are far from advocating their own ascendancy in political life, and hasten for the most part to emphasize that their concern is an expression of what they believe to be their responsibility to the public and government who trained them and who provide financial support for their work.

Their statements are reminiscent of Bacon's support for experiments which shed light which may later bear fruit as well as those having immediate relevance and application. Indeed, modern science's "relevance" is at least as much a product of its attempt to systematically seek out the laws underlying established technical practices as it is an attempt to overcome scholasticism and contemplation for its own sake. The "progress" of science, in other words, is the result not of an effort to be immediately relevant but to contribute theoretical knowledge whose long-term effects might have *exponential* significance for technological concerns. Bacon's object was to mediate between contemplation for its own sake and traditional techniques in the interest of establishing a new relationship of mastery with nature. The contribution of science to modern technology is clear, as Bunge explains:

"We see there is no single road from practice to knowledge, from success to truth; success warrants no inference from [technological] rule to [scientific] law, but poses the problem of explaining the apparent efficiency of the rule. In other words, the roads from [techno-logical] success to truth are infinitely many and consequently theoretically useless or nearly so, that is, no bunch of effective rules suggests a true [scientific] theory. On the other hand, the roads from truth to success are limited in number, hence feasible. This is one of the reasons that practical success . . . is not a truth criterion for the underlying hypotheses. This is also why technology – in contrast to the prescientific arts and crafts – does not start with [technological] rules and end up with theories but proceeds the other way around. This is, in brief, why (modern) technology is applied science whereas science is not purified technology" (Bunge, 1966, 340–341).

Put in summary fashion: "Whereas given a law we may try out the correspond-ing rules, given a rule we are unable to trace the laws presupposed by it" (Bunge, 1966, 340).

While it is no doubt true that a number of politicians and bureaucrats would probably accept this equation of modern technology with technology uniquely science-based, rather than premised on rules of thumb, and perhaps even the central role of basic research for applications, most would likely take issue with the claim that we need continuing contributions in this area in the interests of problem-solving. Their attitude would assume basic research and the theoretical commitment in science to be a luxury which other countries with superior resources ought to carry out, or perhaps an established body of knowledge which can be borrowed from rather than contributed to by Canadians.

Apart from the "colonialism" such an attitude is seen to be giving rise to is the fact that it assumes that problems and possible lines of application remain static, and also that applications can be virtually guaranteed by organizing and structuring the work relations of applied scientists and technologists to this end. Neither one is necessarily the case. One respondent stated the contrary point of view succinctly when he argued that new technological solutions to unsolved problems, which are *both* national and global, demand new contribu-tions of a theoretical kind. Of course, one might argue that these contributions should come from elsewhere, but wouldn't the likelihood of effective solutions be increased if basic research was given greater support in Canada?

The present direction of priorities in Canada is clear from the recent policy shifts of the Ministry of State for Science and Technology and the National Research Council. These shifts clearly constitute responses to the urgent need for what the O.E.C.D. group calls a "technology policy". They stress that success here depends upon the development of "a much more explicit and comprehensive industrial strategy" than has been in evidence since the govern-ment's efforts in 1972 to strengthen industrial R and D by moving a consider-able part of publicly financed R and D from government laboratories to industry (O.E.C.D., 1973, 204–05). No one, least of all the respondents sampled in this study, denies the importance of applied science to technology, though a few may admittedly construe basic research in global rather than in national terms. But such an attitude is precisely where the real strength of science as an intellectual institution and community lies.

It may be necessary to view basic research's contribution "above an amount sufficient to maintain a broad scientific capability" as "an international obligation", as the Senate Special Committee on Science Policy has done. But this Report also recommends that the funding of basic research in Canada "be more or less proportionate to that of other industrially advanced countries." (Senate Special Committee on Science Policy, *Report, Volume 2*, 600.) There is little doubt that, no matter how the priorities are established and maintained in the years to come, the relationship between basic and applied research will depend upon an overall industrial strategy whose technology policy takes account of the perceptions and attitudes of Canada's working scientists.

REFERENCES AND READING

A. Canadian

BÉLOVIC, B. and ALEXANDER, J.
   1974   *Science for What? A Critical Analysis of Trends and Patterns in Canadian Science Policy.* Ottawa: Draft Copy prepared for the Science Council.

DOERN, Bruce
   1973   *Scientists and Policy-Making in Canada.* Montreal: McGill – Queen's University Press.

GRASLEY, Robert H.
   1975   *The Availability of Risk Capital for Technological Innovation and Invention in Canada.* Ottawa: Ministry of State for Science and Technology.

LITHWICK, N. H.
   1969   *Canada's Science Policy and the Economy.* Toronto: Methuen.

Organization for Economic Co-operation and Development
   1974   *The Research System, Volume 3, Canada–United States, General Conclusions.* Paris.

PORTER, John
   1965   *The Vertical Mosaic.* Toronto: University of Toronto.

Science Council of Canada
   1971, October   *Innovation in a Cold Climate*, Report No. 15. Ottawa: Information Canada.
   1971, December   *Basic Research*, Special Study No. 21. Ottawa: Information Canada.
   1971, December   *The Multinational Firm, Foreign Direct Investment, and Canadian Science Policy*, Special Study No. 22. Ottawa: Information Canada.
   1972, September   *Policy Objectives for Basic Research in Canada*, Report No. 18, Ottawa; Information Canada.

Senate Special Committee on Science Policy Report
   1972   *A Science Policy for Canada*, 2 Vols. Ottawa: Information Canada.

WILSON, Andrew H.
   1968   *Science, Technology and Innovation.* Ottawa: Special Study No. 8, Economic Council of Canada.

B. General

BLANKENSHIP, L. Vaughn
   1970   *The Scientist as 'Apolitical' Man*, paper delivered at Northeastern Political Science Assn., Philadelphia, November 12–14.

BOLAND, L. A.
   1971   "An Institutional Theory of Economic Technology and Change," in *Philosophy of the Social Sciences*, Volume 1, No. 3, pp. 253–258.

BUNGE, Mario
   1966   "Technology as Applied Science," in *Technology and Culture*, Volume 7, pp. 329–347.

CALDER, Nigel
   1969   *Technopolis.* London: MacGibbon and Kee.

DAEDALUS
    1973   *The Search for Knowledge*, Volume 102, No. 2 of the Proceedings of the American
            Academy of Arts and Sciences, New York.
GOULDNER, Alvin
    1957–58 "Cosmopolitans and Locals," *Administrative Science Quarterly*, Volume 2, pp.
            281–306, 444–480.
GREENBERG, Daniel S.
    1967   *The Politics of Pure Science*. New York: New American Library.
HABERER, Joseph
    1969   *Politics and the Community of Science*. New York: Van Nostrand.
HABERMAS, Jurgen
    1971   "Technology and Science as Ideology," in Habermas, *Toward a Rational Society*,
            London: Heinemann, pp. 81–122.
HAGSTROM, Warren
    1965   *The Scientific Community*. New York: Basic Books.
JENCKS, Christopher and RIESMAN, David
    1968   *The Academic Revolution*. Garden City, N.Y.: Doubleday.
JUNGK, Robert
    1958   *Brighter than a Thousand Suns*. Harmondsworth: Penguin.
KUHN, Thomas
    1969   *The Structure of Scientific Revolutions*. Chicago: University of Chicago (2nd edition).
LAKATOS, Imre, and MUSGRAVE, Alan (editors)
    1970   *Criticism and the Growth of Knowledge*. Cambridge: Cambridge University Press.
MERTON, Robert
    1957   *Social Theory and Social Structure*, New York: Free Press, part IV.
MOORE, Barrington
    1965   "Tolerance and the Scientific Outlook," in Wolff, Paul, Moore, Barrington, and
            Marcuse, Herbert, *A Critique of Pure Tolerance*. Boston, Beacon, pp. 53–79.
NELSON, William R. (ed.)
    1968   *The Politics of Science*. New York: Oxford.
NIEBURG, H. L.
    1966   *In the Name of Science*. Chicago: Quadrangle.
PELZ, Donald, and ANDREWS, Frank
    1966   *Scientists in Organizations*. New York: John Wiley.
POPPER, Karl
    1944   *The Poverty of Historicism*. London: Routledge.
    1945   *The Open Society and its Enemies*. London: Routledge.
    1959   *The Logic of Scientific Discovery*. New York: Wiley. Originally published 1934–35.
    1963   *Conjectures and Refutations*. London: Routledge.
    1972   *Objective Knowledge*. Oxford: Oxford University Press.
SHROYER, Trent
    1970   "Toward a Theory for Advanced Industrial Societies," in *Recent Sociology*, Volume
            2, New York: Macmillan, pp. 210–234,
STORER, Norman
    1966   *The Social System of Science*. New York: Holt, Rinehart and Winston.
WARNER, Lyle G. and DE FLEUR, Melvin L.
    1969   "Attitude as an Interactional Concept: Social Constraint and Social Distance as
            Intervening Variables Between Attitudes and Action," *American Sociological
            Review*, Volume 34, No. 2, pp. 153–169.
WILSON, H. T.
    1975   *Innovation: The Practical Uses of Theory* (unpublished paper).
    1976   "Science, Critique and Criticism," in *On Critical Theory*, edited by John O'Neill,
            New York: Seabury.
    1977   *The American Ideology*. London: Routledge, Chapters 3–5.
ZIMAN, John
    1968   *Public Knowledge*. Cambridge: Cambridge University Press.

Bureaucracy in the United States and Canada: Social, Attitudinal and Behavioral Variables

ROBERT PRESTHUS and WILLIAM MONOPOLI

York University, Toronto, Canada

Despite THE UTILITY of the Weberian ideal-typical model in analyzing the norms and performance of Western bureaucracy, comparative inquiry suggests that both the role and ideology of modern bureaucracy vary cross-nationally. Two theoretical conditions seem useful in explaining such variations: political culture and political structure. These may be conceptualized as independent, systemic variables. The level of popular participation, resting in part upon educational opportunity in a given society, provides one aspect of political culture that affects bureaucratic responsiveness to popular claims. In turn, the degree of class stratification and attending deferential patterns of authority will bear upon the equality of educational opportunities, the criteria of recruitment to the bureaucratic apparatus, and the extent to which the bureaucracy is representative of divergent social interests. Egalitarian social and political values will tend to militate against the development of an elitist, permanent, higher bureaucracy, as seen, for example, in the British administrative class. The relative weight of such cultural factors in any given context is presently impossible to determine, but one can at least suggest their theoretical relevance.

The impact of political structure is probably easier to demonstrate. The conditions of bureaucratic participation in the parliamentary system seem to encourage a more decisive policy role for the higher bureaucracy than that found in the presidential system. Among the explanations are the relative impotence of backbenchers; the tenuous role of legislative committees; and the extra-functional criteria of recruitment of cabinet leaders, aggravated in turn by the practice of rotating such leaders from one substantive milieu to another. Such tendencies toward amateurism at the top underlie Weber's conclusion that " . . . the power position of a fully developed bureaucracy is always overtowering. The 'political master' finds himself in the position of the 'dilettante' who stands opposite the 'expert,' facing the trained official who stands within the management of administration" (Gerth and Mills: 1946, 228).

In the presidential system, by contrast, with the notable exception of foreign affairs, bureaucratic power is strongly challenged by permanent, substantively-sophisticated legislative committees; individual legislators possessing viable local and state power bases; and the attending seniority system which often enables legislators to develop considerable personal power. As a result, the role of the higher American bureaucracy often seems less one of initiating policy than the subordinate and occasionally negative one of carrying out policy shaped mainly by elected officials and prestigious aides appointed by the President to fill strategic political posts at the secretary, undersecretary and assistant secretary levels. In the Canadian system, different norms and political structure tend to thrust greater policy influence into the hands of permanent deputy ministers. Meanwhile, a more deferential political culture reinforces their autonomy.

In some such a context, we turn to a comparative analysis of certain social, ideological and behavioral characteristics of senior bureaucrats in Canada and the United States.

Data used here were produced by a five-year study of interaction among political elites, including senior civil servants in Washington, D.C. (N = 92) and Ottawa (N = 90) and in British Columbia (N = 36), Ontario (N = 49), and Quebec (N = 39) and in Washington State (N = 57), Michigan (N = 60) and Louisiana (N = 52) (Presthus: 1973, 1974). For the purposes of this paper, both provincial and state samples have been collapsed to ease the analysis.* The bureaucratic samples comprised GS grades 16–18 in the United States and, primarily, deputy ministers and associate and assistant deputy ministers in Canada.

Social Variables

In analyzing the importance of such characteristics as socio-economic status and mobility, we assume that these variables affect the respondents' political attitudes and behavior. At the very least, these variables can be used to differentiate Canadian and American administrators on the salient questions of who the bureaucrats are and what social positions they are likely to have in the societies from which they come.

Socio-economic status as used here is based upon occupation and education, with occupation weighted times seven and education times three (Hollingshead and Redlich: 1958).

The mobility patterns (not shown here) of Canadian and U.S. bureaucrats are quite similar. Nearly 40 per cent of the fathers of Ottawa and Washington respondents rank in the "upper" or "upper-middle" classes. Of the administrators themselves, over 90 per cent rank at these levels.

Canadian and American federal bureaucrats rank very similarly on this scale. State and provincial bureaucrats are less similar but the variation is not statistically significant at .05 in the chi-square test. Among state respondents' fathers, 23 per cent rank in the "upper" or "upper-middle" classes, compared

* We are greatly indebted to the Canada Council for funding the survey.

with 28 per cent of the provincial bureaucrats' fathers. As was the case with the federal administrators, over 90 per cent of the state and provincial officials ranked in the two highest classes. While these data indicate that state and provincial bureaucrats are somewhat more socially mobile than their federal counterparts, they also suggest that the federal administrators come from more privileged backgrounds. This finding is consistent with the concept that executive employment in a national capital appears to be more prestigious or otherwise more attractive to socially-advantaged candidates than similar service at a state or provincial level. An early observer of the Canadian public service noted that the attractiveness of provincial administration has tradition-ally been lower than that of the federal service, although he offered no explana-tion for this phenomenon (Cole: 1949, 273).

The educational achievement levels of bureaucrats in both nations are very high. Fifty-three per cent of Canadian respondents and 45 per cent of the Americans have graduate degrees. Given their high rankings on the Hollingshead scale, there is little question that senior administrators in both countries belong to a highly advantaged elite in terms of education and occupation. Table I provides comparative data.

Table 1

Social Class Status Among Canadian and American Administrators (*per cent*)

| | Administrators | | National* | |
	U.S.	Canada	U.S.	Canada
Upper	49	74	3	7
Upper-middle	48	22	8	11
Middle	3	3	22	28
Lower-middle	.5	0	46	38
Lower	0	0	18	17
	(261)	(214)		

* National data are from Kahl: 1957 and Woods and Ostry: 1962. The cross-national proportions are only roughly comparable.

Closely tied to social class and recruitment criteria in the higher bureau-cracy in Western society is the issue of generalists versus specialists. In Britain and, possibly, to some extent in Canada, the generalist model has often provided a basis for recruitment, following the assumption that intelligent, articulate, liberally-educated individuals are fully capable of administering largescale affairs across substantive fields. (This preference for the nimble amateur re-mains viable in Canadian social science.) In sharp contrast is the American assumption that considerable specialist expertise is required among those who direct programs in modern complex, technologically-grounded government. The generalist model has been severely criticized recently on various grounds, both functional and normative (Chapman: 1962; Estimates Committee: 1965; Nicholson: 1967). Given the salience of British traditions for Canadian institutional development, it is interesting to consider to what extent the higher Canadian service may have adopted the generalist ethos.

Consideration of the respondents' fields of graduate study provides one basis for determining the extent to which administrators are "specialists" or "generalists." The United States is usually thought to have developed a government service in which specialization was the way to success. This contrasts with the British system, where a degree from an elite university and a generalist orientation have been the dominant criteria for recruitment into the higher civil service (Presthus: 1975, 58). It might be expected that the tendency toward specialization would be reflected in the U.S. by a concentration of government officials having completed graduate study in one of the fields thought to be particularly useful in government service: law, economics, political science, or business or public administration. On the other hand, if Canada has followed the British generalist tradition, a relatively low percentage of Canadian administrators would be expected to have degrees in one of those disciplines.

The data appear to support these expectations, particularly at the federal level. Fifty-two per cent of Canadian federal bureaucrats who have graduate degrees have those degrees in areas other than those listed above. The parallel figure for American federal administrators is 31 per cent. Comparative data appear in Table 2.

Of the fields thought to be practically germane for government service, only law attracted a higher proportion of Ottawa bureaucrats than Americans. Of particular interest is that in the specialized areas of business and public administration, the proportion of American bureaucrats having done graduate work is three times higher than the Canadian proportions, at both the federal and state-provincial levels.

Table 2

	U.S.		Canada	
Graduate Canadian and American Administrators, Fields of Study	Federal	State	Federal	Provincial
Law	23	15	29	23
Economics	16	5	12	5
Political Science	8	0	0	0
Business Admin. or Public Admin.	15	20	5	7
Medicine	4	9	0	24
Combination of Two Degrees	4	0	3	1
Other	31	50	52	40
	(52)	(59)	(42)	(72)

Federal v. federal:	Chi-square = 10.62947 with 6 d.f.; significance = .1005; gamma = −.14601
State v. provincial:	Chi-square = 11.92855 with 5 d.f.; significance = .0358; gamma = −.13170

The tendency toward what might be characterized as amateurism in Canada and specialization in the United States is less pronounced at the provincial and state levels, where 50 per cent of state bureaucrats and 40 per cent of provincial respondents did graduate work in a subject other than law, economics or political science or administration. Since health plans are a provincial function, it is not surprising that 24 per cent of provincial administrators did their graduate work in medicine, compared with only nine per cent of state bureaucrats.

The conclusion that federal Canadian administrators are somewhat more inclined to be generalists is not novel. Taylor Cole observed a bias among a powerful group of postwar Canadian federal bureaucrats in favor of creation "of a class of employees in Canada modeled after the administrative class in Great Britain. . . . In fact it has been suggested that these Canadian officials constituted themselves the Canadian counterpart of an administrative class" (Cole: 1949, 270, 271).

Tenure

The length of administrators' government service might be expected to be considerable in both the United States and Canada, in light of the pervasive scope of government bureaucracies in both systems. The development of a civil service career-orientation in both systems can be attributed in part to both nations' high levels of government spending. Nearly 45 per cent of Gross National Product in Canada and about one-third of GNP in the U.S. is spent on government at all levels. For comparative purposes, Canada devotes about 35 per cent more of its GNP to government than the United States.

The data show that Canadian and American bureaucrats have similar lengths of tenure. Twenty-one per cent of those in both nations have been in government service for less than 10 years. Some differences appear between Canadian and American bureaucrats at higher levels of tenure, with 17 per cent of the Canadian respondents, compared with 24 per cent of the Americans, having served for 30 years or longer. The differences between the federal samples and the state-provincial samples are not statistically significant at .05, however. Clearly in both societies, government service is a career, rather than, for instance, a stopping point for those whose primary interests might be in academia or business. As shown elsewhere (pp. 10–11), this condition contrasts sharply with the high turnover and "amateur" character of the typical Canadian legislator.

Attitudinal Variables

Variations in their respective political cultures suggest that Canadian and American administrators might differ on such dimensions as economic liberalism, attitudes towards interest groups, and perceived openness of the bureaucratic process to lobbyists. Canada, for example, has rarely exhibited the individualistic anti-government attitude often seen in the United States. Indeed, from Confederation onward, a close nexus has existed between government and private commerce and industry (Myers: 1968: Naylor, 1975).

If bureaucrats tend to reflect the attitudes of the societies they serve, it might be expected that those in both countries would support "big government" and have faith in the ability of government to solve citizens' problems. It might also be anticipated that Canadian administrators would rank higher on "economic liberalism" than their American counterparts, in light of the fact that social and welfare programs are more pervasive in Canada than in the United States, which tends to resist some such programs (proposals for national health insurance, e.g.) as "socialist." Table 3 presents the data.

Table 3
Comparative Economic Liberalism*

Economic Liberalism	U.S.		Canada	
	Federal	State	Federal	Provincial
High	9	16	29	11
Medium	44	27	30	35
Low	47	57	41	53
	(86)	(160)	(88)	(117)

* This is a multiple-item index defined by agreement or disagreement with these statements: "That government which governs least governs best" (reverse scored); "Economic security for every man, woman, and child is worth striving for, even if it means socialism"; "If unemployment is high, the government should spend money to create jobs"; "A national medicare plan is necessary to insure that everyone receives adequate health care"; "More federal aid to education is desirable if we are going to adequately meet present and future educational needs in this country." A respondent who agreed at the highest level received five points; one who most strongly disagreed received 25 points. The scale used was: High, 5–9; Medium, 10–12; Low, 13–25.

Federal v. federal: chi-square = 11.10293 with 2 d.f.; significance = .0039; gamma = .22041

State v. provincial: chi-square = 2.65171 with 2 d.f.; significance = .2656; gamma = –.02012

Canadian federal bureaucrats scored higher on this dimension, as could be expected. The "lower" scores of the U.S. federal sample probably can be explained by respondent objection to one or two items in the index. For example, U.S. federal bureaucratic resistance to the item on guaranteeing economic security "even if it means socialism" can be understood, given the traditional American belief (in theory if not always in practice) in the virtues of individualism.

Interestingly, larger proportions of both state and provincial bureaucrats rank in the "low" category. One possible explanation for this may be that agreement with at least two of the items (e.g. regarding education or health) would have indicated support for a greater *federal* role in matters which could be seen to diminish the authority of state-provincial administrators.

While a number of factors, such as education, income, or party affiliation,

may explain rankings on the economic liberalism index, one offered for consideration here is tenure. It might be expected in both systems that relatively
new administrators might be more "liberal" on economic issues than their
colleagues who had been in government service for extended periods. Presumably, the longer one serves in an administrative role, the more likely she might
be to develop a view that problems presented by health and welfare issues are
not easily solved by government. Advancing age might also reinforce this
tendency. Table 4 presents the data.

Table 4

Tenure versus Economic Liberalism

Tenure (years)	Economic Liberalism*					
	U.S. Administrators			Canadian Administrators		
	High	Medium	Low	High	Medium	Low
Less than 4	35	6	59	4	18	78
5–9	27	27	46	8	24	68
10–20	14	32	54	15	25	60
21–30	16	35	49	17	39	44
More than 30	14	49	37	14	44	42
	(37)	(67)	(100)	(32)	(81)	(129)

* Index is same as that in Table 3.
   U.S. sample: Chi-square = 17.09460 with 8 d.f.;
                       significance = .0291; gamma = −.28175
   Canadian sample: Chi-square = 13.32640 with 8 d.f.;
                       significance = .1011; gamma = −.03548

In both systems, length of tenure seems to be positively associated with an
inclination to take moderate positions on government's role in economic issues.
It is interesting that in both countries, a preponderance of those administrators
who had been in government service for four years or less rank very low on
economic liberalism, perhaps indicating a lack of faith in the virtues of "big
government." For those for whom bureaucratic norms presumably have had
an opportunity to take firm hold, there seems to a linear movement *away* from
economic conservatism, and especially among the Canadian sample. In both
countries, because of the long tenure and career orientation of senior civil
servants, their attitudes on economic liberalism may be said to exist independently of the ideology of the political party in power. Certainly, they do not
share the unrestrained welfare capitalist preferences of their political masters
(see pp. 14–15 above).

The anti-big government preferences of both sets of bureaucrats bear upon
the interesting theoretical question of the extent to which attitudes are a valid
index of behavior. In the case of higher bureaucrats, whose occupational role
consists essentially of carrying out the vast subsidy and welfare programs that
characterize both national systems, one must conclude that the linkage is
tenuous indeed. How bureaucrats reconcile the resultant role conflict is a
suggestive research question.

Certain federal and state-provincial distinctions may also be made on an index measuring perceptions of political efficacy. It might be assumed that the two federal samples would rank high on this index, considering the central place the bureaucracy occupies in decision-making and the high educational achievement of its members. The results are set out in Table 5.

Table 5
Comparative Political Efficacy*

| | United States | | Canada | |
Efficacy	Federal	State	Federal	Provincial
High	61	45	37	31
Medium	22	28	37	30
Low	17	27	26	39
	(87)	(160)	(89)	(119)

* Efficacy is based on these items: "The old saying, 'you can't fight city hall' is still basically true"; "Most decisions in business and government are made by a small group that pretty well runs things"; "Anyone in this country who wants to, has a chance to have his say about important issues" (reverse scored). The scale used was: Low, 5–9; Medium, 10–12; High, 13–20.

Federal v. federal: Chi-square = 10.08319 with 2 d.f.; significance = .0065; gamma = .35603

State v. provincial: Chi-square = 5.84938 with 2 d.f.; significance = .0537; gamma = −.23612

The results indicate that while both state and provincial administrators perceive themselves as less efficacious than their federal counterparts, Canadian bureaucrats generally rank significantly lower than U.S. bureaucrats. This is somewhat unusual, considering the highly developed nature of the Canadian bureaucracy, its vital role in policy-making, and the comprehensive nature of programs administered by federal bureaucrats. Similarly, the provinces almost surely occupy a stronger position vis-a-vis the federal government than the position occupied by the states in the U.S. federal system. Yet nearly two-fifths of provincial administrators rank low on political efficacy. This finding raises the possibility that the items used evoke differing interpretations in the two national samples. On the other hand, Canadian ministers rank substantially higher than backbenchers on the index, which is consistent with well-known variations in influence in their respective roles in parliamentary systems (Presthus: 1974, 364).

Perhaps the relative differences in the power of the civil service in the two systems, and in the bureaucrats' perceptions of those differences, is better illustrated by responses to the statement that senior administrators are "among the most influential groups in this country." The expectation would be that Canadians would respond more positively to this than Americans, who more obviously share power with a strong executive and with powerful legislative committees. Table 6 supports these expectations.

Table 6

"Senior civil servants are among the most influential groups in this country."

| | United States | | Canada | |
	Federal	State	Federal	Provincial
Strongly agree	2	2	12	9
Agree	33	22	62	50
Don't know	14	20	8	15
Disagree	46	51	16	25
Strongly disagree	5	6	2	1
	(90)	(163)	(89)	(120)

| Federal v. federal: | Chi-square $= 29.300200$ with 4 d.f.; significance $= .0000$; gamma $= .59894$ |
| State v. provincial: | Chi-square $= 40.14297$ with 4 d.f.; significance $= .0000$; gamma $= -.55695$ |

The data indicate that Canadian bureaucrats have much stronger perceptions of the influence of their role than do their American peers. These results are difficult to reconcile with the bureaucrats' rankings on political efficacy presented in Table 5, where Canadians ranked significantly lower than the Americans. One explanation might be that the items in the efficacy index measure perceptions of *citizen* power generally, while Table 6 measures perceptions of the influence of the civil service. Some items in the efficacy index do not directly measure administrators' perceptions of their own *personal* efficacy. A respondent can render an opinion on statements such as, "The average man doesn't really have much chance to get ahead," and "Most decisions are made by a small group," on the assumption that he does not perceive himself as the "average man," and/or that administrators are included in the "small group" that makes most decisions. If this explanation is accurate, the differences between Canadian and American administrators in Table 5 may indicate that Canadian bureaucrats perceive their society as relatively less open to effective citizen participation than American bureaucrats. This would support the belief that Canadian society tends to be less egalitarian and more elitist than American society (Porter: 1969, 49–50).

Canadian and American bureaucrats can also be distinguished by their attitudes towards their colleagues in the legislative branch. Because of the putatively greater policy-making role played by Canadian administrators, as well as the limited influence of the backbencher, it might be expected that Canadian bureaucrats would be less convinced of legislators' competence than their American counterparts.

The variations in Table 7, in which more than half the Canadian sample disagrees with the statement that legislators are competent professionals, may also be traced to differences in tenure and education. Generally, Canadian bureaucrats tend to serve for much longer periods of time than members of national or provincial parliaments (Presthus: 1974, Ch. 13). The comparative differences in tenure might lead to a belief on the part of bureaucrats that

Table 7

"The average member (legislator) is a competent political professional who knows his business."

| | United States | | Canada | |
	Federal	State	Federal	Provincial
Strongly agree	12	4	2	3
Agree	30	24	27	17
Agree slightly	31	24	18	21
Disagree slightly	10	12	6	14
Disagree	15	23	36	30
Disagree strongly	2	13	11	17
	(91)	(162)	(86)	(122)

| Federal v. federal: | Chi-square = 21.71921 with 5 d.f.; significance = .0006; gamma = −.38410 |
| State v. provincial: | Chi-square = 4.29350 with 5 d.f.; significance = .5080; gamma = −.16690 |

legislators simply are not in office long enough to become "professionals" in a career sense. Similarly, that only 58 per cent of Canadian legislators, compared with 86 per cent of Canadian administrators have university degrees, might reinforce any belief by administrators that legislators do not have the necessary academic credentials to become expert in government. While this view surely might be interpreted as elitist, it must be recalled that Canadian bureaucrats represent a highly advantaged group in a nation in which only about five per cent of citizens have such degrees.

The general agreement among administrators in the U.S. that federal legislators are competent is expected, considering the relative power legislators have in the presidential system.* Lower scores for state administrators indicate, reasonably enough, that state legislators, who are more likely than federal legislators to be political amateurs serving part-time roles are not as widely believed to be competent.

In contrast with our findings in Table 7, most administrators in both countries believe *lobbyists* are "competent professionals who know their business." The statement met with 87 per cent agreement among federal administrators in the United States and 81 per cent agreement among Canadian federal bureaucrats. Among state respondents, 87 per cent answered affirmatively. The statement also met with a favorable response – 60 per cent – at the provincial level, although not by the majorities achieved in the state and federal samples. The reason for this difference is not entirely clear, but it should be noted that even among provincial administrators, lobbyists, far more often than

---

* On the other hand, James Burnham argued that senior bureaucrats "do not hide their feeling that Congress is a roadblock that they must somehow bypass if the country is to progress, a kind of idiot boy who must be pushed, teased and cozened." Burnham notes however that there is little published data to support this concept of bureaucratic "arrogance" (Golembiewski, 1966, 76).

legislators, are widely considered competent. The differences between the federal samples were not significant at .05 on this statement, although the state-provincial differences were significant.

Behavioral Variables

Consideration of the frequency with which bureaucrats meet lobbyists may be helpful in explaining why lobbyists are so often considered competent. Among federal respondents in Washington, D.C., 40 per cent said they met with interest group representatives frequently (e.g. twice a week) and 32 per cent met with lobbyists occasionally (e.g. twice a month). Comparable figures for administrators in Ottawa were 33 per cent and 31 per cent. Contact with lobbyists was frequent for 37 per cent of the state administrators and occasional for 29 per cent. For the provincial bureaucrats, the figures were 34 per cent and 30 per cent respectively. Differences between the federal samples and between the state-provincial samples were not statistically significant. Such interaction in both countries is associated with bureaucrats' acceptance of lobbyists as legitimate, and such legitimacy has been demonstrated to translate into polit-ical influence for the lobbyists (Presthus: 1974, 324). Interestingly, this associa-tion does not hold for legislators in either political system (Presthus: 1974, 308).

Contrary to the belief that interest groups are primarily an American phenomenon, our data suggest that Canadian bureaucrats, even more than Americans, respond affirmatively to lobbyists. One measure of this is their responses to a question about which of several conditions "best characterizes the relations of interest groups to your department." The Ottawa and Washing-ton responses were quite similar on this question, with 50 per cent of the Canadians and 49 per cent of the Americans describing their departments' relations with lobbyists as either "almost an integral part of our day-to-day activity" or "usually taken into account during policy-making." Fifty-two per cent of the state administrators responded the same way, as did 68 per cent of the provincial bureaucrats. However, neither the Ottawa-Washington nor the state-provincial variations were statistically significant.

The reasons for extensive interest group involvement in the Canadian bureaucracy again may be traced to the importance of administrators in a parliamentary system. It seems reasonable to suggest that the ministers who ostensibly make policy are not necessarily professionals or specialists and there-fore rely somewhat heavily on senior civil servants. This condition, as noted, is probably aggravated by the policy of rotation of Cabinet members among various ministeries. Senior administrators, who are perhaps more likely to be generalists than specialists, are likely to rely in turn on interest group represent-atives who possess expertise in the several complicated subjects which policy-making involves.

If in fact interest groups are more highly legitimated in the Canadian than in the American system, it would be expected that Canadians would be at least as likely as Americans to characterize interest group access to departmental decision-making as easy.

The data suggest that such is the outcome. Responding to an item asking respondents to characterize interest group access to departmental policy-making, 71 per cent of the Ottawa sample and 65 per cent of the Washington sample rated access as "quite easy" or "fairly easy." Sixty-six per cent of provincial administrators and 62 per cent of their state peers responded similarly. Again, however, neither federal nor state-provincial differences were statistically significant.

The data on access and on the relations of interest groups with the respondents' departments indicate a close relationship between lobbyists and administrators in the U.S. and a marginally closer relationship between them in Canada.

Consistent with this generalization is the finding that in response to the question, "Has your own or any other Department ever created an interest group in order to facilitate the implementation of a policy or program?" a higher percentage of Canadians than Americans answered yes: 50 per cent at the provincial level versus 47 per cent at state, and 45 per cent in Ottawa versus 33 per cent in Washington. One explanation often suggested for an agency creating an interest group is related to the agency's desire to guarantee or strengthen its own existence by having a group make demands upon it. Another explanation is that the agency might need a liaison group with expertise or technical skill that would complement its own capabilities and would facilitate the carrying out of policy. If these explanations are correct, the fact that Canadian agencies more often form their own interest groups than American seems to reinforce the idea that Canadian administrators are more likely to be generalists who require outside expertise. Further, insofar as the creation of interest groups renders indistinguishable the once-assumed difference between "public" and "private" government, this condition is more consonant with a political culture that includes a strong mercantile tradition.

Another reason for the close relationship between Canadian bureaucrats and lobbyists is suggested by responses to a statement that the "formality of the legislative process is a roadblock for lobbyists." It would be anticipated that administrators who believe that lobbying is a legitimate function would be more inclined to welcome lobbyists into their own agencies, in part because of a perception that the legislative arena is too formal. Table 8 presents the results.

As expected, strong majorities in the Canadian samples agree with the statement. Combined with data on access and on the close relationship in Canada between administrators and lobbyists, this can be taken as indicating that the Canadian bureaucracy provides a generally favorable environment for lobbyists. Aware of the lack of clientele relation between legislative committees and interest groups, senior bureaucrats may feel that they should provide an alternative source of group influence.

It also might be expected that Canadian administrators, given their closer ties with lobbyists, will have been influenced more often by them, compared

Table 8

"The formality of the legislative process is often a roadblock for a lobbyist trying to present his position."

	United States		Canada	
	Federal	State	Federal	Provincial
Agree strongly	5	5	8	8
Agree somewhat	17	25	34	35
Agree slightly	17	14	22	22
Disagree slightly	31	25	13	19
Disagree somewhat	24	27	18	12
Disagree strongly	6	5	5	5
	(88)	(154)	(85)	(116)

Federal v. federal: Chi-square = 13.05833 with 5 d.f.; significance = .0148; gamma = .28705

State v. provincial: Chi-square = 14.13328 with 5 d.f.; significance = .0228; gamma = −.27345

with American bureaucrats. On an index weighting the extent to which bureaucrats reported having been influenced by lobbyists (from "beginning to question my position on an issue" to "coming to agree with the lobbyist's position"), one-third of Canadian administrators ranked at the "high" level, compared with 28 per cent of American administrators. The differences between the samples are not statistically significant, however, and no conclusion can be drawn regarding this assumption.

In the Canadian sample, it appears that bureaucrats who are more senior in service are substantially more likely than their colleagues to be influenced by lobbyists. This is clearly not the case for the American administrators, over one-fourth of whom are influenced by lobbyists at a "high" level, regardless of tenure. Table 9 presents the results.

Why such a tendency exists in the Canadian system but not in the American is unclear. One might suggest, however, that the longer the Canadian administrator remains in government service, the more likely he is to adopt its organizational norms, precisely because the socialization process is stronger in ascriptive systems. This explanation is strongly reinforced by the nice linearity of the distribution in the "high" influence column, increasing from almost 20 per cent among those with less than four years service to almost 40 per cent among those with 30 or more years of service. As noted earlier, classical bureaucratic norms of hierarchy, deference, and predictability are strong in Canada, in government, banking, insurance, and academia, which suggests that the socialization process would function in some such fashion. In the United States sample, the tendency might not appear because of somewhat less of a linear disposition to respond positively to group claims. Reasons for this somewhat unconventional finding might also include the following conditions.

Based on their fields of graduate study, Canadian bureaucrats seem to be somewhat less inclined to be skilled specialists in one of the traditional routes

Table 9

*Tenure versus interest group influence**

	United States			Canada		
		Group Influence			Group Influence	
Tenure (years)	High	Medium	Low	High	Medium	Low
Less than 4	37	26	37	19	25	56
5–9	23	50	27	27	31	42
10–20	33	38	29	33	48	16
21–30	24	47	28	37	48	16
Over 30	25	31	33	39	36	25
	(65)	(97)	(72)	(68)	(78)	(58)

* Weighted index of responses to these items: "How often have you been influenced by a lobbyist to the extent that you began to question your position on an issue?" (frequently, occasionally, hardly ever, never); "Influenced . . . to the degree of changing your position . . . and have come to lean more toward his view?"; "Influenced . . . to the extent of coming to agree with his position?" The second question was given twice the weight of the first, and the third question was given three times the weight of the first. Recording was as follows: High, 6–12; Medium, 13–18; Low, 19–30.

U.S. sample: Chi-square $= 5.50699$ with 8 d.f.;
                 significance $= .7023$; gamma $= .05301$
Canada sample: Chi-square $= 14.34555$ with 8 d.f.;
                 significance $= .0732$; gamma $= -.21766$

to government service, such as economics or administration, and, perhaps partly for that reason, are more likely to rely upon and to include interest groups and lobbyists in the formation of policy alternatives. Political culture may also be involved, in the sense that Canadian corporatism, contrasted with the individualist social ethic of the United States, might explain why interest groups and lobbyists seem to be more favorably received by Canadian administrators, and might also account for some of the social, attitudinal and behavioral differences found between them and American bureaucrats.

REFERENCES

BURNHAM, James
    1966 "Some administrators unkindly view Congress," pp. 75–80, in Robert T. Golembiewski (ed.), *Public Administration*. Chicago: Rand McNally.
CHAPMAN, Brian
    1962 *British Government Observed*. London: Allen and Unwin.
COLE, Taylor
    1949 *The Canadian Bureaucracy*. Durham, N.C.: Duke University Press.
GERTH, H. H. and MILLS, C. W.
    1946 *From Max Weber*. New York: Oxford University Press.
Estimates Committee
    1965 *Recruitment to the Civil Service*. London: H.M.S.O.
HOLLINGSHEAD, A. B. and REDLICH F.
    1958 *Social Class and Mental Illness*. New York: John Wiley.
KAHL, Joseph
    1957 *The American Class Structure*. New York: Holt, Rinehart.

MYERS, Gustavus
    1968   *Canada Wealth.* New York: Argosy-Antiquarian.
NAYLOR, R. T.
    1975   *The History of Canadian Business.* Toronto: James Lorimer.
NICHOLSON, Max
    1967   *The System: The Misgovernment of Modern Britain.* London: Hodder and Stoughton.
PORTER, John
    1969   "Canadian National Character," 5 *Cultural Affairs.*
PRESTHUS, Robert
    1973   *Elite Accommodation in Canadian Politics.* London: Cambridge University Press.
    1974   *Elites in the Policy Process.* London: Cambridge University Press.
    1975   *Public Administration.* New York: Ronald Press.
WOODS, H. D. and OSTRY S.
    1962   *Labour Policy and Labour Economics in Canada.* Toronto: University of Toronto.

NAME INDEX

SUBJECT INDEX

Academics, Canadian, 3, 4, 178
Affirmative Action, 112–113
Alberta, 92
American Revolution, 8
Anglicans, in Canada, 55
Anti-Americanism in Canada, 48–49, 91, 103, 105
Appalachia, 144
Aristocracy, 17
Ascription, in Canada, 3, 8, 9, 103, 104, 188
Assimilation
    in Canada, 104–105, 106–107
    in the United States, 105, 106
Atlantic Provinces
    (see also Maritime Provinces), 92
A. G. Canada v. Lavell, 114, 122–124
Austria-Hungary, 105
Authority
    attitudes towards
    in Canada, 5, 8, 9, 65, 176–177
    in United States, 8, 64, 65

Banks, in Canada, 9, 61, 92
Barron v. Baltimore, 108
Belleville, Ontario, 63, 64, 65, 67, 74, 75, 77, 78, 79
Bicultural-Bilingual Commission, 15
Biculturalism, 104–105, 114
Bilingualism, 59, 91, 104
Bill of Rights
    Canada, 102, 103, 107, 114, 116–124
    Section 1(b), 102, 114, 119–124
    United States, 108, 113, 117
Blacks, in the United States, 108–113
Bourgeois society, 83
Branch-plant managers, Canada
    (see also Managers)
British Columbia, 20, 27, 31–32, 92, 177
British heritage
    of Canada, 2, 8, 90–91, 96, 102, 103, 105, 178–179
    of United States, 102, 105
British North America Act, (BNA Act), 103, 116–117, 119
Brown v. Board of Education, 110–112, 115
Bureaucracy
    in Britain, 176, 178–179, 180
    in Canada, 8, 14, 177–189
    in the United States, 177–189
Bureaucrats
    Canada, 177–189

attitudes, 180–186
background, 177–180
economic liberalism, 180–182
education, 178–180, 188–189
lobbies and interest groups, relations with, 185–188
political efficacy, 183–185
tenure, 180, 182, 184–185
United States, 177–189
attitudes, 180–186
background, 177–180
economic liberalism, 180–182
education, 178–180
lobbies and interest groups, relations with, 185–188
political efficacy, 183–185
tenure, 180–182

Cabinet
    Canada, 70, 140, 145–146
    United States, 70
Canada
    anti-Americanism, 48–49, 91, 103, 105
    ascription, 3, 8, 9, 103, 104, 188
    assimilation, 104–105, 106–107
    authority attitudes to, 5, 8, 9, 11, 64–65
    banks, 9, 61, 92
    biculturalism and bilingualism, 59, 91, 104–105, 114
    Bill of Rights, 102, 103, 107, 114, 116–124
    Branch-plant managers, 3, 46
    British Heritage, 2, 8, 90–91, 96, 102, 103, 105, 178–179
    British North America Act, 103, 116–117, 119
    bureaucracy, 8, 14, 177–189
    bureaucrats, 1, 177–189
    Cabinet, 8, 10, 70, 140, 145–146
    class, 5, 8, 88, 99
    conservatism, 2, 4, 8, 59, 103, 106, 107
    counter-revolutionary tradition, 103, 107
    discrimination, 114, 119–124
    economic development, 14, 92, 93
    economic Liberalism, 13–15, 21, 64–65, 141, 148–149, 180–182
    education, 1, 3–4, 5, 9, 26–27, 31, 54–56, 96, 107, 141–142, 178–180, 188–189
    "elite accommodation", 5, 9, 10, 15, 20
    elites, 5, 10, 49, 50, 55, 60, 65, 87–88, 177, 185
    elitism, 2, 3, 47, 64, 104, 184

CONTRIBUTORS

Nathaniel BECK is Assistant Professor of Political Science at Washington State University. He received his Ph.D. from Yale University. His research has been published in *Public Choice, The American Political Science Review, Political Methodology*, and as chapters in several books. His current research interest includes models of partisan choice in multi-party systems.

Colin CAMPBELL is Assistant Professor of Political Science at York University, Toronto. He received his Ph.D. at Duke University. His articles have appeared in *Comparative Political Studies, American Review of Canadian Studies*, and the *Social Science Journal*. He served from 1973–75 as an editorial intern with the *American Political Science Review*. His major research interests are in legislative behavior and the policy influence of the Prime Minister's Office. His book, *The Lobby From Within: Canadian Senators*, Macmillan, is in press.

Carl J. CUNEO, Assistant Professor, Dept. of Sociology, McMaster University, Hamilton, Ontario. Ph.D., University of Waterloo, 1973. Current research interests are in social class and social mobility, and in the social, economic and political relations between Canada and the United States.

Ronald G. LANDES, Associate Professor of Political Science, Saint Mary's University, Halifax, Nova Scotia, currently teaches courses in Canadian and Comparative Government. Receiving his Ph.D. (1973) from York University, Toronto, Landes has presented three papers at the annual meetings of the Canadian Political Science Association and currently has several articles forthcoming, including pieces in the *Dalhousie Review*, the *International Journal of Comparative Sociology*, and a reader on the political socialization process in Canada.

Craig MCKIE is an Assistant Professor in the Department of Sociology at the University of Western Ontario in London, Ontario. He received his Ph.D. in sociology from the University of Toronto in 1974. His current research interests are in social class and social mobility, and in social, political and economic relations between Canada and The United States.

William V. MONOPOLI received his A.B. from Hamilton College in 1971. In 1974 he entered Boston College Law School where he will receive a J.D. degree in 1978. He has an M.A. in political science from York University.

John C. PIERCE is presently Professor of Political Science, Washington State University. He received his Ph.D. from the University of Minnesota. His research has been published in *The American Political Science Review, The American Journal of Political Science, Polity*, and *The Public Opinion Quarterly*. He is also the co-editor of several books, including *Cross-National Micro-Analysis*. His current research interests include the relationship of personal values to political choices.

Robert PRESTHUS is University Professor of Political Science, York University, Toronto, Canada. His research has focussed upon organizational and political behavior, as reported in *The Organizational Society; Men at the Top: A Study in Community Power; Elite Accommodation in Canadian Politics; Elites in the*

Policy Process; and *Interest Groups in International Perspective.* His articles have appeared in *Journal of Politics, International Journal of Comparative Sociology, American Political Science Review, Canadian Journal of Political Science* and *Public Administration Review.*

H. T. WILSON is Associate Professor of Administrative Studies and Law, York University, Toronto. His writings on administrative behavior and science policy have appeared in the *Canadian Journal of Political Science, Canadian Review of American Studies. International Journal of Comparative Sociology, Canadian Public Administration* and *Queen's Quarterly.* His forthcoming book, *The American Ideology,* is being published by Routledge, Kegan and Paul.